San Diego Christian College
2100 Greenfield Drive
El Cajon, CA 92019

CULTURAL PSYCHOLOGY

PATH IN PSYCHOLOGY
Published in Cooperation with Publications for the
Advancement of Theory and History in Psychology (PATH)

Series Editors:
David Bakan, *York University*
John M. Broughton, *Teachers College, Columbia University*
Robert W. Rieber, *John Jay College, CUNY, and Columbia University*
Howard Gruber, *University of Geneva*

CHOICES FOR LIVING: Coping with Fear of Dying
Thomas S. Langner

COGNITIVE SCIENCE AND GENETIC EPISTEMOLOGY: A Case Study of Understanding
David Leiser and Christiane Gillièron

A CRITICAL PSYCHOLOGY: Interpretation of the Personal World
Edmund V. Sullivan

CULTURAL PSYCHOLOGY AND QUALITATIVE METHODOLOGY: Theoretical and Empirical Considerations
Carl Ratner

CULTURAL PSYCHOLOGY: Theory and Method
Carl Ratner

DEVELOPMENTAL APPROACHES TO THE SELF
Edited by Benjamin Lee and Gil G. Noam

HUMANISTIC PSYCHOLOGY: Concepts and Criticisms
Edited by Joseph R. Royce and Leendert P. Mos

MANUFACTURING SOCIAL DISTRESS: Psychopathy in Everyday Life
Robert W. Rieber

THE MASS PSYCHOLOGY OF ETHNONATIONALISM
Dusan Kecmanovic

THE PROCESS APPROACH TO PERSONALITY: Perceptgeneses and Kindred Approaches in Focus
Gudmund J. W. Smith

PSYCHOSOCIAL THEORIES OF THE SELF
Edited by Benjamin Lee

REGIONAL IDENTITY AND BEHAVIOR
Max Sugar

THEORETICAL PSYCHOLOGY: The Meeting of East and West
Anand C. Paranjpe

WILHELM WUNDT IN HISTORY: The Making of a Scientific Psychology
Edited by Robert W. Rieber and David K. Robinson

CULTURAL PSYCHOLOGY

THEORY AND METHOD

CARL RATNER

KLUWER ACADEMIC / PLENUM PUBLISHERS
New York, Boston, Dordrecht, London, Moscow

ISBN 0-306-46660-0

© 2002 Kluwer Academic / Plenum Publishers
233 Spring Street, New York, New York 10013

http://www.wkap.nl/

10 9 8 7 6 5 4 3 2 1

A C.I.P. record for this book is available from the Library of Congress

PREFACE

This book seeks to deepen our understanding of the cultural aspects of human psychology. These are aspects of psychology that originate in, are formed by, reflect, perpetuate, and modify social processes and factors outside the individual mind. My motivation in pursuing cultural psychology is both scientific and political. I believe that construing psychology as a cultural phenomenon is the scientifically correct way to understand psychology; a cultural analysis of psychology can also provide crucial insights for political action to improve human life.

The scientific and political aspects of cultural psychology are interdependent and reciprocally reinforcing. The scientific identification and explanation of cultural aspects of psychology can identify societal changes that will enhance human psychology—to help people become more intelligent, far-sighted, logical, harmonious, helpful, moral, and secure, and less stressful, disturbed, prejudiced, competitive, aggressive, lonely, insecure, depressed, mystified, and irrational. Conversely, the political orientation of cultural psychology to enhance psychological functioning through comprehending and improving the social fabric advances the scientific understanding of psychology as a cultural phenomenon. Social goals direct cultural psychology to devise special theories and methods that investigate cultural origins, formation, characteristics, and functions of psychology. Traditional theories and methods are not necessarily applicable because they are informed by a vision of psychology as individual, biological, or universal.

The scientific study of cultural psychology is a check on political analyses. Without independent scientific information about the effects of culture on people, political analyses are subject to self-confirming, erroneous thinking. History is replete with fervent ideas for improvement which wind up debilitating people. A scientific cultural psychology can help to overcome such errors.

This book develops a scientific, politically useful theory and methodology that can investigate the cultural origins, formation, characteristics, and functions of psychological phenomena.

My theory rests on a conceptual approach called activity theory. Activity theory is the most coherent and profound articulation of the cultural nature of human psychology that I know of. It was introduced by Vygotsky and his Russian colleagues, Luria and Leontiev in the decades following the Russian revolution. I seek to advance their approach by adding points that will make activity theory a more complete and useful theory for cultural psychology.

I also seek to advance the methodology of cultural psychology. I explain the principles of a methodology that can elucidate the distinctive and complex subject matter of cultural psychology. In addition, I develop qualitative methods—especially interview techniques and content analysis—as empirical tools for exploring this subject matter.

This book has benefited enormously from discussions I have had with Paul Dillon, Gil Perez, Luis Zarzoza, Diana Moreno, Olivia Tena, Carlos Kölbl, Sonia Carbonell, and Ruben Rodriguez. Lumei Hui has supported me in many ways which I gratefully acknowledge by dedicating this book to her.

Trinidad, CA
http://www.humboldt1.com/~cr2

Contents

Part 1: Theory 1

Introduction 3

1. *Cultural Psychology from the Perspective of Activity Theory* 9

   The Influence of Cultural Activities on
      Psychological Phenomena 12
   The Influence of Cultural Artifacts on
      Psychological Phenomena 31
   The Influence of Cultural Concepts on
      Psychological Phenomena 34
   The Dialectical Relationship Among Cultural
      Activities, Artifacts, Concepts, and
      Psychological Phenomena 54
   Agency from the Perspective of Activity Theory............. 59
   Advantages of Activity Theory for Cultural Psychology 67
   Notes 71

2. *Individualistic Approaches to Agency: A Critique* 75

   The Individualistic Conception of Agency
      and Culture... 75
   Critique of the Individualistic View 82
   The Scientific and Political Value of Conceptions
      of Agency 95
   Notes 99

Part 2: Method 103

3. *Implications of Activity Theory for Cultural
    Psychological Research* 105

    The Researcher Must Possess a Comprehensive,
      Detailed, Profound Understanding of Social
      Activities, Artifacts, and Concepts to Relate Them to
      Psychological Phenomena 108
    To Elucidate the Specific Cultural Character of
      Psychological Phenomena the Researcher Must
      Construe Them in Concrete Rather than Abstract Terms ... 112
    The Cultural Features of Psychological Phenomena
      Must Be Gleaned from Investigating the Phenomena
      Themselves 113
    Experimental Procedures Are Powerful Tools for
      Indicating the Association Between Psychology,
      Activities, Artifacts, and Concepts 116
    Qualitative Methods Are Necessary for Discerning
      the Cultural Character of Psychological Phenomena 121
    The Qualitative Methods that Investigate Cultural Facets
      of Psychological Phenomena Must Be Rigorous and
      Systematic in Order to Draw Warranted Conclusions 129
    Cultural Features of Psychology Must Be Discerned by the
      Cultural Psychologist Through Skillful, Probing Analysis
      Because People Are Ordinarily Not Aware of Them........ 135
    The Foregoing Principles of Cultural Psychological
      Research Are Applicable to Studying Cultural
      Aspects of Psychological Phenomena in All Societies...... 138
    Notes 140

4. *Interviewing Techniques for Eliciting Cultural–Psychological
    Information* 145

    The Value of Interviews................................. 145
    Formulating Interview Questions........................ 153
    Conducting the Interview 158

5. *A Procedure for Analyzing Cultural Themes in Verbal Accounts* 167

    A Phenomenological Procedure for Identifying
      Psychological Themes in Verbal Accounts 168
    An Application of the Phenomenological
      Procedure to Cultural Psychology....................... 172

A Cultural Analysis of Psychological Themes 177
Objective Determination of Meanings 179
Quantification 183
Notes 185

6. *An Empirical Investigation into the Cultural Psychology
of Children's Moral Reasoning* 187

Theoretical Framework 187
Procedure 194
Results 201
Notes 203

References 205

Index 215

CULTURAL PSYCHOLOGY

Part 1

THEORY

INTRODUCTION

After many decades of self-imposed insulation from cultural issues, psychologists belatedly and reluctantly have been forced to recognize that psychological phenomena are constituted in certain ways by cultural processes. This recognition has led to the development of a field of studies called cultural psychology. Broadly conceived, it seeks to comprehend the ways in which psychological phenomena are part of cultural life and are interdependent with other cultural phenomena. In 1910 Dewey wrote a statement that expresses a central tenet of cultural psychology. He said that the processes that animate and form consciousness lie outside it in social life. Therefore, the objective for psychologists is to use mental phenomena (e.g., perception, emotions) as clues for comprehending the life processes that they represent. This task resembles the paleontologist's who finds a number and variety of footprints. From these he goes to work to construct the structure and the life habits of the animals that made them. Just as the paleontologist would be remiss to restrict his attention to describing footprints themselves, analyzing their elements, comparing them to each other, and discovering the laws of their arrangement in space—while failing to explore the living organisms and habits that they represent—so psychologists are remiss in restricting their attention to describing states of consciousness, their elements, and interactions, while failing to link consciousness to real-life processes of human beings. "The supposition that these states [of consciousness] are somehow existent by themselves and in this existence provide the psychologist with ready-made material is just the supreme case of the 'psychological fallacy'" (Dewey, 1910, p. 250; see also Vygotsky, 1997a, pp. 272–273, 327 for a remarkably similar statement).

Of course, psychological phenomena have a more complex relationship to social life than footprints have to forces that form them. However, Dewey is metaphor correctly emphasizes the social formation of the psyche.

3

Studying cultural processes in order to understand psychology is a daunting task. It requires a specific, comprehensive conceptualization of what culture is and how it encompasses human psychology (see Ratner, 2000a).

Progress in this area is difficult for several reasons. The structures of modern societies militate against scientifically understanding psychology as a cultural phenomenon. Social life in contemporary societies appears to be a myriad of diverse factors that have no ostensible relationship to each other. Furthermore, each individual occupies diverse social positions, is exposed to diverse information, and has substantial freedom of choice. Given this dizzying diversity, how can there be anything coherent we can call "culture"? And how can a dizzying diversity of cultural factors be related to human psychology in any meaningful way, especially when human psychology appears to be dizzyingly diverse? Individuals seem to differ enormously in their perceptions, emotions, reasoning, memory, and intelligence. If culture and psychology are indefinite, incoherent, and ineffable then no systematic relationship could exist between them.

Difficulties in relating psychology to culture are compounded by the institution specialization of psychology as an academic discipline. Segregated from social sciences such as sociology, anthropology, history, and political science, psychology appears to be unrelated to the social issues that are covered by these disciplines.

An additional factor that obscures the cultural nature of psychology is Western ideology. It tends to regard human psychology as an individual or universal phenomenon, equally unrelated to social factors.

These obstacles have impeded the development of cultural psychology (see Ratner, 1993a, 1997b, 1999 for examples). Most cultural psychologists manifest little interest in formulating a specific and thorough conception of culture to guide their work. They often satisfy themselves with casual, incomplete, and implicit notions such as "Psychological processes take place in cultural settings," "Psychological processes are socially constructed and shared," "Psychological processes are mediated by cultural tools" (Wertsch), and "Cultural psychology is the study of intentional worlds" (Shweder). Cultural psychologists rarely consult sociological or historical research concerning the formation, maintenance, and change of social organizations, classes, conditions, norms, and systems. Most cultural psychologists express the belief that they are abandoning psychology if they systematically study culture. Many anthropologists and psychologists tend to regard culture as a platform on which psychology stands. The platform model acknowledges that people in New Guinea and Germany behave, reason, remember, feel, and perceive in different ways. It tells us *that* these phenomena are cultural; however, it does not tell us *how* they are cultural—that is, what they have to do with the particular societies in which they occur. The very connection between culture and psychology is suspended although psychology is recognized as occurring in (or on) culture. This kind of research requires no familiarity with social systems because it describes psychological phenomena per se.

Even research from the positivistic standpoint, which attempts to correlate specific cultural factors with psychological phenomena, generally overlooks the internal relationship, between them. It discovers that commercial activity, for example, is associated with depression. However, it does not disclose how depression recapitulates commerce, or how the characteristics of depression reflect commerce. Thus, the *cultural character* of depression is obscured even though its correlation with a cultural factor has been identified.

Lacking a specific and thorough conception of culture has led to eclecticism in cultural psychology. Virtually any topic, theoretical viewpoint, and methodology are accepted within the rubric of cultural psychology. There is little integration of hypotheses or findings. In addition, many crucial components of culture are overlooked or discounted. The result is little agreement or understanding about the cultural aspects of psychology—or what it means to say that psychology is cultural.

The disinterest in culture reaches its apex in postmodernist notions of culture, agency, and psychology. Postmodernism renounces culture as a set of shared psychological phenomena that are grounded in organized social life. Postmodernists construe society as inchoate, indefinite, and incapable of providing a structure to psychological phenomena. They also construe society as depersonalized and deleterious so that individuals must find fulfillment in personal acts apart from social influence. In this view, individuals must form their own personal psychologies on the basis of unique needs and choices. This antisocial view of psychology has squelched the promise of cultural psychology to deepen our understanding of cultural aspects of psychology.

To be worthy of its name, cultural psychology must penetrate beneath apparent fragmentation, incoherence, and disorder to discover regularities and relationships. This, after all, is the task of all science. Just as natural science has discovered parsimonious principles and laws that integrally explain an enormous diversity of seemingly disparate phenomena—the falling of an apple and the revolving of planets are all forms of gravity—so social science can discover that culture is an organized, coherent system; psychological phenomena are socially shared and distributed; and psychological phenomena have definite social origins, characteristics, and functions. As Hegel said, the real is rational.

Developing the science of cultural psychology requires a renewed commitment to deeply understand culture both in general terms ("What is human culture?") and in specific terms ("What is Polish culture?"). A concentrated analysis of culture is necessary to provide a conceptual basis to cultural psychology that will explain the cultural origins, formation, and function of psychological phenomena. An analysis of culture will also elucidate the active role of human agency within social life.

In the first part of this book I articulate a specific and comprehensive conception of culture. I identify its crucial components, the manner in which they are integrated together, and the role of psychological phenomena within them. My theoretical perspective draws on Vygotsky's activity theory. I seek to develop its philosophical and political underpinnings in new ways that can guide cultural psychology to become a scientific discipline with practical importance.

In Part 2 I develop methodological procedures for testing the theoretical issues raised in Part 1. I explain the principles of a methodology that can elucidate the distintive and complex subject matter of cultural psychology. I explain how interview techniques can be refined to probe for cultural themes in psychological phenomena. I also explain how narrative statements can be analyzed to elucidate cultural themes. The final chapter designs an empirical investigation into the cultural psychology of moral reasoning in children. It conceptualizes cultural aspects of moral reasoning which are typically overlooked in structuralist accounts such as Kohlberg's. It then describes a procedure for identifying cultural aspects of moral reasoning. This project brings together theoretical and empirical issues that have been discussed in earlier chapters.

The theoretical and methodological approach I outline is not meant to apply to every aspect of human psychology. My approach is confined to describing and explaining the specific cultural content that is embedded in psychological phenomena shared by members of a particular society (or subsociety). In other words, I seek to describe and explain the characteristics of psychological phenomena that originate in, are formed by, and function to promulgate particular cultural activities, artifacts, and concepts that comprise a definite social system. Other aspects of psychology are comprised of idiosyncratic features that originate in unique experiences and biological processes of an individual. For example, a boy who is raised by a soft-spoken mother may grow up to be soft-spoken. His manner is more a function of his idiosyncratic experience than of prevalent social activities. Or a girl whose father committed suicide in her presence becomes insecure and paranoid. These psychological phenomena are the province of clinical psychology, not cultural psychology.

In addition, there are general aspects of human psychology that are common to all people. These psychological universals include the fact that all humans engage in self-reflection and volitional action, are profoundly open to experience and learning, understand the nature of things and use this understanding to solve problems intelligently, communicate via language, think and remember in symbolic terms, organize emotions and perceptions around cognitive interpretations, and engage in logical reasoning. These universal, general aspects of human psychology are devoid of content and they do not reflect particular social activities, artifacts, or concepts. They evidently depend on some social experience, as its absence impedes the development of these general psychological features (Ratner, 1991, pp. 11–68). However, they seem to reflect general aspects of social experience rather than specific characteristics. For instance, parental regulation of behavior may be necessary to foster self-control, volition, planning, and self-consciousness. The general occurrence of parents interrupting, guiding, and encouraging behavior fosters these in all children, regardless of the specific manner in which parents exercise this regulation. The specific manner in which regulation is exercised—for example, by verbal threats, physical constraint, patient explanation, tolerance for continued impulsiveness on the part of the child—would affect the specific content of the child's self-concept, volition, and emotional expression (Ratner, 1991, pp. 113–198).

The cultural psychology that I outline in this book is confined to describing and explaining specific, content-laden characteristics of psychology. I concentrate on this domain because it has tremendous (but undeveloped) potential for enhancing our understanding of human psychology. It also contains the greatest potential for practically improving psychological functioning. We can alter cultural factors that affect the psychology of many people, whereas general aspects of psychology (e.g., emotions depend on cognitive appraisals) cannot be altered, and individual aspects can be altered only in piecemeal fashion, and even this is difficult as long as social activities, artifacts, and concepts continue to foster them.

1

CULTURAL PSYCHOLOGY FROM THE PERSPECTIVE OF ACTIVITY THEORY

Culture is a system of enduring behavioral and thinking patterns that are created, adopted, and promulgated by a number of individuals jointly. These patterns are social (supraindividual) rather than individual, and they are artifactual rather than natural. Psychological phenomena are cultural insofar as they are social artifacts, more specifically, insofar as their content, mode of operation, and dynamic relationships are:

- Socially created and shared by a number of individuals.
- Integrated with other social artifacts.

For example, modern romantic love has certain qualities—being intense, sensual, disorienting, and personal—that are cultural because (a) they were initially developed by a group of people, namely the rising middle class of the 18th century in England; and (b) the qualities of love were fostered by, and reflected, the increasingly popular notion of an individualistic self, the free market, the pursuit of material pleasure, and the opposition of personal/family affairs to public activities. Thus, romantic love was socially created and shared by a number of individuals, and it depended on, embodied, and perpetuated various cultural concepts/values and activities.

Cultural psychology studies the content, mode of operation, and interrelationships of psychological phenomena that are socially constructed and shared, and are rooted in other social artifacts. It investigates the cultural origins, formation, and characteristics of psychological phenomena as well as the ways that psychological phenomena perpetuate and modify other cultural artifacts.

9

Vygotsky enumerated three cultural factors that organize psychology:

1. *Activities* such as producing goods, raising children, educating the populace, devising and implementing laws, treating disease, playing, and producing art.
2. *Artifacts* including tools, books, paper, pottery, weapons, eating utensils, clocks, clothing, buildings, furniture, toys, and technology.
3. *Concepts* about things and people. For example, the succession of forms that the concept of person has taken in the life of men in different societies varies with their system of law, religion, customs, social structures, and mentality (Mauss, 1938/1985, p. 3).

These three factors interact in complex, dynamic ways with each other and with psychological phenomena. The system of cultural activities, artifacts, concepts, and psychological phenomena is culture. Vygotsky emphasized that social activities exert more influence on the system than the other factors do. The reason is that humans survive and achieve self-realization through socially organized activities. To eat, a number of people have to organize together in a coordinated pattern of behavior to gather, hunt, or produce the food. In addition, they must socially coordinate ancillary tasks such as making requisite tools, containers, storage and cooking facilities, and means of transportation. The manner in which we organize food production and distribution determines how many people work in that undertaking, the kind and level of remuneration they receive, the kinds of routines and interactions they have, the tools they employ, how much food is provided to particular individuals in society, and thus the physical survival and health of whole sections of the population. Possessing such vital importance for existence, activities are basic to the ways in which an individual interacts with the world of objects, other people, and even himself (Vygotsky, 1997b, pp. 5, 53–54, 133; see Malinowski, 1944, pp. 36–54).[1]

Vygotsky explained the formative influence of activities on psychology as follows: "The structures of higher mental functions represent a cast of collective social relations between people. These [mental] structures are nothing other than a transfer into the personality of an inward relation of a social order that constitutes the basis of the social structure of the human personality" (Vygotsky, 1998, pp. 169–170; see Ratner, 1997a, Chap. 3, 1999, pp. 10–12, 2000a,b for discussion of this approach).

Leontier (1981, p. 222) similarly stated that "changes take place in the course of historical development in the general character of men's consciousness that are engendered by changes in their mode of life." (see also Leontier, 1979)

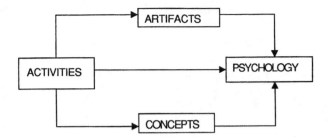

FIGURE 1.1. Psychology, activities, artifacts, and concepts according to Vygotsky.

Vygotsky's activity theory can be represented in Fig. 1.1.

Figure 1.1 emphasizes the dependence of psychology on the other cultural factors and the dominance of activities over all the factors. The real situation is more complex and dynamic. It contains reciprocal influences among the factors, and it is animated by intentionality, teleology, or agency. Vygotsky (1997a, p. 206) emphasized that "Man's relationship to his surroundings must always bear the character of purposefulness, of activity, and not simple dependence."

Vygotsky outlined the foregoing points about culture and psychology. Unfortunately, he never developed them in depth. He made scattered, general comments about the importance of culture, activity, social environment, social system, social role, social relationships, social class, social conditions, tools, and ideology in forming psychological phenomena. However, he failed to rigorously define these terms or demonstrate their relation to psychology. Activity theory is thus more of a conceptual framework than a specific theory regarding connections between sociohistorical processes and individual functioning (Gauvain, 1993, p. 94). Vygotsky's research rarely scratched the surface of institutional and ideological influences on psychological formation. His research primarily concerned interpersonal influences (between caretaker and child) on psychological development (see Ratner, 1997a, chap. 3, 1999, pp. 12–14 for discussion of this point).

For cultural psychology to advance, Vygotsky's points must be developed. We must comprehend the nature of cultural activities, artifacts, and concepts, the manner in which these organize psychological phenomena, and the complex, reciprocal relationships among these four factors. The role of agency in these factors and interrelationships must also be explored.

Exploring activity, artifacts, and cultural concepts in a work on psychology may appear excessively sociological to the psychologically oriented reader. However, as Dewey explained in the Introduction, this is the only way to comprehend the cultural aspects of psychology. If cultural factors and processes constitute the content, mode of operation, and dynamics of psychological phenomena, then we must look outside the individual mind to comprehend the content, mode of operation, and dynamics of psychological phenomena. If we focus exclusively on consciousness itself, we will fail to understand the manner in which it is constituted by cultural factors and processes.

THE INFLUENCE OF CULTURAL ACTIVITIES ON PSYCHOLOGICAL PHENOMENA

Cultural Activities

Lacking biological determinants of how to behave, humans produce their existence by devising actions. We construct actions to realize ourselves—i.e., make ourselves real. Constructed actions are first and foremost designed to satisfy fundamental needs. These "existential needs" include the need for means of subsistence, raising and educating children, treating disease, deriving entertainment, defense against attack, esthetic and spiritual fulfillment, gathering and disseminating information. Actions that address these general needs are what we designate as family, economy, education, medicine, recreation, military, news reporting, art, and religion. Such actions are coordinated among large numbers of people because collective action is far more effective than individual behavior. Thus, we find that a particular mode of economic production and distribution, education, family, medical care, government, mode of receiving information, and form of entertainment is dominant throughout a population of people. Widely shared, socially organized actions which address fundamental needs of existence I call cultural activities.

Cultural activities are the categories of social life—social life is categorized into education, family, politics, medical care, religion, law, production of material goods. Their general forms are universal—all people raise and educate children, produce material goods, etc. However, in practice, cultural activities are carried out in specific ways in different societies. Indeed, a society is defined by the specific ways in which cultural activities are conducted and existential needs are met. A cultural activity is defined by the social relations and rules of conduct that govern it. Within a particular society there may be variations in a particular activity—education may take different forms in private schools and in public schools, cooperative businesses may co-exist with capitalist corporations. However, one form of an activity normally dominates the other forms of that activity.

Cultural activities are forms of social life that a population constructs to satisfy fundamental, existential needs. Cultural activities are not mundane, personal acts; nor are they non-descript instrumental, intention, tool-mediated acts. Cultural activities may exist at different degrees of formal institutionalization. Economic, political, educational, medical, military, and religious activities are tightly organized with definite leaders, explicit rules, supervisors who oversee whether rules are obeyed and mete out sanctions for violating them. Family relations, at least in modern capitalist societies, are less formally organized. There are general rights and obligations which are mandated by government policies and laws (Cott, 2000), however, these do not prescribe specific behaviors in the way that work rules are prescribed by a manager or religious observances are prescribed by the church hierarchy. Friendships and dating are even less formally institutionalized—although, we shall see that they are governed by definite norms.

Activities are social products that transcend individual people. Although they are formed and maintained by individuals, activities are not individual acts. Rather, as Durkheim emphasized, people form collective activities which transcend any individual because the final product is a compromise among numerous people (cf. Ratner, 1999, pp. 21–22; Harre, 1984; White, 1949, pp. 121–145).

The fact that activities are socially constructed does not mean that they are democratically constructed and controlled. Most activities are controlled by powerful elites rather than by the majority of people who engage in them.

The social nature of activities gives them coercive power over individuals. Once regular, regulated, interlocking patterns of behavior become established, individuals must conform to their requirements. (Later on I shall discuss the fact that individuals can alter social activities.) Individuals who do not cooperate are punished in two ways. They are excluded from rewards that accrue to those who perform successfully. In the competitive market place, for example, the businesswoman who does not engage in competitive business practices (expanding market share, lowering prices, etc.) loses money until she withdraws from the activity. When an activity has been formally institutionalized in an organization (a school, factory, laboratory, military unit, government agency), nonconformers can be punished by administrators of these enterprises. University professors, for example, can be deprived of travel funds, research grants, and publishing opportunities if their behavior does not conform to standards set by university administrators and journal editors.

Activities possess certain general, universal features as well as specific, variable ones. The general features of all activities are:

- They aim at various objectives, for example, to provide a social service, or make a profit for the owner.

- They are divided into particular tasks.
- Each task entails status, rewards (including remuneration), opportunities, rights, and responsibilities.
- Each task is governed by norms that are enforced formally or informally.
- The norms for each task govern physical behavior (e.g., how rapidly or frequently a certain behavior is to occur) and social relationships among participants (how they treat each other).
- Qualifications (such as experience, education, ethnicity, class, gender, age, appearance) are stipulated for engaging in particular tasks.
- They are related to other activities in a division of labor.

These general, universal features of an activity take specific and distinctive forms in particular historical periods. Farming, for example, is a basic, central activity for all peoples; however, its specific characteristics differ greatly in different societies. It is important to explore these specific social characteristics because they impart distinctive features to psychological phenomena, as we shall soon explain.

In subsistence farming, which was widespread in colonial North America, food products were home grown by a family. Growing food was integrated with family life; food products were directly consumed by the producers and they were not usually exchanged for money on a commercial market. Family members did the work without financial remuneration. There was little internal division of labor of tasks, and each family member contributed to a wide range of jobs. The work occurred through direct personal relationships among the family members; these relationships were cooperative, as everyone was working for a common purpose to produce more food for the family. The food that was produced by labor was shared among all the family members without regard for the amount of labor that anyone had contributed; and the rewards, rights, and responsibilities of all the workers were similar.

Today, farming in the United States is an entirely different kind of activity. It is organized primarily by huge corporations that are privately owned by a small number of individuals, who also own the natural resources and instruments. Farming is internally differentiated into an enormous number of specialized positions, from corporate executive to farm manager to secretary to farm worker; farm hands and secretaries have limited responsibilities while owners/managers have more extensive responsibilities. Owners/managers have the right to set the conditions of work for the thousands of employees who work under them; rewards and opportunities are limited for the workers, but are great for the owners and managers. Work is routine and sometimes dangerous for workers whereas it is more creative, interesting, and safe for owners/managers. All individuals in this activity are afforded a great deal of legal independence—entrepreneurs and workers are legally free to sell their goods and services on the market, are free to decide where to look for jobs, how long to work at a job, and what kind of enterprise to establish.[2] For owners/managers, the main objective of producing food is maximizing profit for themselves; they treat food as a commodity—that is, as a means to earn money. Owners/managers treat employees as a commodity to be bought at an appropriate price for a temporary period to serve as a means for generating profit. The main objective of workers is earning money for themselves. Relationships between workers and owners are competitive; relationships among workers themselves are also often largely competitive although solidarity is occasionally manifested. Owners of farms also generally compete with one another although they occasionally form alliances. Work is remunerated by a monetary wage. Qualifications to be an owner of a farm include financial expertise. The production of food is segregated from the production of other goods (such as steel, airplanes, and books) and from other activities such as art, education, entertainment, and the family.

Activity theory maintains that sociohistorical aspects of an activity impart a distinctive content and mode of operation to participants' psychological phenomena. The ways in which people treat each other, as well as their ways of treating and being subject to things, structure emotions, perceptions, memory, intelligence, personality, and other psychological phenomena. Tomasello (1998, pp. 221–222) states this well in regard to children: "Human children participate in a variety of social practices that antedate their arrival in the culture—including games, scripts, rituals, instructional formats, and other forms of prepackaged communal activities (often involving artifacts). These social practices serve to motivate children toward certain goals, to instruct them in the pursuit of those goals, and, in general, to potentiate cognitive skills that would not develop in social isolation."

Gerth and Mills (1953) provide a detailed account of how social activity influences psychology. The authors state that any activity is internally divided into roles and that each role entails distinctive rights, responsibilities, norms, opportunities, limitations, rewards, and qualifications. For instance, the activity of law includes the roles of judge, defense attorney, prosecuting attorney, jury, and defendant. The activity of art includes roles of artist, director/owner of art galleries and museums, art viewers, and buyers. Higher education includes roles of administrators, teachers, students, and governing boards. (This kind of analysis falls within the rubric of the sociology of institutions; see Powell & DiMaggio, 1991.) It is these distinctive characteristics of a role that shape the occupants' psychology (Gerth & Mills, 1953, p. 11). "By his experience in enacting various roles, the person incorporates certain objectives and values which steer and direct his conduct, as well as the elements of his psychic structure" (ibid., p. 22). "Expertness at fulfilling some role often involves psychic training: it involves learning what to look for as well as the meaning of what is seen" (ibid., p. 70). "His memory, his sense of time and space, his perception, his motives, his conception of his self, his psychological functions are shaped and steered by the specific configuration of roles which he incorporates from his society" (ibid., p. 11).

The social role is the link between activity and psychology. It is the site where an individual enacts a particular portion of an activity and structures his psychology in accordance with this action. "The concept of role, the key term in our definition of the person, is also the key term in our definition of institution. It is, therefore, in our definitional model, the major link of character and social structure" (ibid., pp. 22–23; see Bhaskar, 1989, pp. 40–41). Bourdieu (2000, p. 134) also emphasizes social role as the point of contact at which the individual meets the social system: "Social agents ... are situated in a place in social space, a distinct and distinctive place which can be characterized by the position it occupies relative to other places (above, below, between, etc.) and the distance that separates it from them" (see also Nadel, 1957).

The social role may be the "unit of analysis" of activity theory—the locus where psychology takes on a cultural form. In other words, when we wish to analyze the cultural quality of an emotion, a personality trait, a cognitive ability, or a perceptual phenomenon, we must (provisionally) conceive them as being aspects of social roles. We would investigate the (possible) interdependence between the specific aspects of specific roles and psychological phenomena. In Bourdieu's terms we would ascertain the extent to which psychological dispositions are a function of social positions (Bourdieu, 1993, p. 30).

Social role is useful for cultural psychology because it designates a historically specific set of norms, rights, responsibilities, and qualifications. Thus, student, child, farmer, soldier, politician, and wife are not abstract roles undertaking general actions such as "learning," "growing up," "growing crops," "defending territory," "making policies," and "caring for a husband," respectively. Roles are specific, distinctive ways of acting and interacting, as we have seen in the case of farming. These ways comprise the cultural character of a role.

One of the determinants of role specificity is its position vis-à-vis other roles *within* an activity. Merton (1968, pp. 422–438) calls this "the role set" of any given role. The role set of a medical student, for example, is the relationships he or she has with teachers, nurses, patients, social workers, and other students. All of these interactions in the role set determine the nature of a given role, for example, medical student. Occupants of a role set may have differing expectations and treatments of a role occupant. Parents, school board members, students, and the principal may have different expectations and treatments of a teacher, for example. This introduces great complexity, instability, and stress into the teacher role.

Another factor that introduces cultural specificity to a role is its position vis-à-vis roles in *other* activities. Activities stand in an external division of labor to each other, and the particular relationship of a given activity to others affects the roles within it (see Bourdieu, 1998a, p. 39; Engestrom, 1993, pp. 72–74; Ratner, 1997a, pp. 54–57, 64–66, 77–78, 154–157; Swartz, 1997, Chap. 6). The roles of doctor and patient within medical activity have become dramatically altered in recent years as a result of external corporate pressures by pharmaceutical companies and insurance companies.

In the external division of labor among activities, a particular role or activity may be influenced to a greater or lesser extent by particular other activities. In capitalist countries, politics is influenced more by economic activities than it is by family activities. (The influence that any one activity has on particular others may vary with class, ethnic group, and gender.) Activities differ in the extent of their autonomy from other fields (Bourdieu, 1996, pp. 217–223). In capitalist countries, natural science is an activity that commands a great deal of autonomy from other activities. Scientists pursue their research with little ideological interference. The social sciences, in contrast, are thoroughly dominated by social and political ideologies.

The degree of autonomy an activity has is determined by a social struggle. Businessmen in the 19th century desired economic freedom and they worked to exclude personal issues from work. They relegated personal issues to the family, which became a distinct activity for the first time in history. Business and political leaders similarly worked to separate religion from government.

Members of an activity may also work to incorporate features of another activity. Women seek to correct power imbalances in the family by utilizing commercial calculations of labor time to equalize the housework that husbands and wives do. Workers attempt to restructure their relationship with managers by infusing political forms of democracy into the workplace. Students seek to enliven their educational activity by requesting that entertainment programs be incorporated into classrooms and recesses. Children request that parents express love by buying commercial products from the economic realm. Increasing or decreasing the distinctiveness of roles/activities alters their character. It also alters the psychology of the participants.[3]

The entire system of activities including the internal and external division of labor depends on an active struggle among competing interest groups. Whether businessmen and -women can successfully commercialize education, the media, politics, medical care, science, and family life depends on a struggle with groups who oppose this. Whether university presidents and trustees can successfully eliminate tenure and usurp decision-making authority from professors depends on the strength of resistance from the latter (Bourdieu, 1996, pp. 223–227, 1998a, pp. 40–41). Recognizing the active struggle involved in constructing and maintaining a system of activities, Vygotsky said, "The social environment comprises an inexhaustible collection of the most diverse aspects and elements which are always in the most outright contradiction with each other … We should not think of the environment as a whole as a static, elemental, and stable system of elements, but rather as a dialectically developing dynamic process" (Vygotsky, 1997a, p. 205). Although struggle is continuous and change is always possible, at any given time one interest group is dominant and imposes its will on the others. Capitalistic economic relationships are dominating all countries in the world right now despite the resistance of labor and environmental groups. Of course, these groups may eventually become more powerful and alter the existing economic activities; however, business activities are clearly dominant over most other activities at this time.

The fact that an individual occupies different roles in different activities makes one's social experience diverse. The characteristics of one's psychological phenomena are heterogeneous as well. A worker may be emotionally constrained at work yet expressive at home. She may conform to work rules yet be independent with friends. An individual who occupies a prestigious, interesting job may be poorly educated. Others who occupy menial jobs may have been well educated. Consequently, not all poor people, rich people, doctors, factory workers, farmers, or secretaries as a group have the same experiences or psychology.

While diversity in an individual's social experience and psychological organization exists, it is limited by factors that promote consistency. One such factor is the uniformity of different activities. Many activities have fallen prey to commodification, competition, alienation, materialism, the profit motive, and individualism. Thus, participants of many activities will nevertheless encounter similar treatments and experiences.

Another factor that promotes consistency of experience is the fact that one role may be more influential than others and may shape a person's experience throughout many roles/activities. The demands of the worker role may be so powerful that they lead the factory worker to be unemotional at home as well as at work. Likewise, workers whose economic role provides them with relatively little income and limited intellectual skills will live in inferior housing, speak and dress poorly, and will be treated with condescension in stores, real estate offices, police departments, and credit agencies. *One's working role may thus determine one's class position* in other activities. This relatively homogeneous pattern of experiences would foster a relatively consistent psychology throughout numerous activities.

Social psychological consistency extends across generations from parents to children. One's class position imparts a uniform character to many experiences and psychological phenomena of one's children. Class position structures children's early family interactions and education which ultimately shape their qualification for adult occupation. In a study of business elites in France and Germany, Hartmann (2000) found that adult members of the upper class provide their children with "cultural capital" in the form of educational experiences and personality traits—a "class-specific habitus." Elite youngsters are then able to successfully obtain prestigious jobs that the economy presents. In France and Germany, 80% of senior business executives are recruited from the social elite, which comprises only 4% of the population. Young people from the middle and lower classes are not provided the cultural capital (including psychological capabilities) to obtain these jobs. This evidence indicates that substantial homogeneity of experience exists throughout children's family, educational, and subsequent occupational activities.

Additional evidence comes from studies on the school success of American and British children. The school success of English 10-year-old children relates strongly to their preparedness for literacy on entry to school at age 5, which in turn relates directly to early literacy practices in the home before the age of 5 (e.g., parents' playing alphabet games, reading books aloud with great affect, asking children pictures about pictures in books, encouraging children to pretend they can read before they actually can, letting children manipulate magnetic letters on a refrigerator, watching educational television programs), all of which relate most directly to children's social class (Gee, 1992, p. 124). Gee explains how literacy socialization actually serves a broad social function of preparing the child for an entire life style that continues the life style of the parents: "When a parent asks a young child 'What's that?' of a picture in a picture book, the parent is not, in fact, trying to teach the child the skills of how to answer 'what questions.' Rather, this is merely a small part of what the parent does with the child in order to introduce the child into a characteristic (socially and culturally specific) *way of doing things*, into a particular *form of life*, in the case, how people 'like us' approach books (talk about, read, value, use, and integrate them with other activities)." "What is happening is that the child is being *socialized* into certain ways of being in the world, ways intimately connected to the sociocultural identity of the child's group, as well as to their power and status in the world" (ibid., p. 124). The way of being in the world encompasses a variety of activities that share a common character.

Eckert (1989) reports similar evidence that class position shapes adolescents' social and educational styles. High school students who dress fashionably, participate in school activities (including student government and sports), and study hard and get good grades are generally from the middle class whereas disaffected students who have poor study habits and grades, eschew school activities, dress sloppily, and get into trouble are typically from the working class. These two styles, which Eckert labels "Jocks" and "Burnouts," respectively, are proxies for social class in adolescent school behavior. Furthermore, these two styles implicitly prepare the participants to remain in their class positions by cultivating class-appropriate perceptions, emotions, cognitive processes, and personality attributes. "A conspiracy of factors conspires to lead the children of parents of different socioeconomic statuses into strikingly different roles in adolescence, and these roles in time prepare the individuals for their places in adult society" (ibid., p. 175).[4]

The form of activity is the way in which the participants actually act, not the way they are supposed to perform. Often, official pronouncements of activity obscure real practices by leaders and subordinates. Laws are often unequally enforced despite official proclamations of uniformity. Politics are often controlled by rich people despite official proclamations of democracy. Education is often treated as a commodity despite official proclamations that it fosters a regard for pure knowledge. Marriage is often conflictual and depersonalizing despite official proclamations of harmonious love and devotion. Workers may sabotage work and produce inferior products despite the fact that work is supposed to be efficient and of high caliber. Government programs may disenfranchise people despite official proclamations that they empower people. Psychotherapy may work to control and mystify patients despite official proclamations of therapeutic empowerment.

The real character of an activity, including its specific roles and its independence or dependence on other activities, must be empirically ascertained (Bourdieu, 1996, pp. 181, 199). Whether "wage laborer" is a social role depends on how homogeneous the social relationships of wage laborers are. If the vast majority of wage laborers do, in fact, have similar social relationships that circumscribe their work experience then the wage laborer is a heuristic construct. However, if it turns out that wage laborers comprise a wide range of social relationships—from factory worker to salesperson to executive secretary to farm worker to professor to account executive to movie actress to computer engineer—that have little in common, then the wage laborer would be an abstraction that has no useful empirical referent. The same holds for "woman," "mother," and other purported roles.

The construct of a social role denotes a position in an organized activity. However, people engage in numerous informal activities that are not structured into formal roles. Talking with a friend, shopping, dating, watching a movie, reading a newspaper, and going on a picnic are examples. However, these informal acts are nevertheless greatly affected by formal activities (Gerth & Mills, 1953, p. 434). In the first place, the very fact that these actions occur in the interstices of organized activities imparts a particular cultural quality to them. The fact that friendships and dating occur outside of economic activity (rather than within work as was more common in earlier times, when marriages were arranged for economic purposes based on economic calculations and criteria) imbues them with a highly personalized, escapist, antisocial quality. Thus, the social position of informal actions outside formal institutions affects their quality.

In addition, class background inculcates attitudes, cognitive processes, motivation, perceptions, emotions, personality attributes, and particular skills that carry over into informal activities. Eckert describes how friendship groups, dress styles, and drug use (including cigarettes) reflect socioeconomic class. Moreover, informal actions draw upon a host of cultural models that are generated by organized activities. These include all sorts of cultural concepts such as individualism, competition, achievement, and wealth. Informal roles that involve several individuals are governed by informal norms. A person who violates norms of friendship or dating is quickly shunned by others.

Finally, leaders of institutionalized activities constantly strive to influence informal activities that are outside their direct control. A case in point is shopping. Although consumers are not organized in an institution that sanctions particular behaviors, they are heavily influenced by a bombardment of advertising messages that effectively control their behavior. There is little difference between the regularity and predictability of informal shopping during Thanksgiving and Christmas that is inspired by advertising and the formally sanctioned behaviors of people in organized institutions. Actually, being a consumer is partly an institutionalized role. While shopping, purchasing, or returning an item the individual occupies the role of a customer. Although this role is quite marginal and of very short duration (unlike that of employees and managers), it entails rights, responsibilities, qualifications, opportunities, and restrictions. The customer has the right to expect truthful information about the product and the right to return the product if it is defective; she is obliged to wait on line to purchase the product; she must pay her bill on time; interact with sales people in a certain manner; cannot smoke in most shops; restaurants, or airplanes; and cannot talk in a movie theater. Thus, a given action such as consumerism may include a noninstitutionalized component (in which individuals decide whether, when, and what to buy outside of institutional norms) and an institutionalized component (in which individuals participate in established procedures while shopping, purchasing, and returning items).

Cultural Activities Structure Psychological Phenomena

The foregoing discussion of cultural activities was designed to illuminate their full, rich character that they impart to psychological phenomena. Cultural activities give form to psychological phenomena by imparting a specific content and mode of operation to them. Social activities are "cultural amplifiers" of general human capabilities. They structure our unformed capacity for intelligence, learning, memory, reasoning, perceiving, feeling, imagining, and language in particular ways. Ogbu explained this quite profoundly with regard to intelligence:

> Cultural activities are amplifiers when they require, stimulate, increase, or expand the quantity, quality, and cultural values of adaptive intellectual skills. Some obvious cultural amplifiers in Western middle-class eco-cultural niches include handling technology, participation in a large-scale economy, negotiating bureaucracy, and urban life. These cultural activities require and enhance intellectual skills such as abstract thinking, conceptualization, grasping relations, and symbolic thinking that permeate other aspects of life. Each eco-cultural niche presents a wide array of cultural amplifiers of the intellectual skills that are required for success in that particular niche. Different eco-cultural niches require different repertoires of intellectual skills. Some skills enhanced by activities specific to one niche may also be of value in other eco-cultural niches. Other examples of cultural amplifiers and the associated intellectual skills found in various eco-cultural niches are pottery making–conservation, market trading–mathematics, foraging–spatial perception, video games–spatial perception, and verbal games–verbal abilities.
>
> Cross-cultural studies of cultural amplifiers of intelligence suggest at least two conclusions. First, intellectual skills prevalent or considered important are not the same in all populations. They depend on the cultural amplifiers in the eco-cultural niche. Second, normal members of all human populations can acquire new intellectual skills, including those included in IQ tests because all normal human beings possess the panhuman genotypic ability to do so. We observe this capability when individuals enter new eco-cultural niches through migration, when formal Western schooling is introduced, and when social and economic circumstances change. (Ogbu & Stein 2001, pp. 8–9)

Social activities (along with artifacts, and cultural concepts) organize psychological phenomena in two broad ways. They directly mold psychological phenomena by treating individuals in particular ways. They also act indirectly as models which individuals draw on to construct their psychology.

Examples of direct treatment of people include requiring them to work in particular ways (e.g., quickly, without questioning, without considering personal needs); firing them summarily; making them wait a long time to receive medical service; performing medical services impersonally without explanation; discriminating against certain categories of people; cramming hundreds of college students into huge lecture halls to listen to a professor's lecture; imposing educational requirements on students and punishing them for not complying; treating children consistently and patiently; forcing children to solve problems on their own to become independent; punishing children for using other people's things; placing babies in separate rooms to sleep; devoting attention to and smiling at pretty girls; instructing children not to talk with their mouths full of food; doctors directing patients to change their patterns of exercise, work, and eating; telling boys that crying is something only girls do and criticizing boys when they do cry; placing green and blue color chips in different piles before babies to show them that the two colors form two color categories rather than one.

Social activities (and artifacts and cultural concepts) also affect psychology indirectly by serving as models to imitate. The manner in which parents treat each other is a model that children use in interacting with people. Gender images in the media are another indirect social influence on psychology. These images present activities, artifacts, and concepts as images or models that viewers utilize in fashioning psychological phenomena. Viewers of the media are not directly forced to act in particular ways by these images; they are not even directly told that they should act in those stereotypical ways or threatened with punishment if they do not. Rather, the images serve as models that viewers strive to imitate. The more pervasive a particular model is—in advertisements, television programs, movies, magazine articles, educational materials—the more influence it has. People do not freely choose the models they adopt. Their choices are influenced by the pervasiveness of the model and also its congruence with their role in activities.

One psychological competence that activities organize is reading. Cressy (1983) shows that reading is inspired by socially organized activity. Historical evidence from the 16th through the 18th centuries reveals that "literacy was…an appropriate tool for a particular range of activities" (p. 37). The most important social activities for inspiring reading were economic ones: "The social distribution of literacy in preindustrial England was more closely associated with economic activities than with anything else" (ibid., p. 37). Cressy presents a clear activity theory account of reading in showing concentrations of literacy in geographical places where reading and writing were especially applicable economically, and among social groups whose economic need for literacy was likewise developed. There are of course exceptions and counterexamples, but the central tendency is clear.

> In France, for example, the north and east were more accomplished than the south and west. The far north of England was more illiterate than the area around London, while the English settlers of Massachusetts Bay were much more fluent with reading and writing than their contemporaries in the outlying parts of New England or in the southern colonies. Cultural and ideological pressures were certainly influential, but the factor which ties together these pathfinder regions for literacy was their level of economic development. Their overall environment was more demanding of literacy. This is even more clear at the local level. Farming communities were less literate than trading communities, while within the world of agriculture there were cultural, educational, and economic differences between commercial grain growers and family subsistence farms, between suppliers of meat for the urban market and upland or marshland shepherds. (Cressy, 1983, p. 35)

In preindustrial England and New England, reading was inspired by, and correlated with, particular occupations.

> The gentry, professional men, and merchants were virtually all in possession of literacy, and they used reading and writing in all their affairs—to get rich and stay that way, to solidify ideas and gain access to others, and to service and extend their hegemony ... In the next cluster, at some distance, would be found yeomen and tradesmen, who in turn maintained a solid superiority [in the rate of literacy] over humbler artisans, husbandmen, and laborers. (Cressy, 1983, p. 37)

The activity basis of reading for different occupational groups was as follows:

> As the complexity of one's dealings increased, so did the advantage of being able to decipher writing and record things on paper. The farmer who could jot down market prices and compare them from week to week or season to season could secure a commercial advantage over his illiterate neighbor who relied on his memory ... Reading and writing would become useful and thereby worth knowing. (Cressy, 1983, p. 29)

Cressy notes that educational efforts to promote literacy were effective only when there was practical economic need for the skill. For people who had no practical economic need for literacy, "however persuasive the rhetoric, it foundered on the indifference to literacy of the bulk of the population who saw no practical need for those abilities. Where people needed little literacy to manage their affairs ... it was difficult to persuade them to embrace a skill which was, for all practical purposes, superfluous" (p. 40).

Commerce also stimulates cognitive competencies such as farsightedness and flexibility. Producers of commodities for the market must be farsighted to predict future rates of productivity, market share, consumer demand, and purchasing power in order to know whether their investments will be profitable. Producers must also continually alter their techniques to reduce costs, and must invent new products and expand their market share in order to remain competitive and maximize profit. Workers must refine their skills to keep up with changes in production (Haskell, 1985).

House (1981) presents similar evidence that personality traits such as openness to new experience (both social and physical), the assertion of independence from authority, ambition for oneself and one's children, a concern for promptness, and a concern for international issues are greatly influenced by "modern," that is, commercial, social activities.

Fabrega (1989, p. 61) explained how schizophrenic symptoms are grounded in cultural activities: "Changes in the political economy of early modern societies were associated with a transformation in the structure and content of the self, on the demands placed on it, and on the supports available to it from the social environment. A consequence of this was a change in the appearance, interpretation, and treatment of disease states like 'schizophrenia' that affect the self in a central way."

An outstanding experimental demonstration of the influence that activity has on psychology is the study of Sherif, Harvey, White, Hood, and Sherif (1954/1988) of intergroup conflict and cooperation. The authors matched 11-year-old boys on demographic, cognitive, and personality factors. They then assigned the boys to two groups at a camp in Oklahoma. The activities of both groups were manipulated in ways that had a powerful effect on their cognitive functions, personalities, stereotypes, and interpersonal behaviors.

The activities studied were competitive athletic contests and cooperative problem solving. Competition and cooperation were the ways the activities were socially organized. They were the shared principles/norms that guided behavior and determined the distribution of rewards and opportunities. When the two groups competed against each other the children quickly become hostile, aggressive, self-serving, and socially distant from and prejudiced toward each other. In addition, cognitive processes such as memory were affected by the competitive activity. As a case in point, after a tug-of-war that lasted 48 minutes, the losing group overestimated its duration by 12 minutes while the winning group underestimated its duration by 18 minutes. The median judgment (of duration) for the losing group was twice that of the winning group's—one hour vs. 30 minutes (pp. 118–119).

After competing for several days, the researchers had the two groups cooperate with each other, in solving problems that affected all of them. In one case, the water tank, which supplied water to the entire camp, was turned off by the researchers, thereby confronting all the boys with a common plight. The boys joined together to find out why the water had stopped and to get it running again. After several of these cooperative problem-solving activities, "Reduction of the conflict and hostility was observed in reciprocally cooperative and helpful intergroup actions, in friendly exchanges of tools," and in increased mingling and camaraderie of children from the two groups. "The reliability of these observations is established by sociometric indices that showed increases of friendship choices from the erstwhile antagonists and also in the sharp decrease of unfavorable stereotypes toward the outgroup. Favorable conceptions of the outgroup developed ..." (p. 211). Specifically, at the end of the competitive stage, 53% of the ratings by one group of the other had been unfavorable; but after the series of cooperative problem-solving tasks, only 4.5% of the ratings were unfavorable and 86% were favorable (pp. 194–195).

A very important finding of the study was that overcoming the negative effects of competition required a series of cooperative activities. Mere contact with the out-group had no effect in altering behavior (pp. 152–160). Between the termination of the competitive games and the start of the cooperative phase, the boys had the opportunity to freely associate with each other in the dining hall during meals. However, during this time, members of the two groups continued to eat in separate groups and to engage in hostile actions toward each other. The social distance and hostility broke down only after the boys engaged in cooperative activities that utilized new principles of solving problems and a new basis for distributing rewards and opportunities among the groups. Sherif's experiment demonstrates the centrality of socially organized activity for numerous psychological phenomena.

Additional demonstrations that psychological phenomena are grounded in social activities come from research that correlates participation in activities with an attendant psychological phenomenon. This research takes the form of "as people engage in X activity they tend to have higher levels of Y phenomenon." Such quantitative correlations sometimes disregard the specific ways in which psychological phenomena embody the content of activities, or what the internal relationship or qualitative congruence is (Ratner, 1997a). However, this research at least demonstrates that activities and psychological phenomena are related.

At a time when most psychologists overlook this vital fact, positivistic studies provide useful information.

Research on childrearing reveals an interesting link between mothers' participation in educational activities and their children's cognitive performance. LeVine, Miller, Richman, and LeVine (1996) found that the school experience of Mexican mothers led to adopting beliefs about their infants' readiness for conversational interaction which in turn led to engaging their infants in reciprocal vocalization that influenced their language development. Specifically, more highly educated mothers believed their children could interact linguistically several months after birth; these women initiated conversations 5 months after birth, and their children consequently developed high language performance at 31 months of age.

Gerris, Dekovic, and Janssens (1997) found a similar relationship between Dutch parents' social class, parents' ability to take the perspective of their children ("parental perspective taking"), and childrearing style. The higher the parents' social class—that is, their position in social and educational activities—the more they believed in considering their children's needs and interests, and the more child-oriented their childrearing style was (e.g., affectionate, considerate, supportive, reasoning, and encouraging independence). Social class correlated 0.48 with parental perspective taking which, in turn, correlated 0.75 with parents' child-oriented style.

Kagan goes so far as to state that social class is the most significant influence on psychological functioning. He cites several studies that find that social class is the only robust predictor of a child's IQ and reading skill. Biological variables such as attentiveness and activity level did not predict cognitive performance. Bee et al. similarly found that, compared with psychophysiological measures, "at most ages the total HOME [family environment] score was the single best predictor of IQ or language" (cited in Ratner, 1991, p. 35).

In a fascinating, broadly conceived investigation of social influences on IQ, Sameroff, Seifer, Barocas, Zax, and Greenspan (1987) concluded that socioeconomic class, as measured by parents' occupation and mother's educational level, was the strongest predictor of children's IQ. Socioeconomic class was more important than the mother's psychological health–anxiety, the amount of interaction (touching, smiling, and vocalizing) between mothers and children, and even the presence of stressful life events such as job loss, death in the family, or physical illness. Parents' occupation correlated 0.58 with children's IQ, mother's education correlated 0.56 with IQ, and minority ethnicity correlated −0.51 with IQ. In contrast, mothers' interaction with children correlated only 0.39 with their children's IQ, stressful life events correlated −0.26, and mother's anxiety correlated −0.24 with children's IQ. The importance of activity is demonstrated in the fact that high vs. low maternal education made a difference of 16 IQ points in the children, high vs. low occupation produced an 18-point IQ differential, and minority status also produced an 18-point differential. High or low mother's anxiety, on the other hand, made a difference of only 7.5 points in IQ score; the mother's interaction also only effected a 10-point IQ difference in the children. Another indication of the importance of socioeconomic class is the fact that lower class children with four or more social risk factors averaged an IQ of 90, while upper class children with the same number of risks factors averaged IQs of 100. Social class thus mediates the impact of other factors such as stressful life events, mother's interaction with children, mother's anxiety, and mother's mental health.

Sameroff et al. (1987) conclude that the factors that are most amenable to psychologists' amelioration—mother's anxiety and mother's interaction with children—are the factors that account for little variance in children's IQ. To improve intellectual levels, psychologists must consequently engage in broad social action beyond the narrow domain of professional psychology.

This conclusion is supported by additional studies on poverty and IQ. Brooks-Gunn, Klebanov, and Duncan (1996) compared IQ scores of 5-year-old black and white children who had been followed from birth with data on neighborhood, family poverty, family structure, family resources, maternal characteristics, and home environment. On a simple comparison of IQ scores, the white children scored 18 points higher than the blacks. However, black children live in worse environments than whites: 66% of black children but only 26% of white children live in poverty for 1 out of 5 years; and 40% of black children chronically live in poverty all of their lives while only 5% of white children do. In addition, 57% of black children live in poor neighborhoods (defined as having 20% or more neighbors living in poverty) as compared with 8% of white children. Astonishingly, almost one half of all black families who are *not* poor reside in poor neighborhoods compared with less than 10% of comparable white children. When Brooks-Gunn et al. selected black and white children who were equally poor, the 18-point differential in IQ scores dropped to 8.5 points. When the children were further matched on the opportunity for learning in the home environment, the ethnic difference in IQ dropped to 3 points! (Maternal education, female head of family, maternal verbal IQ score did not reduce the children's IQ differential.) The authors conclude that ethnic differences in IQ score are due to differential rates of family poverty and associated limited opportunities for learning at home. When these social differences are eliminated, IQ differences are virtually eliminated as well.

Research concludes that neighborhood residence, which is a proxy for social class, has psychological effects. These studies compare psychological outcomes of families having similar characteristics (such as income, education, literacy, motivation) but living in different neighborhoods. As summarized by Leventhal and Brooks-Gunn (2000), living in more well-to-do neighborhoods (affluent, high employment, job stability, intact families, low welfare, institutional resources such as libraries and community centers, sports and art programs, good child care) leads to higher scores on IQ tests, a greater chance of completing high school and attending college, better mental health, and better behavior (less anti-social behavior). For example, adolescent boys who moved to middle-class neighborhoods were less likely to be arrested for violent crimes than were their peers (matched on family characteristics) who stayed in public housing in poor neighborhoods or peers who moved out of public housing to poor neighborhoods. Unemployment and the presence of few professional workers in the neighborhood leads to increased risk of adolescent and nonmarital pregnancy and childbearing. Poor, dangerous neighborhoods lead parents to engage in more hostile, controlling, and aggressive treatment of their children. Such parental practices may be an important mediator of neighborhood effects on children's psychology. Leventhal and Brooks-Gunn observe that the positive effects of good neighborhood on psychology are not uniform across all social groups. Blacks do not benefit as much because they remain segregated from many of the institutional resources (ibid., p. 328). This is an important example of how social influences on psychology are modulated by specific positions (occupied by ethnic groups and genders) within activities.

Naoi and Schooler (1990) and Schooler (2001) found a causal influence of occupational activity on a host of psychological factors. Occupational self-direction engendered intellectual flexibility, self-confidence, independence, personal responsibility for actions, anti-authoritarian attitudes, modern attitudes toward living with older children and with elderly parents (e.g., not willing to take parents into one's own home, or keep elderly children at home), and low stress. Path analysis revealed that while the path from occupational self-direction to psychological factors is significant, the path from psychological factors to occupational self-direction is insignificant.

Position in social activity is a major determinant of mental disorder (Belek, 2000; Brown, Susser, Jandorf, & Bromet, 2000; Ratner, 1991, pp. 247–263, 287). Harris, Brown, and Bifulco (1987) found that class substantially determines the impact of other risk factors. For example, residing in an institution such as a children's home had a stronger relationship with later depression in working class than in middle-class women. Fifty-six percent of institutionalized working class women later became depressed compared with only 15% of institutionalized middle-class women. The relationship between premarital pregnancy (PMP) and depression was similarly mediated by class. Sixty-eight percent of PMP working class women suffered later depression while only 7% of PMP middle-class women suffered depression.

The psychological effect of coping strategies to PMP also varied with social class. Among working class women who were ineffective copers with PMP, 69% became depressed, in contrast to 25% of middle-class ineffective copers. Among effective copers (defined as aborting the pregnancy, marrying the father only if marriage was intended before pregnancy, or marrying a more suitable man if the father was unsuitable), 66% of working class women became depressed (the same proportion as among ineffective copers), in contrast to 0% of middle-class women. It is clear that social class is a more important determinant of depression than coping strategy is. The working class social position is so powerful that it overrides coping effectiveness and makes good and poor copers equally depressed. Moreover, middle-class ineffective copers are far less likely to suffer depression than effective working class copers are.

Mirowsky and Ross (1989, pp. 173–176) found depression monotonically related to social class (low income, education, and employment), gender, and minority group membership. Members of the lowest decile of social factors experienced 72% more symptoms than members of the highest social decile.

Domestic violence and child abuse are similarly inversely correlated with social class. In the United States, the incidence rate of child abuse and neglect is more than five times higher among children from families below the poverty line than above it. Only 6% of the cases are from families earning the median income for all U.S. families. In the narrower category of physical abuse, 89% of the cases are in families below the poverty line. Seventy-seven percent of cases of emotional abuse are among poor families. Eighty percent of child sexual abuse cases are from poor families and only 2% of such cases are in families earning above $25,000 in 1979 (Pelton, 1994).

Werner's (1989) study of at-risk children exemplifies how social class powerfully affects psychological development. Werner found that "rearing conditions were more powerful determinants of outcome than perinatal trauma" (p. 108).

> Prenatal and perinatal complications were consistently related to impairment of physical and psychological development at the ages of 10 and 18 only when

they were combined with chronic poverty, family discord, parental mental illness or other persistently poor rearing conditions. Children who were raised in middle-class homes, in a stable family environment and by a mother who had finished high school showed few if any lasting effects of reproductive stress later in their lives. (Werner, 1989, p. 109)

The Influence of Cultural Artifacts on Psychological Phenomena

Vygotsky stated that culture includes artifacts as well as socially organized activities. He emphasized the effects that tools have on consciousness. However, he considered only very general effects produced by general properties of tools. For example, he observed that tool use is mediated action rather than direct action on things. This mediation entails some distancing from things and reflecting about how to act on them. Tools also expand the types of action one can engage in—a particular goal can be accomplished in a variety of ways using a variety of tools. Tools thus promote flexibility, imagination, and planning (see Ratner, 1991, pp. 47–57 for discussion of the importance of artifacts/tools for Vygotsky's sociocultural theory of psychology).

In addition to these general psychological effects, artifacts impart a specific content and mode of operation to psychological phenomena. The architecture of houses has been observed to structure interpersonal interactions, self-concept, and the relationships among daily chores. Medieval houses consisted of large, general-purpose rooms in which cooking, eating, socializing, and sleeping all occurred among children, adults, relatives, and friends indiscriminately. Likewise,

A typical house in the tobacco-growing region of Tidewater Virginia and Maryland in the seventeenth century was a one-story frame dwelling of two rooms, with additional space in the attic. In such tight and relatively undifferentiated quarters, dwellers did not have the luxury of setting aside special spaces for particular tasks or individual use. Nor did they have many specialized pieces of furniture. Only one in four families owned a table to sit at; only one in three had chairs and benches—and only one in seven both. Most of necessity were 'squatters or leaners,' slumping on the floor or crouching on boxes and chests in the waking hours ... They lacked not only bedrooms; less than one in seven owned a single bedstead. Most took mattresses and blankets and slept on the floor in groups. (Kasson, 1990, pp. 20–21)

The architecture of medieval and Tidewater houses objectified interconnectedness of people and function. "Such households did not encourage a highly individuated sense of self with its characteristic need for privacy" (ibid., p. 21).

Modern houses are divided into separate rooms occupied by different people for different functions. The husband and wife have their own bedroom, as does each child. This physical separation of individuals promulgates psychological differentiation among individuals. Having to separate from one's parents in the evening to sleep in one's own bedroom with the door closed, and having to call/cry loudly and alone for many minutes in order to get parents to come and assist in case of difficulty, gives the child a sense of distinctive individuality. The creation of a physically separate bedroom privatizes a personal space for changing clothing (preparing one's appearance), nudity, sex, and sleep. Modern kitchens were downsized, which had the effect of isolating the wife from social contact: "Modern architects broke up the 'unhealthy' communality of the kitchen by designing tiny, one-woman kitchens, where the housewife undertook her lonely, Taylorized tasks. Space for eating was provided in a small dining room, and for socializing, the middle-class parlor was installed in diminutive form" (Gartman, 2000, p. 91).

The architecture of residences has been found to affect people's perception. The geometrical forms of buildings provide cues that shape perceptual expectancies and even neural growth. Consequently, Navajo Indians brought up in curvilinear homes are significantly less susceptible to the Muller–Lyer illusion than Navajos reared in rectilinear homes (Ratner, 1997a, pp. 29–30).

Clocks and watches are other cultural artifacts whose physical characteristics shape psychology. Clocks and watches indicate time in precise, separate, equivalent units (seconds, minutes, hours). This physical objectification of time greatly affected people's conception of time. Before the invention of clocks, time was construed as a smooth continuum or cycle in which qualitatively different moments (depending on the event) were integrated. There was little interest in precisely specifying when an event had occurred. Even people's ages were not precisely known. The advent of mechanical clocks in the late 13th century (with only an hour hand, as the minute hand was not invented until the mid-17th century) fostered a new conception of time as composed of discrete, homogeneous (equivalent) units (Gauvain, 1998a & b). This conception is objectified further in digital clocks that display only the current minute and second.

The physical characteristics of certain artifacts objectify social activities, imparting the character of these social activities to the psychology of people who use them. Maynard, Greenfield, and Childs (1999) demonstrated these points in a sophisticated research project on the cultural history of textiles in a Mayan hamlet in Chiapas, Mexico. The authors compared woven garments from 1970 and 1993. They found that this artifact changed substantially in the two decades. Later textiles were much more individuated than the earlier ones. Shawls and ponchos from the later period contained unique embroidered designs and colors. In contrast, earlier shawls were more uniform. Greater individual differences in textiles were fostered by economic changes: a subsistence, collective, agrarian economy was transformed into a commercial, free market economy in which individuals owned their own instruments and trucks and sold goods on the open market. The authors conclude that the individuation of the market economy generated individualized tastes for individuated textiles. In addition, the way that youngsters learned to weave became much more individualized. In 1970, parents closely assisted and guided their children. They remained physically close to their pupils, often with their arms around the learner's back. Two people wove the cloth as one body; both pairs of hands were on the loom at the same time. In 1993, teachers were physically distant from the pupils and supervised and guided them much less closely. Pupils had to learn on their own by trial and error. They also had more freedom to innovate. Educational activity and the woven artifact pivoted around commercial economic activity.

The physical design of modern Western houses similarly objectifies the individualized free market and corresponding social distinctions among behaviors and people (Kasson, 1990, pp. 170–171).

Gartman explains how modern Western architecture embodies the standardization, efficiency, cost-saving, time-saving, and depersonalization of capitalist socioeconomic relationships: "In the 1920s modern architects such as Walter Gropium, Mies van der Rohe, and Le Corbusier pioneered a new architectural aesthetic to support and testify to the technocratic project to rationalize power and consumption...Known as the 'new objectivity' or 'machine aesthetic,' their style was generally characterized by simple, undecorated, geometric forms, usually of severe rectilinearity, constructed of industrially produced building materials like steel, glass, and concrete." "This aesthetic dimension of the 'machine style' promoted the technocratic project by ideologically symbolizing the domination of abstract, instrumental reason over humans and nature...To integrate people into rationalized mass production, their housing had to glorify its instrumental reason." The aesthetics of modern architecture symbolized and glorified instrumental reason in several ways. Modernists used simple, elementary shapes because these reflected the standardization and mechanization of mass-production technology. "And the straight line was preferred to the curve both because of its labor-saving predominance in mass-produced machines like automobiles and because it symbolized the precise, instrumental reason underlying mass-production technology." "Abstract, flexible space facilitated the mobility of business tenants in and out of office buildings in the fast-paced urban real estate market.

Modernists created residential spaces that were also universal and non-specialized to allow the rapid turnover of workers ... " "The abstract, homogeneous, mobile space of modernist architecture was really a metaphor for the commodity in the age of technocracy, a vessel emptied by new technologies of any qualitative uses to become a mere holder of quantitative exchange value" (Gartman, 2000, pp. 87–89).

In the foregoing cases, the physical characteristics of artifacts impart a single, definite content and mode of operation to psychology. Anyone who lives in a modern house will be inclined to regard herself as a distinctive individual whose rest, nudity, and sexuality are functions differentiated from socializing. The physical design of the house makes it difficult to develop a different psychology while living within its architecture. A more collective, integrated sense of self and behavior would require a different architecture akin to the medieval one that could accommodate many people performing a variety of tasks together. The geometrical forms of a house's structure would also have to be altered in order to modify perceptual experiences & effectiveness. Similarly, the physical appearance of clocks and watches makes it difficult to conceive of time other than as discrete, homogeneous, precise units.

Not all artifacts affect psychology through their physical properties. Many artifacts affect psychology through the content that is inscribed on/in them rather than through their physical properties, per se. Paper, for example affects psychology through the content of what is written on it. The physical character of paper has no known psychological effect. A musical instrument similarly affects psychology through the kind of music that is played on it, not by the physical dimensions of the instrument.

Whether an artifact has an intrinsic, fixed effect on psychology or a variable effect has consequences for changing psychological phenomena. Artifacts whose physical characteristics intrinsically organize psychological phenomena in fixed ways need to be physically transformed to foster novel psychological features. Musical instruments, paper, pencils, computers, and many machines do not need to be redesigned to foster new psychological features. They only need to be used in different ways for different purposes in order to foster new psychological features.

THE INFLUENCE OF CULTURAL CONCEPTS ON PSYCHOLOGICAL PHENOMENA

Cultural Concepts

Another cultural factor that organizes people's psychology is concepts about the nature of things and people. Cultural concepts, objectified in linguistic terms, have been considered to be the major cultural organizers of psychology by most cultural psychologists. Some notable representatives of this symbolic approach to cultural psychology are Sapir, Whorf, Geertz, Shweder, D'Andrade, Lutz, and M. Rosaldo. Symbolic cultural psychologists have demonstrated that cultural concepts impart a specific content and mode of operation to emotions, perception, memory, logical reasoning, aggression, childrearing, developmental processes (such as the acquisition of language), and mental illness. Before presenting examples in the next section, it is necessary to explore the character and origins of cultural concepts to gain a sense of what they impart to psychological phenomena. We must delve into the world of sociology, as we did earlier in exploring the nature of activities, to better understand cultural aspects of psychology.

Cultural concepts are collective products. That is, they emerge from social processes of negotiation and transcend any one individual's idea (see Flick, 1998a, esp. Chaps. 6, 7; Harre, 1984).

Saxe (1999, p. 30) explains this production of a collective product as follows: "[Social] occasions provide opportunities for reciprocally appropriating features of one another's constructions. In such appropriations, new forms are born as particular representations become valued and institutionalized as regularized ways of representing and accomplishing problems linked to collective practices. The process of diffusion and institutionalization of individuals' microgenetic constructions into the activities of others constitutes a sociogenesis of knowledge."

Activity theory maintains that cultural concepts are formed in and reflect the social organization of activities. In contrast to idealist views that regard concepts as originating in the mind apart from social relationships, activity theory construes concepts as dependent on real-life activities by which people govern, educate, and procreate, and produce their means of subsistence. Vygotsky clearly explained how concepts, which mediate between the (physical and social) environment and psychology, are grounded in social activities:

> Environment does not always affect man directly and straightforwardly, but also indirectly through his ideology. By ideology we will understand all the social stimuli that have been established in the course of historical development and have become hardened in the form of legal statutes, moral precepts, artistic tastes, and so on. These standards are permeated through and through with the class structure of society that generated them and serve as the class organization of production. They are responsible for all of human behavior and in this sense we are justified in speaking of man's class behavior. (Vygotsky, 1997b, p. 96, 211)

Volosinov (1973, p. 13) similarly emphasized that "Consciousness takes shape and being in the material of signs created by an organized group in the process of its social intercourse." In the same vein, Leontiev (1978, Chap. 4) stated that "Behind linguistic meanings hide socially developed methods of action (operations) in the process of which people change and perceive objective reality. In other words, meanings represent an ideal form of the existence of the objective world, its properties, connections, and relationships, disclosed by cooperative social practice, transformed and hidden in the material of language. For this reason meanings in themselves, that is, in abstraction from their functioning in individual consciousness, are not so 'psychological' as the socially recognized reality that lies behind them."

Gerth and Mills (1953, p. 54) explained how a particular psychological phenomenon, emotion, is structured by conceptual meanings that, in turn, are structured by social activities: "The meaning of a situation to a person sets the experience and the nature of emotion. These meanings vary according to the person's past experiences; these experiences, in turn, must be explained in terms of the person's position and career within given kinds of social structure." This account is congruent with Fig. 1.1.

These scholars all followed Marx's idea that social concepts, consciousness, philosophy, and ideology ultimately serve social activities. Less well known is the fact that Durkheim also linked collective representations to socially organized activities. In *Suicide* he said that, "A people's mental system is a system of definite mental forces ... related to the way in which the social elements are organized. Given a people consisting of a certain number of individuals arranged in a certain way, there results a determinate set of collective ideas and practices that remain constant so long as the conditions on which they depend are unchanged" (cited in Harre, 1984, p. 933). "If categories are essentially collective representations, as I think they are, they translate states of the collectivity, first and foremost. They depend upon the way in which the collectivity is organized, upon its morphology [structure], its religious, moral, and economic institutions, and so on" (Durkheim, 1915/1995, p. 15; see also House, 1981, pp. 536–554; Smail, 1994, pp. 5–7; see Ratner, 1991, pp. 96–99, 1997a, Chap. 3, 1997b, p. 199). For example,

> Rights and liberties are not things inherent in the nature of the individual as such. Analyze the given constitution of man and you will find there no trace of the sacred character with which he is today invested and form which his rights are derived. He owes this character to society. It is society that has consecrated the individual and made of him the thing to be respected above all. The progressive emancipation of the individual thus does not imply a weakening but a transformation of the social bond. (Durkheim cited in Giddens, 1995, p. 120)

The internal and external division of labor of activities (their morphology) lead occupants of different positions to form different conceptions of things. "Complementary learned meanings refer, in large part, to the status/role systems within a society" (Rohner, 1984, p. 122). Individuals within a position in an activity also develop idiosyncratic connotations to concepts. However, a basic equivalence exists in the sense that participants share a core connotation despite minor individual variations.

Many concepts reflect activities because they are formulated through the auspices of established institutions such as government agencies, religious organizations, courts, foundations, advertising agencies, scientific and artistic societies, and the news and entertainment industries. Certain concepts are modified by institutions that disseminate them. Publishers of newspapers, magazines, and books; advertising agencies; educational bureaus; and television, radio, and music companies all modify concepts that may have originated outside these organized activities. Even concepts about things that are not directly implicated in institutionalized activities are ultimately influenced by activities. This is true for concepts of sex, pollution, food, the body, odors, birthdays, the elderly, capital punishment, abortion, homosexuality, God, women's rights, intelligence, marijuana, friendship, and death. Identifying elements of social activities that are incorporated into diverse concepts is vital for understanding people's cultural psychology. For cultural concepts impart content and operations to psychological phenomena, and this content originates in social activities. Accordingly, the more we understand the activity basis of concepts, the better we understand the cultural content of psychological phenomena.

Historical and sociological research has elucidated the activity basis of certain concepts. One example is the modern American concept of masculinity that emerged in the 1920s. In a detailed historical study of magazine articles, Pendergast (2000) has concluded that Victorian ideals of masculinity—emphasizing self-control, discipline, frugality, industry/hard work, character, honesty, and fairness—were abandoned in the 1920s and replaced by an emphasis on appealing personality, superficial appearances, self-expression, sexual attractiveness, wealth, recreation, and self-gratification. For example, the male athlete was originally portrayed as having a strong character that consisted of being disciplined, playing by the rules (honest), fair, learning about himself through suffering defeat, loyal, cooperative, and self-sacrificing for the team. This emphasis on character and teamwork was displaced by an emphasis on winning, attracting fans, becoming a celebrity, gaining commercial endorsements, earning large sums of money, and becoming influential outside of sports in politics and business. Of course, the language of Victorian character was sometimes retained in the modern era, although usually in the service of commercial ends. For instance, 1924 advertisements for billiards equipment touted the game as building character, patience, concentration, and an even temper. However, the objective of these ads was consumerism, not building character (ibid., p. 132). Traditional values were used by advertisers to sell billiard equipment in the same way that beautiful models were used to sell cosmetics and clothing. Responding to the ads and buying equipment on the basis of stylized images (including traditional ones) itself undermined traditional virtues of patience, self-reflection, and frugality—just as buying a book because the model in the advertisement appears intellectual, successful, or popular undermines serious appreciation of good literature.

Pendergast concludes that Victorian masculinity was tied to the ownership of property in a petty capitalist economy. Modern ideals of manhood were spawned by the corporate capitalist economy: "The growth of modern masculinity created roles for men that suited them to a corporate consumer culture ... The rise of corporate consumer culture largely shaped the masculine roles within which we operate even today" (ibid., p. 3). Specifically, modern masculine personality attributes motivated men to become consumers of mass produced products, to become efficient salesmen of products at work, to sell themselves to bureaucratic enterprises, to work their way up the job ladder and continually strive for a higher salary, to look out for oneself in a competitive, impersonal economy, and to enhance one's exchange value (the value of things that one can command) regardless of one's intrinsic character or "use value" (ibid., pp. 145–147). Dale Carnegie expressed the commercial utility of superficial personality attributes in his 1936 book *How To Win Friends and Influence People*: "I find that smiles are bringing me dollars, many dollars every day."

Modern ideals of manhood were fostered by modern capitalist economic activities that demanded new roles for working men. These ideals were refined and explicated by the information industry (e.g., magazine and advertising companies). Pendergast explains this confluence of influences as follows: "Modern masculinity was at once the creation of advertisers eager to create customers and editors and writers eager to offer understandings of masculinity that were consonant with larger cultural changes" (ibid., p. 166).

Further evidence of the activity basis of masculine ideals is the fact that they were originally promulgated among white middle-class men who occupied a distinctive position in the capitalist economy. Among black men Victorian ideals of masculinity persisted until the 1940s. Given their social position, blacks were primarily concerned with finding jobs and winning equal social and political rights (Pendergast, 2000).

Pendergast explains that while masculinity was definitely shaped by social activities, this shaping was not a mechanical process that circumvented the participation of ordinary people. The men who adopted the new ideals did so actively. Yet their agency was definitely guided by social activities and concepts. The process is aptly described as follows: "As men increasingly came to work in large, bureaucratic corporations rather than small shops; as they sought leisure in large, impersonal cities rather than in small towns, and as they viewed the world through mass-circulation magazines rather than local newspapers, they began to devise new ways to think about their identity as men. The masculinity that evolved alongside this modern culture came to emphasize personality, sexuality, self-realization, and a fascination with appearances, all traits that made men well suited to participate in the social and economic institutions of the period" (Pendergast, 2000, p. 13).

A related cultural concept that was organized around social activities is the ideal of a thin body. Stearns (1997) documents the birth of this concept in American magazines around 1890 (it arrived earlier in Europe). Before this date, the ideal North American body image was plump. The ideal of thinness was formulated by the middle class, and by 1920 both men and women endorsed it as the dominant ideal for middle-class women—both men and women believed that thinness was much less important for men. Stearns (ibid., p. 89) observes that, "The preoccupation with weight and dieting did not catch on among African American women, either as a matter of practice or in the cultural signals generated. The pages of *Ebony* magazine from 1943 onward were singularly spare in their treatment of weight problems, compared to their middle class white counterparts" (see Grogan, 2000, p. 140 for supporting evidence). This social circumscribing of the thin body image to a particular class, race, and gender (white, middle-class women) at a particular historical time indicates that it was fostered by particular activities (and roles) occupied by the middle class.

Although Stearns does not enumerate the specific activities that fostered the thin body ideal for middle-class women, a plausible speculation is that the concept reflected a combination of dynamic middle-class commercial activity as well as the lingering low domestic status of women. By the turn of the 20th century, traditional fixed life styles of the colonial period had been largely displaced by dynamic business activity. The free market emphasized innovation, mobility, boldness, unpredictability, quick decision-making, assertiveness, and self-direction or self-control over activity. Slimness objectified this dynamic, energetic middle-class economic activity. Capitalist work valued expending energy to produce things, and a slim body objectified an energetic person who was expending energy rather than accumulating it. The traditional ideal of plumpness now connoted lethargy, passivity, immobility, and inflexibility (see Grogan, 2000, p. 140). These were all antithetical to energetic middle-class work. Middle-class men were influenced to value slimness because it objectified crucial work behaviors. Women were influenced to value slimness partly through their association with their husbands, but partly through their domestic role, which was quite different from their husbands' social role. Slimness in women connoted weakness, delicacy, diminutiveness, demureness, and youthful immaturity associated with middle-class women's subordinate domestic role. Women's thinness thus had a different basis and meaning from men's. Whereas male thinness represented role-appropriate activity, boldness, self-direction, and speed, women's thinness represented the opposite qualities and roles. Weakness and delicacy were further objectified in the middle-class feminine ideal of a smooth body. It was in the 1920s that North American women began to shave their underarm and leg hair (Stearns, 1997, Chap. 4). Thus, the thin body concept may have reflected both the active life style and the domestic, subordinate role of middle-class women.

The black embracing of large women lay in the fact that black women were often heads of households who worked. They provided the most stable income even when husbands were present. Their work was largely routine and menial, in contrast to the dynamic, innovative, adventurous work of the middle class. A large body connoted the power and durability to work amidst difficult conditions. A diminutive appearance was incongruent with the family and economic activities of black women.

In many countries, men and women of African descent regard corpulence in women as symbolizing wealth—the ability of the family to buy large quantities of food and escape poverty. Afro-Caribbean women are likely to report higher desired body weight, larger desired body shapes, and fewer weight concerns than white women. In Niger there is a festival at which women compete to be the most corpulent. They train for the festival by gorging themselves on millet, and they drink quantities of water the morning of the competition. Many women take steroids to gain bulk, or pills to sharpen their appetites. Some women even ingest feed or medications designed to beef up animals! Among the Calabari people of Nigeria, brides go to fattening farms before their weddings (*The New York Times*, Feb. 12, 2001, p. A4).

Luker (1984) provides another example of a concept that is derived from social activities. She found that different views about abortion reflect positions in social activities. Luker compared the social positions of pro-choice and anti-choice activists in California. She found (ibid., Chap. 7) that anti-choice activists were economically poorer, less educated, less involved in work outside the family, and more religious than pro-choice activists. When anti-choice activists worked outside the home they earned little money and worked at traditional female jobs such as teaching, social work, and nursing. In contrast, 94% of pro-choice activists worked and their jobs were well-paid professional jobs. The vast majority held secular, nonreligious views (73% professed either religion or a personal one, in contrast to only 5% of the anti-choice activists). Anti-choice women also held more traditional views of the relationship between the sexes. They endorsed the dominant status of men as productive agents, and they endorsed a domestic, compliant, maternal role for women. In addition, anti-choice women regarded sex as primarily for procreation, while pro-choice women regarded sex as primarily for pleasure. These findings indicate that although concepts of abortion do not directly refer to socially organized activities they are rooted in economic, familial, and religious activities, and cultural concepts about related issues. Luker explains the social activities associated with the pro-choice position: "Abortion permits women to engage in paid work on an equal basis with men. With abortion, they may schedule pregnancy in order to take advantage of the kinds of benefits that come with a paid position in the labor force..." (ibid., p. 204). Opposing abortion is associated with different positions in family and economic activities: "The more limited the educational credentials a woman has, the more limited the job opportunities are for her, the more attractive motherhood is as a full-time occupation... All the circumstances of her existence will encourage a pro-life woman to highlight the kinds of values and experiences that support childbearing and childrearing and to discount the attraction of paid employment. Her circumstances [i.e., activities] encourage her to resent the pro-choice view that women's most meaningful and prestigious activities are in the 'man's world'" (ibid., p. 206).

Another interesting concept that derived from activity was that of the individual that arose in England during the 17th and 18th centuries. The "middling sort" of artisans and yeomen in the late 17th and early 18th centuries emphasized egalitarian attitudes about the worth of all individuals. This egalitarian ideology "was shaped by socioeconomic reality... The central feature of the social and economic structures that persisted in Halifax throughout the seventeenth century was an economy that was fluid enough to allow individuals to increase or decrease the stock with which they had started out in life but at the same time set limits, especially at the upper end, to the mobility that was possible" (Smail, 1994, p. 36). The limits on wealth created relative homogeneity in peoples' standard of living. Moreover, the textile industry was dominated by small independent artisans who worked in their own homes along with members of their family and with their own materials. The restricted commercial economy forced these clothiers to earn a relatively similar income (ibid., pp. 20–25). Thus, "Egalitarianism was a feature of the socioeconomic reality of the parish throughout the seventeenth century" (ibid., p. 36) and it formed the basis of the middle sort's egalitarian ideology.

Other classes of people who engaged in other kinds of economic activity—or other positions in the field of economic activity—developed different concepts. A case in point was the new class of manufacturers and merchants who emerged out of the middling class. "In Halifax, manufacturing—direct involvement in the production of woolen cloth on a large scale as distinct from any mercantile or professional activity—was an important factor in shaping the middle-class culture that originated there, because it gave rise to a new set of social relations between manufacturers and their workers and helped to change the values and outlook of the manufacturers" (ibid., pp. 14–15). The social relationships of the burgeoning market led the bourgeoisie to formulate values about people, morality, sex, and religion that were more cosmopolitan, individualistic, flexible, and critical than those of the middling class.

The primacy of activity over concepts is expressed in the fact that there was a time lag between socioeconomic activity and the conceptualization of middle-class identity: "It took time to develop a 'vocabulary' of class identity that matched the practical reality ... In time a coherent conceptualization of middle-class identity was constructed" (ibid., p. 230). The more institutionalized (crystallized) bourgeois socioeconomic practices became, the more substantial middle-class identity and ideology became: "As the practical reality of class relations endured, those relations came to be conceived and expressed in a more abstract [general] but also a more coherent form" (ibid., p. 230).

Another cultural concept that was organized around economic activities is the notion of time:

> Throughout the whole medieval period, there was a conflict between the cyclic and linear concepts of time. The scientists and scholars, influenced by astronomy and astrology, tended to emphasize the cyclic concept. The linear concept was fostered by the mercantile class and the rise of a money economy. For as long as power was concentrated in the ownership of land, time was felt to be plentiful and was associated with the unchanging cycle of the soil. With the circulation of money, however, the emphasis was on mobility. In other words, men were beginning to believe that "time is money" and that one must try to use it economically and thus time came to be associated with the idea of linear progress. (Whitrow, 1973, p. 402)

The linear concept of time was institutionalized in coercive work rules throughout capitalist industries: Through "division of labor, the supervision of labor, fines, bells and clocks, money incentives, preachings and schoolings, the suppression of fairs and sports—the new labor habits were formed and a new time-discipline was imposed" (Thompson, p. 90).

Legal concepts were similarly transformed after the American Revolution by merchant and entrepreneurial groups to support economic activities.

> By around 1850 that transformation was largely complete. Legal rules providing for the subsidization of enterprise and permitting the legal destruction of old forms of property for the benefit of more recent entrants had triumphed. Anticommercial legal doctrines had been destroyed or undermined and the legal system had almost completely shed its eighteenth century commitment to regulating the substantive fairness of economic exchange ... Law, once conceived of as protective, regulative, paternalistic and, above all, a paramount expression of the moral sense of the community, had come to be thought of as facilitative of individual desires and as simply reflective of the existing organization of economic and political power.
>
> This transformation in American law both aided and ratified a major shift in power in an increasingly market-oriented society. By the middle of the nineteenth century the legal system had been reshaped to the advantage of men of commerce and industry at the expense of farmers, workers, consumers, and other less powerful groups within the society. (Horwitz, 1977, pp. 253–254)

American religious beliefs in the early 19th century are another cultural concept that was organized around economic activities. The two predominant religious doctrines—Evangelicalism and Unitarianism—were adopted by two distinctive social classes. Evangelicals espoused traditional Calvinist ideals—including the omnipotence of God, reliance on the literal truth of scripture, and saving people from sin. Unitarians, in contrast, gave greater value to developing ethical principles on the basis of reason. They adopted Enlightenment ideals into religion, and they repudiated the idea of uncritically relying on a literal interpretation of religious dogma. Unitarians conceived God to be a benevolent figure rather than a punishing one. They also tolerated some diversity of opinion concerning religious and ethical beliefs. These contrasting religious beliefs were adopted by two distinctive social groups of people who engaged in different kinds of economic activity. Evangelicals came primarily from the class called the "petty bourgeoisie" (small property holders, artisans, shopkeepers) joined by some members from the laboring class. Unitarians were primarily members of the bourgeois class (merchants, bankers, realtors, industrialists) and professionals, and "almost completely lacked adherents who were servants, laborers, or factory operatives" (Cayton, 1997, p. 94). The Unitarians were centered in Boston, where they formed a cohesive "Unitarian mercantile oligarchy" that dominated the economic, political, judicial, educational, and intellectual landscape of Boston (Howe, 1970, pp. 4–12). Of course, not all capitalists were Unitarians, nor were all small property holders Evangelicals. However, those people who were attracted to the doctrines of Unitarians were most likely to be from the bourgeois class while the vast majority of Evangelicals were from the petty bourgeoisie. This class division indicates that the kind of social activities people participated in made particular religious concepts appealing to them. People outside those activities were unlikely to adopt those concepts.

These examples demonstrate that an activity can influence the content of concepts that are not directly concerned with that activity.

Another concept that is rooted in activities is the way people think about emotions. Many Americans regard emotions as distinct from cognition, irrational, impulsive, personal, and primitive. This belief stems from the manner in which emotions are treated in various activities. Emotions are suppressed in many cultural activities in which "cold" calculations take priority over personal relationships. Calculations are impersonal, serious, and mechanical. This is true at work, in politics, and even in medicine, where decisions are made primarily on the basis of the monetary value of people, things, and procedures. Emotions have been relegated to family activities and personal relationships outside of work, politics, and other cultural activities. In the personal domains, emotions are to be expressed freely; reason and calculation are impugned as impersonal, serious, and rigid, because of the connotation they have in public institutions. This social compartmentalizing of emotions and cognition in separate activities has led to conceptually differentiating them as separate, antithetical phenomena. Emotions seem to be noncognitive, irrational, antisocial, impulsive, and primitive because they have been divorced from reason, calculation, and control in social life (Ratner, 2000b).

The foregoing examples demonstrate that particular cultural concepts originate in, embody, and perpetuate social activities. The influence of activities on concepts extends beyond such particulars and encompasses entire conceptual systems. Research has demonstrated that entire languages evolve under the impetus of changes in social activities. Kulick (1992) conducted a fascinating detailed study of "language shift" in a small community, Gapun, in Papua New Guinea. Gapun is a "tidy, windless slit in the jungle." It is 500 meters long by a few hundred meters wide and is surrounded on all sides by rainforest. Villagers live in houses that are 12 meters by 9 meters. Until recently, Gapuners spoke a language called Taiap. They were the only people in the world to speak it. In recent decades Taiap has been replaced by Tok Pisin, which is a form of pidgin English that arose in the mid-19th century and has gradually been replacing most of the Papuan languages. The language shift in Gapun began during World War I, when several men temporarily migrated out to work in other areas where Tok Pisin was spoken. The shift intensified during the 1950s, when virtually every unmarried male spent at least a year working in other villages (ibid., p. 72). Another reason for the language shift was the introduction of Tok Pisin into the village by Christian missionaries. Finally, in the late 1950s Gapuners relocated their village closer to Wongan, a Tok Pisin-speaking village. Commercial contact expanded, children attended Wongan schools, and intermarriage between the two villages became commonplace (ibid., p. 81). These changes in social activities led Gapuners to shift their language (see ibid., pp. 9–10 for an additional example).

Kulick studied every member of Gapun and found that the language shift was related to the contact that an individual had with the new economic, educational, religious, and family activities. Tok Pisin was spoken only by males during the first decades of its absorption into the village verbal repertoire because men learned it in their migratory work, which women did not engage in (ibid., p. 71). The language shift also varied with people's ages. All Gapuners older than 10 are currently bilingual because they have participated in a combination of traditional and modern activities. However, none of the 1- to 9-year-olds speaks Taiap. All are monolingual speakers of Tok Pisin, and most do not even understand Taiap (ibid., pp. 70–71). The reason is that conversations with children are conducted primarily in Tok Pisin, especially those involving important topics that elders want a child to attend to (ibid., pp. 194–195).

The strong, systematic association of language shift with gender and age groups indicates that linguistic symbols rest upon social processes for their formation and distribution. Gapuners did not individually create idiosyncratic personal symbols, nor did they negotiate semiotic constructs; likewise other villagers throughout Papua New Guinea did not coincidentally decide to renounce their native vernaculars in purely intellectual acts that were removed from social life. In fact, parents do not even understand why they and their children have shifted from Taiap to Tok Pisin. Parents are unaware of the fact that they have developed new forms of linguistic interchange with their children (ibid., pp. 7, 223). Their use of language unconsciously flows from the manner in which their social lives are organized.[5]

Both the construction and reception of cultural concepts are circumscribed by activities. Thus, when organizations such as advertising agencies, educational bureaus, religious organizations, labor unions, scientific and artistic societies, political parties, and entertainment companies promote concepts that they wish to be adopted by the populace, their success depends on whether the concepts are congruent with the life styles of the people they are reaching. Advertisers know that people's receptivity to marketing messages is affected by their social roles, which structure their interests and skills. Advertisers devise different styles of advertisements to appeal to occupants of different roles. Because ads are delivered through programs in the media, advertisers pressure the media industries to gear their entire programming to specific role occupants.

Advertisements will generate behavior only if people have the means to purchase products. In the United States business people created a massive change in life activities around the turn of the 20th century to support the new ideology of consumerism. National corporations cooperated with banks, advertisers, department stores, promoters, display artists, fashion designers, the entertainment industry, publishers of books and magazines, corporate lawyers, model agencies, credit advisers, business schools (e.g., Harvard Business School), and government agencies to promote consumerist buying and thinking habits. For example, businessmen such as John Wanamaker and Marshall Field lobbied the mayors and city planners of New York City and Chicago—and even sat on traffic committees—to ensure that zoning ordinances created a space for retail stores apart from noisy and dirty manufacturing enterprises, to ensure that old buildings could be torn down and replaced by department stores, and to ensure that subway lines converged on department store and hotel locations (Leach, 1993, pp. 173–176). Businessmen also promoted new retail practices such as installment buying and credit to enhance customers' abilities to buy. Electric signs and show windows were invented to call attention to products. Pageants and holidays were transformed into consumer rituals. Newspapers and magazines were turned into advertising vehicles when in 1893 Frank Munsey lowered the price of his magazine, *Munseys*, below market value to 10 cents and had advertisers subsidize the cost of production. Advertisements as well as magazine articles successfully promoted consumer thinking, imagination, motivation, and behavior because they were supported by these multiple changes in life activities (Garvey, 1996; Ohmann, 1996; Schmidt, 1995).

Political advertisements, endorsements, and slogans are similarly effective because they fall on a fertile field of activities: The populace has little in-depth information about, or participation in, political activity and thus is receptive to superficial messages as valid information.

If concepts are not supported by activities, they become impotent and irrelevant. If the ideal of democratic voting is contradicted by the reality that political activity is controlled by elite wealthy individuals (in the form of financing candidates and determining legislation by lobbying/bribing legislators), then the populace will reject the ideal and will not vote. In certain cases, *multiple activities* must support a concept (that is proposed by social leaders) for individuals to accept it. The idea that education is valuable will be accepted by the populace only if *educational activity* provides meaningful instruction in a solicitous manner *and* if *economic activity* provides opportunities to utilize education.

Concepts, like activities, are the result of struggles among the constituent groups of an activity. Although the outcome may be a compromise of competing meanings/definitions, it is usually dominated by the more powerful group(s) just as activities are. In contemporary United States, a dominant concept that reflects the interests of the social and economic elite is the notion that the United States is a classless, or single-class, society in which everyone is middle class. This concept obfuscates extreme socioeconomic inequality and the dominance of the rich elite. Another dominant concept is that everyone has the same opportunities to succeed. A corollary to this is that differences in wealth and power are due to individual hard work and/or natural talents rather than to an advantageous position one occupies in the social system (Gee, 1999, pp. 67–68). Concepts that contradict these dominant ones are rarely encountered in public discourse or in the media. Dominant cultural concepts that reflect the interests of powerful groups are called "hegemonic" (see Lears, 1985).

Powerful elites ensure conceptual hegemony in two ways: through controlling the actions of people in institutionalized activities and through controlling the dissemination of information (see McChesney, 1999; J. Thompson, 1990, pp. 193–205).

An important complexity in the area of cultural concepts is that a concept in one field may draw upon concepts and activities in another field of activity. An example is scientific concepts that incorporate concepts from economic or political activity. Dewey observed that:

> Every science in its final standpoint and working aims is controlled by conditions lying outside itself—conditions that subsist in the practical life of the time. With no science is this as obviously true as with psychology. Taken without nicety of analysis, no one would deny that psychology is specially occupied with the individual; that it wishes to find out those things that proceed peculiarly for the individual, and the mode of their connection with him. Now, the way in which the individual is conceived, the value that is attributed to him, the things in his make-up that arouse interest, are not due at the outset to psychology. The scientific view regards these matters in a reflected, a borrowed medium. They are revealed in the light of social life. An autocratic, an aristocratic, a democratic society propound such different estimates of the worth and place of individuality; they procure for the individual as an individual such different sorts of experience; they aim at arousing such different impulses and at organizing them according to such different purposes, that the psychology arising in each [society] must show a different temper. In this sense, psychology is a political science. While the professed psychologist, in his conscious procedure, may easily cut his subject-matter loose from these practical ties and references, yet the starting point and goal of his course are none the less socially set. (Dewey, 1910, pp. 242–243)[6]

Several scholars have concluded that natural science and philosophy in the 14th century was inspired by concepts and ways of thinking in the nascent capitalist economic and political activities. The preeminent historian of science Joseph Needham states that "The scientific revolution had not happened in a vacuum, but that it had been bound up so intimately that no one could fully detect the connections, with the rise of capitalism and the Reformation" (in Zilsel, 2000, p. xii). Specifically, early capitalism calculated and measured, introduced bookkeeping, and used machines. The rise of economic rationality furthered development of rational scientific methods. The emergence of the quantitative method, which is virtually nonexistent in medieval theories, cannot be separated from the counting and calculating spirit of capitalistic economy. The mathematical writings of the 15th and 16th centuries first deal in detail with problems of commercial arithmetic and, second, with the technological needs of military engineers, surveyors, architects, and artisans. The modern sign to denote mathematical equality was first used in an arithmetical textbook to promote the continual increase of commodities. The rationalization of politics and law also had its counterpart in the 17th century scientific idea that all physical processes are governed by rational natural laws. Furthermore, the individualism of the competitive marketplace was a presupposition of scientific thinking—it provided the inspiration for scientists to independently and critically assess evidence without relying on traditional authorities (Zilsel, 1939/2000, pp. 8–10; see also Hadden, 1994; Kaye, 1998, pp. 2, 201, 226–227, 229, 235–236).

Although cultural concepts are grounded in practical cultural activity, they are not necessarily accurate representations and understandings of activity. Concepts about social reality are fallible just as concepts of physical nature are. Just as people erroneously believed that the Earth was flat or that it was the center of the universe, so cultural concepts often misrepresent and obscure the social reality that generates them. (Bourdieu, 1990b, p. 122; Ratner, 1994, 1997a, pp. 107–108). Marx called these fallacious concepts "ideology." He explained that they have two sources.

1. Many concepts represent partial aspects of social life. They are true as far as they go but they do not represent the total character of social life. For example, individualism reflects real aspects of capitalistic social life including the private ownership of resources, private decisions about how to manage these, and private benefits from such ownership and control. However, individualism also obscures the real social connections and processes that constitute activities, concepts, and psychological phenomena. In the same vein, the notion that wealthy individuals have earned

their money through hard work is partially true, as they do accumulate capital, try to predict the market, and establish enterprises. However, such a notion is not entirely accurate because it obscures the fact that profit is generated by workers who do not fully receive the fruits of their labor.

These ideological concepts are believed by the populace because their partial truth describes and explains some portion of life events. As long as the populace does not think too deeply, comprehensively, or critically, these ideological concepts possess a veneer of sensibility.

2. Many cultural concepts are simply unadulterated propaganda that is deliberately manufactured by leaders to obscure problems and con-tradictions in society. For example, the concept that China is "a People's Republic" is a fiction that contradicts its totalitarian form of government and the disenfranchisement of Chinese people. Similarly, the American government's definition of its military interventions in Vietnam and other sovereign states as "preserving freedom and democracy" is mere propa-ganda that contradicts the imperialist intent and consequences of these interventions.

Activity theory ascertains the extent to which concepts about social life accurately comprehend it. In this sense, social science has the same goal as natural science—which also tests the validity of scientific concepts. If social science did not do this and instead accepted concepts at face value, it would be as remiss and useless as if natural scientists accepted the flat Earth view at face value.

Cultural Concepts Structure Psychological Phenomena

The foregoing lengthy discussion of cultural concepts was designed to illuminate their full, rich content which they impart to psychological phenomena. We shall now examine the content, modes of operation, and dynamics of psychological phenomena that embody the content of cultural concepts.

Cultural psychologists have investigated the manner in which cultural concepts serve as filters that mediate perception, memory, self-concept, and other psychological phenomena. One fascinating line of research found that perception of one's body is structured by cultural ideals of body image. The cultural ideal of a slim female body leads women to misperceive their body size. In a survey of women free of eating disorders, 95% misperceived their body size and overestimated it as one fourth larger than it was. In a survey of 33,000 women,

75% perceived themselves as too fat despite the fact that only one fourth were overweight according to standard weight tables and 30% were underweight according to the tables (Bordo, 1993, pp. 55–56). The ideal of a thin body is primarily directed at and accepted by white, young, middle-class, Western women. Consequently, they suffer dissatisfaction, misperception, and psychological disorders over body image and eating more than men and women of other ethnic groups and social classes. When white and Asian women of the same body size are asked to estimate the size of parts of their bodies, white women perceive their stomachs, thighs, and bottoms as significantly larger than Asian women do. Emotionally, white women are more dissatisfied with their body size than Asian women are (Grogan, 2000, p. 134). Black Americans, both men and women, are more positive about overweight in women than are white Americans. Black men are more likely than white men to want to date an overweight woman and to consider an overweight woman sexually attractive. Obese black women have a more positive body image than obese white American women and are less likely to want to lose weight. Black girls (14–18 years old) in the United States are four times less likely to diet or exercise as a way to control weight than white girls, and they are six times less likely to use diet pills or vomiting to control their weight. By age 9, ethnic differences in ideal body sizes are apparent, with black boys and girls selecting significantly heavier ideal body sizes for themselves than white boys and girls do (Grogan, 2000, pp. 133–137). Earlier we saw that magazines targeted at white and black women represented slimness and obesity differently. Contemporary psychological studies reveal that these differences have spilled over from magazine pages into the minds and bodies of black and white Americans.

A great deal of research demonstrates that the quality of emotions is significantly structured by cultural concepts. For example, the Buddhist concept of suffering and sorrow imbues sadness with a distinctive quality. Buddhists accept suffering and sorrow as everyone's common fate. They are usual, expected, understandable, and shared. They testify to human frailty and humility. Accepting this state of affairs defines one as a good person. Striving to avoid or alter one's fateful position is a manifestation of *hubris*. As a result of this concept, sadness is enobling and, paradoxically, pleasurable. It testifies to one's strength of character and to one's commonality with other people. Sadness rarely degenerates into depression because it is socially shared, understood, and accepted. North American sadness has quite different qualities because of its conceptual underpinning. Sadness is regarded as a deviant state that contradicts our normative values of success, pleasure, and optimism. In addition, sadness is regarded as a personal state caused by personal misfortune and is shared by few other people. This conceptual basis makes sadness a soli-tary, lonely, unusual, disturbing, unpleasant, pitiful, helpless ("What shall I do?"), overwhelming state of failure that one anxiously seeks to over-come. However, these qualities make it difficult to overcome and lead to degeneration into depression (Ratner, 1997a, pp. 106–107). The difference between the two forms of sadness is not simply the situations that trigger sadness, but rather the nature of the feeling itself. The feeling of sadness is a different experience for a Buddhist in Sri Lanka and for an American. Of course, there is some common element that makes both of them forms of sadness, but it is shot through with specific differences.

Shame is another emotion whose very quality depends on and varies with cultural concepts. Shame that rests upon Taoist concepts has a different quality from shame that rests upon modern concepts of self, suc-cess, material wealth, and social relationships. Ancient Taoists believed shame to be an intrinsic human frailty, namely the inability to achieve Tao. Tao was an ideal state in which the individual relinquishes intellectual reasoning and achieves an intuitive awareness of the unity of subject and object. The near impossibility of achieving this state of self-fulfillment causes shame. Shame is a universal, ontological, permanent condition that results from the inability of the human being to relinquish his own consciousness and merge with the world. It is a socially shared bond that unites people together and is infused with sympathy and compassion. This emotion is qualitatively different for a modern Korean who feels shameful because of her poor dress, for example. For her, shame is a personal lapse at a specific time and situation. It is a failure to employ reason and self-control (rather than relinquish them). Modern shame is theoretically possible to avoid by greater personal resolve (e.g., work harder and live better), and it has nothing to do with human nature or with overcoming the distinction between subject and object. In addition, modern shame is a negative condemnation by others that ostracizes the individual; it is not a shared feeling infused with bond-ing and commiseration. The two kinds of shame share a similar sense of inadequate capability; however, the feeling of inadequacy is quite dif-ferent as a result of the different mediations that modulate it (Ratner, 2000b, p. 11).

Symptoms of mental illness are also organized by cultural concepts (Ratner, 1991, pp. 264–278). A phenomenological account of schizophrenic symptoms reveals a dichotomized self that is split into a public "false" part that conforms to social demands and a private "true" self that fears and despises social relationships (and the public self that caters to them). The true, inner self believes that it is superior to other people, independ-ent of them, hidden from them, and able to be and do anything that it so desires. These specific features—which are overlooked and obscured by simplistic, abstract descriptions of schizophrenia as "out of touch with reality," "delusional thought disorder," and "flat affect"—are homologous with the Western concept of the individual as a private, self-made person, independent of society, with the capability to become whatever one wishes. The schizophrenic inner self also draws upon the individualistic notion that social life is a system of hypocritical social conventions that interfere with personal freedom and that must be circumvented in order to realize freedom.

Although general features of schizophrenia, such as vulnerabilities in processing information and regulating attention, may exist in numerous populations, their specific form and content vary with cultural concepts, social activities, and related psychological phenomena such as the self.

Bourdieu has provided a fascinating explanation of how artistic sensibility is grounded in cultural concepts and practices. His work is directly relevant to cultural psychology because artistic sensibility is a form of perception (see Bourdieu, 1977, Chap. 2, 1990a, pp. 76–86, 91, 1990b, Chap. 3, 1998b, pp. 6–8 for Bourdieu's cultural analysis of psychological phenomena). Speaking of artistic sensibility of the 15th century, Bourdieu said, "The Quattrocento eye is nothing other than the system of schemas of perception and appreciation, of judgement and of pleasure, which were acquired through the practices of daily life (schools, church, marketplace) by listening to lectures, speeches or sermons, measuring piles of wheat or lengths of cloth, or by resolving calculations of compound interest or maritime insurance, and which were put to work in ordinary existence and also in the production and perception of works of art" (Bourdieu, 1996, p. 318).

In the 15th century, the mathematical notion of geometric form underlay artistic perception and appreciation. Mathematical calculations of form were developed by Italian merchants who needed to measure strictly the volume of differently shaped containers in order to calculate prices. Merchants had to convert unstandardized containers into standard, regular forms that could be compared. Particular figures were hence redefined as cones, rectangles, cylinders, and polygons whose volume could be calculated in standardized units.

Baxandall (1988) explains the commercial basis of mathematical concepts that were utilized in 15th century Italian painting. His account is worth following because it illuminates the activity basis of perception. The transfer of concepts/schematas from commerce to painting was easily accomplished because many of the Italian painters were merchants (Baxandall, 1988, p. 87). Piero della Francesca was a painter/merchant and "The skills that Piero or any painter used to analyze the forms he painted were the same as Piero or any commercial person used for surveying quantities" (ibid., p. 87). "In both cases there is a conscious reduction of irregular masses and voids to combinations of manageable geometric bodies" (ibid., pp. 88–89). Painting compositions recapitulated commerce in emphasizing regular geometric forms such as circles, cones, cubes, cylinders, and polygons.

Art viewers had been educated in these geometrical skills and used them in looking at pictures. For example, they knew that a hexagon was a regular figure that repeated a particular form six times. When viewers recognized that the front view of a crown was a portion of a hexagon, they knew what the hidden remainder would look like (ibid., p. 91).

Another commercial concept that was incorporated into esthetic perception and presentation was exact proportionality. Merchants developed mathematical rules for calculating proportionality: A is to B as C is to D. They needed such rules in order to compare (equilibrate) amounts of commodities that had been measured in different systems and priced in different currencies. Two ounces at 30 cents had to be equilibrated with a number of liters priced in francs. These mathematical proportions were employed by painters in their design of objects. Using precise proportional relationships among parts of figures gave the paintings a sense of lucid solidity that strike us as remarkable now.

Linear perspective was another artistic perceptual competence that arose with commercial activity in the 15th century. Goldstein (1988) explains that linear perspective rests on distinctive concepts of space:

1. Physical space is continuous, infinite, and three dimensional.
2. Space is homogeneous.
3. Space is quantifiable.
4. The picture painted using linear perspective assumes that the viewer stands in a privileged position from which the painting is painted. The vision of a single pair of eyes viewing from a particular point of view at a particular moment supercedes other possible perspectives.

These Renaissance concepts of space were quite novel. They contrasted with the ancient and medieval notions of space as composed of discontinuous, qualitatively different, finite areas occupied by diverse people. These older views of space precluded thinking about diverse objects in the same space from a single point of view.

Goldstein argues that the "new way of viewing reality depended upon a new way of living" (ibid., p. 21). Specifically, the new view of space as homogeneous, infinite, and quantifiable reflects the economic conversion of qualitatively different products and processes into abstract,

homogeneous monetary value. The economic landscape that the entrepreneur purviewed was a homogeneous, infinite space of value. This was
recapitulated in concepts of physical space as homogeneous, infinite, and
quantifiable. The additional underlying concept of linear perspective—
privileging a particular position and viewpoint of a single individual—is
also based on new features of Renaissance economic life. This concept
reflects the freedom of the entrepreneur to construct his own point of
view of how to conduct business (ibid., pp. 74–82).

Although Quattrocento artistic sensibility derived from commercial
activities and concepts, it was not a strict duplication of them. Rather, it
was a sensitivity to forms and proportions that omitted much of the detail
of commercial calculations. As Baxandall explained,

> It would be absurd to claim that all these commercial people went around
> looking for harmonic series in pictures. The point to be made is less forthright.
> It is, first, that ... . These people ... used [their mathematical speciality] in
> important matters more often than we do, played games and told jokes with
> it, bought luxurious books about it, and prided themselves on their prowess in
> it; it was a relatively much larger part of their formal intellectual equipment.
> In the second place, this specialization constituted a disposition to address
> visual experience, in or out of pictures, in special ways: to attend to the struc-
> ture of complex forms as combinations of regular geometrical bodies and as
> intervals comprehensible in series. (ibid., p. 101)

Baxandall's statement of this relationship between commercial activity, mathematical concepts, and artistic perception indicates the nuanced
relationship between psychology and activity which warrants discussion
in the next section.

The Dialectical Relationship Among Cultural Activities, Artifacts, Concepts, and Psychological Phenomena

I have endeavored to prove that psychology is cultural. I hope to
have demonstrated that psychological phenomena possess a definite content that originates in cultural factors, is formed by them, embodies, and
perpetuates them. The cultural factors that constitute psychology are
social activities, artifacts, and cultural concepts. Social activities have a predominant influence that affects the content of artifacts, cultural concepts,
and psychological phenomena. To prove these rather unfamiliar, contro-
versial, and threatening points I have documented causal relationships
between two factors at a time. I have documented the influence of social
activities over artifacts, the influence of activities over cultural concepts,
the influence of activities over psychology, the influence of artifacts on

psychology, and the influence of cultural concepts on psychology. While this strategy documents each of these crucial causal relationships, it obscures some important issues. These include distinctive properties of concepts, artifacts, and psychological phenomena that are irreducible to the factors that influence them and that react back on these factors.

To fully understand the cultural character of psychology, we must understand activities, artifacts, concepts, and psychological phenomena as dialectically related. In a dialectical relationship, factors are interdependent AND distinct. They are neither independent nor reducible to each other. Hegel and Marx called a dialectical relationship a unity of differences, or differences within unity.

A dialectical relationship between social activities and cultural concepts means that there is an internal, intrinsic interdependence between the two. This connection is developed in various ways under various influences, but it always exists. Activities depend on and are influenced by concepts just as the reverse is true. Concepts are always part of activities. Activities never preexist concepts and then generate concepts as a later byproduct. People do not blindly initiate activities and then later develop concepts. People obviously conceive activities before and during their implementation. In addition, concepts motivate people to adopt activities. The concept of "individual equality" motivated women to achieve the same political, educational, and economic rights (to act) that men had. This power of concepts is so strong that it motivates vitriolic ideological struggles. Individuals strenuously advocate and oppose cultural concepts to promote certain activities. Business owners and university presidents seek to limit union propaganda from entering their institutions. University faculty often exhort students and administrators to reject commercial values in education because they alter the students' way of approaching education.

Smail cogently explained the dialectical interchange that existed between concepts and activities during the rise of industrialism in England. "On one hand, the economic changes could not have occurred without changes in attitudes toward work; on the other hand, attitudes were forced to change as economic practice evolved" (Smail, 1994, pp. 71, 80).

Within this dialectic of activity and concepts, activity had the leading role. "The cultural differences between clothiers and manufacturers did not exist beforehand; they developed along with the differences in economic practice and influenced the development of those practices" (ibid., p. 74). When concepts preceded activity, their function was to plan, motivate, and implement it. The fact that two things are interdependent and mutually influencing does not mean that their power is equal. Although activities do not determine concepts mechanically, they do structure concepts in a dialectical fashion (see Ratner, 1997a, pp. 110–115, 1997b).

A similar dialectical relationship holds among psychological phenomena and activities, artifacts, and concepts. Psychological phenomena are inherently part of activities, artifacts, and concepts. The latter three do not preexist psychology or cause it as a secondary byproduct. On the contrary, activities develop through the active participation of psychological phenomena. As Bourdieu (1993, p. 64) said, "The objective probabilities inscribed in the field [of social activities] at a given moment only become operative and active through 'vocations', 'aspirations', and 'expectations', that is, insofar as they are perceived and appreciated through the schemes of perception and appreciation that constitute a habitus." For individuals of a particular class to engage in class-related activities they must become equipped with corresponding psychological capabilities. For upper-class individuals to occupy positions of political and economic power they must have the correct cognitive competencies, social skills, and personality traits. In the section on activities I cited Hartmann's and Gee's findings that upper- and middle-class parents systematically inculcate these competencies in their children to prepare them to participate in appropriate activities. The existence of educational, economic, and political opportunities is irrelevant to the vast majority of the population who lack the activity-based psychological competencies to successfully compete for them.

Psychological phenomena make a difference to cultural life by facilitating homologous cultural factors and impeding incongruous cultural factors. Jealousy makes cooperative activities difficult because it resists sharing possessions, ideas, and even friends.

In the dialectic of psychological phenomena, social activities, artifacts, and cultural concepts, the former are formed by the latter while also being distinctive entities which modify them. Romantic love, for example, embodies elements of artifacts, activities, and concepts (Ratner, 2000b). At the same time love is also an emotion whose visceral quality is palpably different from the qualities of activities, concepts, and artifacts. The real disorientation that is part of romantic love tangibly disrupts social action and thinking even though it was inspired by activities and concepts. Motives, needs, anticipations, perceptions, imaginations, recollections, and hallucinations are additional psychological phenomena whose *qualia*, or qualities, are different from activities, cultural concepts, and artifacts and which significantly affect them.

Mental processes affect the form and intensity with which cultural factors are expressed. As Freud, Shakespeare, and other keen observers of human psychology have pointed out, mental processes repress cultural content, sublimate it in novel forms, compartmentalize it, exaggerate it (as when feelings of frustration or anxiety make us hypersensitive to irritations so that we respond more negatively than we otherwise would), compensate for cultural deficits (as when a child who receives little recognition stridently calls attention to herself, or seeks a father figure), rationalize it (with false labels and explanations), and rigidify it (as when an abused child adopts protective behaviors and refuses to give them up even in situations where they are unnecessary and deleterious). These mental processes make psychological phenomena distinctive from, and irreducible to, cultural activities, artifacts, and concepts. These mental dynamics testify to the fact that the mind is not like a tape recorder that records and mechanically replays inputs from the environment.

While recognizing that psychological phenomena are real and irreducible and affect other cultural factors, we must reiterate that they are always circumscribed and structured by the other cultural phenomena. Even Freud realized that repression, sublimation, displacement, and rationalization originate in social situations such as frustration, trauma, and neglect. Thus, the very mental processes that modify cultural aspects of psychology are themselves cultural products. Moreover, the manner in which individuals cope with social traumas ultimately draws upon social activities, artifacts, and concepts. Examples of such compensatory behavior are overeating, overworking, aggressiveness, egoism, and promiscuous sex. All of these are exaggerations of normative behavior.[7] In addition, our level of confidence, which guides selection of opportunities in the cultural environment, is the result of social experience. Social deprivation leads to developing "learned helplessness," "low self-efficacy," "external locus of control," "fatalism," low motivation, low self-confidence, and low aspirations (for occupations, school curricula, and social interactions, etc.). These psychological phenomena perpetuate the initial deleterious social position (see Martin-Baro, 1994, pp. 198–220). Social experience affects self-confidence in another, indirect way. Aspirations for oneself are constructed by observing the successes and failures of people similar to oneself (in appearance and background)—what social psychologists call "social comparison."

The fact that active, distinctive psychological phenomena are shaped by social factors was vividly demonstrated in Bartlett's research on memory. He found that memory often condenses material, unifies it, and adds and deletes elements to make it more familiar and understandable. This "effort after meaning" is directed by social schemes: "the specific bias ... in the group awakens in the individual too an acute tendency to notice, retain and construct specifically along certain directions" (Bartlett, 1932, pp. 254–255).

The dialectical relationship among cultural factors holds true on the phylogenetic and ontogenetic level. The phylogenetic development of activities requires the corresponding development of artifacts, concepts,

and psychology. Likewise, the phylogenetic development of psychological phenomena requires the corresponding development of cultural activities, artifacts, and concepts. The same mutual support is necessary for the
ontogenetic development of any of these components. Psychology develops in a baby to the extent that he or she participates in activities, utilizes
artifacts, and acquires cultural concepts (Tomasello, 1999). Conversely, the
baby can participate in family activities only if he or she acquires shared
concepts; utilizes artifacts such as spoons, chairs, napkins, clothing, and
tables; and develops psychological phenomena such as emotions, perceptions, memory, and reasoning.

A dialectical relation of cultural factors requires revising the unidi-
rectional model diagrammed in Fig. 1.1. While that model usefully depicted
the major lines of influence in cultural psychology, it (deliberately)
obscured the full, complex interrelationships among the factors. A revised
model portrays the factors as overlapping in a "quadruple helix." Each
helix of activities, artifacts, concepts, and psychological phenomena comprises a cultural field. The cultural field of work denotes the norms, positions, rights, responsibilities, rewards, and qualifications entailed in the
activity of work plus concepts, artifacts, and psychological phenomena
(including perception, reasoning, memory, emotions, imagination) that
are fostered by the practice of work. The fields of politics, education,
medicine, sports, religion, entertainment, law, art, religion, and the family
are each similarly comprised of activities, artifacts, concepts, and psychological phenomena. "The culture of poverty" likewise denotes definite
socioeconomic activities that produce insufficient jobs, skills, and salaries,
along with associated concepts about things (likelihood of success, trust in
people) and psychological phenomena (self-esteem, motivation, reasoning,
intelligence).

The dialectical model of cultural factors integrated into cultural
fields may be depicted as in Fig. 1.2.

Figure 1.2 indicates that a cultural field is comprised of four components that are interdependent, interpenetrating, and unified, yet also distinctive and irreducible to each other (see Ratner, 1997a, pp. 110–116).
Each component of a cultural field is a system of elements: An activity
consists of heterogeneous positions, responsibilities, rights, rewards, and
norms. "Concepts" consist of numerous concepts about things. And "psychological phenomena" consist of diverse functions such as perception,
logical reasoning, problem solving, memory, motivation, emotions, self-
concept, and imagination. We must keep in mind that the quadruple helix
is dominated by social activities; the four components are not equally
powerful although each exerts some influence over the others.

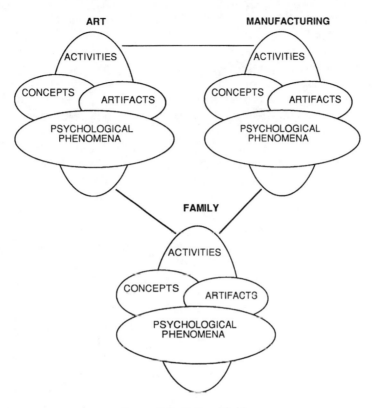

FIGURE 1.2. Cultural fields.

AGENCY FROM THE PERSPECTIVE OF ACTIVITY THEORY

Agency is the animating force that constructs, maintains, and transforms cultural activities, concepts, artifacts, and psychology. Agency can be defined as the intentional causal intervention in the world, subject to the possibility of a reflexive monitoring of that intervention (Bhaskar, 1989, p. 81).

From the perspective of activity theory, agency is dialectically related to cultural factors. This means they are inseparable yet distinct. Agency is real and has a determining effect on the others, yet it is also dependent on them, facilitated by them, and constrained by them. Human agency produces social activities, artifacts, cultural concepts, and psychological phenomena in order to survive and develop (see Ratner, 1991, Chap. 1). Its products then react back on it and determine its capabilities. For example, the machines (instruments) that human agency produce determine the speed, strength, and precision that human actions can have. Although agency produces the machines, the latter still determine the capabilities that people have. In the same way, the socially organized activities, concepts, and psychological phenomena that agency produces determine the capabilities that people have. Human agency is mediated (facilitated and constrained) by its own products. It is not a supreme, transcendental force that acts on its own. Agency has the power to see beyond the given and to create new products—that is the definition of agency. However, its creativity is always "conditioned" by existing mediations. It is not free to imagine and invent any- and everything at a given time. The process is a spiral where situated, mediated agency is enabled by its conditions to imagine certain new phenomena, it invents them, and is then enabled to imagine and invent additional phenomena.

This dialectical view of agency has been articulated by eminent scholars. Bhaskar said that "Society provides necessary conditions for intentional human action, and intentional human action is a necessary condition for it" (Bhaskar, 1989, pp. 36–37). Agency always operates within and through a social structure. "The social cannot be reduced to (and is not the product of) the individual [and] society is a necessary condition for any intentional human act at all ... Society is both the ever-present *condition* and the continually reproduced *outcome* of human agency" (ibid., p. 34). From a cultural perspective, agency is "the temporarily constructed engagement by actors of different structural environments which, through the interplay of habit, imagination, and judgment, both reproduces and transforms those structures in interactive response to the problems posed by changing historical situations" (Emirbayer & Mische, 1998, p. 970). Bourdieu employed the concept of *habitus* to denote intentional action that is socially constrained: "The notion of habitus restores to the agent a generating, unifying, constructing, classifying power, while recalling that this capacity to construct social reality, itself socially constructed, is not that of a transcendental subject but of a socialized body, investing in its practice socially constructed organizing principles that are acquired in the course of a situated and dated social experience" (Bourdieu, 2000, pp. 136–137).

Agency is cultural in two senses: It forms culture and is formed by culture.

Agency is indispensable to culture because it forms ("causally intervenes in") activities, artifacts, concepts, and psychological phenomena. Activity theorists from Marx and Engels on have recognized the vital role that agency plays in forming, maintaining, and altering social activities. Marx and Engels stated that "History does nothing, it 'possesses no immense will,' it 'wages no battles.' It is man, real living man who does all that, who possesses and fights; 'history' is not, as it were, a person apart, using man as a means to achieve its own aims; history is nothing but the activity of man pursuing his aims" (Marx & Engels, 1845/1975, p. 93).

Bourdieu acknowledged agency in his account of the genesis and structure of the literary field. He emphasizes "how much Flaubert contributed, along with others, notably Baudelaire, to the constitution of the literary field as a world apart, subject to its own laws." "Baudelaire effects for the first time the break between commercial and avant-garde publishing … " (Bourdieu, 1996, pp. 48, 55–56, 67). Specifically,

> Even though it [the new differentiated art field] is inscribed in a potential state in the very space of positions already in existence, and even though certain of the romantic poets had already foreshadowed the need for it, those who would take up that position cannot make it exist except by making the field in which a place could be found for it … They must therefore invent against established positions and their occupants, everything necessary to define it, starting with that unprecedented social personage who is the modern writer or artist … (Bourdieu, 1996, p. 76)

Agency actively constructs activities, artifacts, concepts, and psychological phenomena. This process prevents each from being mechanical replicas of the others. Agency requires that each be investigated in its own right to ascertain precisely what has been utilized from the others (Bourdieu, 1990b, pp. 52, 55).

The fact that agency causally intervenes to create culture means it is culturally oriented. It is so because human beings depend on social activities, artifacts, and concepts to develop/realize themselves (see Ratner, 1991, Chap. 1, 1993a,b, 1994, 1997a,b, 1998, 1999). Just as thought is objectified and realized in social language, so agency is objectified and realized in culture. As merely an individual wish or action, agency is as ineffable and impotent as thought without language. Consequently, agency has *social intentionality*.[8]

History provides real examples of agency realizing itself by creating institutionalized social activities, artifacts, and cultural concepts. Speaking about the rising English bourgeoisie in the 17th and 18th centuries, Smail tells us that "They had to create their own institutions and these institutions helped to create class identify" (Smail, 1994, p. 121). "The associations, the disputes, and involvement in national politics were means by which the commercial and professional elite at once constructed their middle-class consciousness and expressed this class identity vis-à-vis other groups" (ibid., p. 122). "These men exerted their dominance as a group, for their efforts to achieve their common goals required them to work together" (ibid., p. 122).

In the same vein, new artistic viewpoints are institutionalized in social activities if they are to endure (Bourdieu, 1996, p. 61). "The constitution of art as art is inseparable from the constitution of a relatively autonomous artistic field" (Bourdieu, 1990b, p. 113). An entire system of art producers, sellers, displayers (galleries, museums), publicists, and critics must endorse artistic viewpoints or they remain marginalized, or disappear.

Whether agency is more or less original, fulfilling, and humane depends on the social organization of activities and concepts that people experience. Where social activities are democratically controlled by the majority of citizens, their agency is stimulated in the process of deciding important, complex issues. Unfortunately, most societies are dominated by a small group of powerful individuals who wrest control of social relationships from the majority of people. The agency of the resulting classes then reflects their positions in the social system. The agency of the powerful rulers runs the major social institutions and makes wide-ranging decisions about fundamental issues. The agency of the populace is much more limited because it has been subjugated by the ruling elite and deprived of the ability to control major life activities (see Marx's *Economic and Philosophic Manuscripts* for the classic statement of this alienation). In contemporary capitalist society, the agency of most people is limited to individual mundane tasks such as finding a job, a friend, a house to buy, a vacation spot, a hobby, a movie to watch, a candidate to vote for, and to interpersonal interactions with individual friends and relatives. The agency of most people does not control the manner in which social activities such as work, religion, education, government, and medical care are socially organized (Ci, 1999a & b).[9]

The difference between creative, fulfilling agency and conformist, debilitating agency is not that one can choose and one cannot. The difference lies in the kind of choices that are available. Therefore, choice in alienated conditions does not eliminate alienation.

Agency that concentrates on individual mundane tasks is a historically situated, culturally specific form of agency. Individualistic agency is not natural or universal. The fact that individualistic agency is fostered by, adapts to, and functions to perpetuate specific social relationships demonstrates that, like all agency, it is socially intentional.

Because agency has a social character that depends on social activities, it is not intrinsically creative, fulfilling, or empowering. It becomes so only by creating social activities that promote these characteristics. In this sense, *agency is a historical project*. It needs to be realized and perfected through historical processes. Agency is akin to language. Like language, agency exists as mere potential in the infant. It is actualized only through participation in social interactions (see Marcuse, 1964, 1987). The specific kind and level of language that a person expresses depends on her position in a particular society. The same is true for agency. Throughout the world, individuals no more possess the same kind of agency than they speak the same language.

If culture comprises the character of agency, then enhancing the creativity, fulfillment, and power of agency requires constructing activities, artifacts, concepts, and psychological phenomena that call for such characteristics. If one tries to alter agency by focusing exclusively on the individual, one will fail because one has neglected its cultural constituents. The more one narrowly focuses on changing agency by itself, the more it will conform to social relations because these constituents of agency remain intact. Vygotsky put it well when he said that "Life becomes creation only when it is finally freed of all the social forms that distort and disfigure it" (Vygotsky, 1997a, p. 350).

Barber (1984, p. xv) amplified this point in an eloquent statement:

> Autonomy is not the condition of democracy, democracy is the condition of autonomy. Without participating in the common life that defines them and in the decision-making that shapes their social habitat, women and men cannot become individuals. Freedom, justice, equality, and autonomy are all products of common thinking and common living; democracy creates them ... We are born in chains—slaves of dependency and insufficiency—and acquire autonomy only as we learn the difficult art of governing ourselves in common ... we acquire equality only in the context of socially sanctioned political arrangements that spread across naturally unequal beings a civic mantle of artificial [cultural] equality.

Even understanding and improving oneself requires understanding and improving one's social relationships. Each person must understand the manner in which his ideas and actions reflect social practices and concepts. He must repudiate adverse social practices and concepts in his own life, and he must engage in social action to uproot them from society at large so that they no longer influence himself and other people.

The question is, how can stultified, alienated agency understand its social world and work to create a new one that will promote creative agency? Freire used the term *concientizacion* to denote this process. The term "supposes that persons change in the process of changing their relations with the surrounding environment and, above all, with other people" (Martin-Baro, 1994, p. 41). Through critically understanding their social system, people grasp the constraints on their psychology and behavior. This awareness opens up the horizon to new possibilities for social action and for new forms of identity and other psychological processes. The process is a kind of spiral in which alienated agency (collectively) takes initial steps to humanize its social relationships, then these improved social relationships foster enhanced agency which then takes greater steps toward reforming social relationships which then promote enhanced agency (see Martin-Baro, 1994, p. 218). People can overcome alienation if they develop a new form of agency that comprehends and humanizes their social world. Their existing individualistic agency cannot accomplish significant personal or social improvement because it is stultified and misdirected.

Activity theory helps to identify whether agency is alienated and conformist or is improving life. Activity theory distinguishes genuinely novel behavior (which surpasses prevailing cultural activities and enhances the fulfillment of people) from acts that are superficial variations of the status quo (see Williams, 1977, p. 123). It does so by examining the social content and mode of operation that psychology/behavior possesses and identifying whether these recapitulate existing activities, artifacts, concepts, and psychological, or whether they point toward a better cultural system.

Richard Wright performed this kind of analysis on petty theft that Southern blacks carried out against their white employers in the 1920s. While many blacks believed that black petty theft was a liberating act of defiance against white oppressors, Wright revealed this behavior to be quite individualistic. Stealing by one individual from another had no potential of improving the subordinate position of blacks. The black thief dared not directly confront his employer or the system of oppression. Petty thievery perpetuated the subservient, sneaky, irresponsible stereotype that whites held of blacks. Consequently, many whites accepted this behavior by blacks. As Wright explained, "The southern whites would rather have had Negroes who stole, work for them, than Negroes who knew, however dimly, the worth of their own humanity. Hence, whites placed a premium upon black deceit; they encouraged irresponsibility" (Wright, 1945, p. 219).

Many contemporary psychological phenomena that appear to be innovative and liberating similarly recapitulate crucial features of the status quo. For example, many women who adopt the personality trait of assertiveness believe they are realizing their true selves. However, an analysis of the cultural activities that underlie this trait lead to a different evaluation. Activity theory reveals that this change in women's personality was induced by economic pressures to join the labor force. With real wages of men declining from the 1970s until today, a family could maintain its standard of living only if women entered the labor force. Participating in the bourgeois economy, with its competitiveness, materialism, depersonalization, alienation, and individualism led women to become assertive in the same way that men had become (Risman, 1987, p. 27). From this perspective, assertiveness among women is not a form of self-fulfillment, but conformity to economic roles.

Derne (1994, p. 218) arrived at the same conclusion after analyzing the concepts and practices that Indian women devise to enhance their subordinate position. She concludes that paradoxically, "Women respond to structural constraints by creating meaning systems that reconstitute that social structure" (ibid., p. 222). Kandiyoti (1988, p. 275) similarly concludes that women strategize within a set of concrete constraints that reveal and define the blueprint of a "patriarchal bargain." Patriarchal bargains exert a powerful influence on the shaping of women's gendered subjectivity. They also influence the specific forms of women's active or passive resistance in the face of their oppression (see Gaudio, 1998; Jackson & Oates, 1998, Chaps. 7 and 8 for a similar assessment of homosexual relationships as recapitulating heterosexual relationships).

Brison extends this line of thinking and concludes that most cases of suffering lead individuals to adopt coping strategies that recapitulate social norms and values. Suffering does not usually lead to challenging the conditions that provoke it. Nor does suffering lead to improved coping skills. For example, bereaved Kwanga (New Guinea) women and men

> unwittingly followed cultural scripts that allowed them to work through diffuse pain by defining and expressing their emotions in ways that won communal approval. But in doing so, women internalized a view of themselves as helpless victims while men took on the personas necessary to exercise leadership in the village. In short, in the attempt to maintain a positive sense of self, individuals were drawn to think and feel in ways that ultimately supported male dominance in Kwanga society. (Brison, 1998, p. 372)

Psychological disorders are another example of acts that are active constructions which appear to transcend social norms, but actually recapitulate normative social activities, concepts, and psychological phenomena. Disorders are highly creative constructions in the sense that the individual creates mental states that are unusual. Nineteenth century women suffering from hysteria, for example, deadened their senses and immobilized their limbs in extraordinary ways. However, a careful cultural analysis reveals that these symptoms embodied stereotypical characteristics of the female gender role. Hysterical conversion reflected the middle-class feminine ideal of a weak, spiritual person. Normal middle-class women were expected to shun physical work, take no interest in bodily pleasure, and even avoid mentioning bodily functions. This dephysicalized feminine ideal became the basis for the sensory and motor deadness of hysteria (Ratner, 1991, pp. 273–274).

Another example of an innovative behavior that recapitulates social norms is teen motherhood. Teenage motherhood elicits cultural condemnation and entails high social, economic, and personal costs. It appears to exemplify an innovative, antisocial behavior. However, Luker (1996)

observes that teen motherhood is socially constrained. It is predominant-
ly a phenomenon among very poor girls (80% of teen mothers are from
extremely poor backgrounds). It also ultimately ties young mothers
to those conditions and prevents their transcending them. Moreover,
teen motherhood seeks to obtain socially valued gratifications despite
the unusual age at which it occurs. Luker tells us that teen mothers are
using their babies to establish self-esteem, respect, and a stable, intimate
interpersonal relationship. In this regard, teens recapitulate the "cult of
motherhood" that is a common value throughout Western society.
Utilizing conventional means to obtain conventional ends, and perpetu-
ating a life style of extreme poverty and alienation do not constitute
genuine agency despite the fact that teen motherhood violates social
taboos against early sex and parenthood (see Ratner, 1998 for a further
discussion). Such behavior appears to manifest creativity and agency only
if one disregards the social activities and concepts it reproduces.

Creative agency introduces more substantial change into the given
than conformist agency does. However, it is not more autonomous from
social life in the sense of disregarding it and marching to its own beat.
Actually, creative agency is more deeply aware of social life than conformist agency is. It also works on social life more systematically.

According to activity theory even truly creative actions are exten-
sions of prior conditions and values. Creative actions utilize possibilities
that exist in the given social order for qualitatively new things. Such
actions are creative because they perceive potentials in existing social life
that are not obvious. Creative agency does not invent things on its own,
out of the blue. Its creativity is shaped by problems and potentials inherent within given conditions.

Consider the rise of capitalist economic activity in Western Europe
from the 14th to the 18th centuries. The capitalistic social relationships
that the merchants organized were made possible by the prior expansion
of trade under feudal lords. This expansion spurred commodity production and it increased the numbers and strength of the merchant class
(Dobb, 1963). Without this historical foundation, commodity production
would have remained primitive and the bourgeois class would have
remained small and weak. The merchants were genuinely creative in
devising new social relationships of production, but it was the old feudal
system that prepared them for this possibility. The incipient commercial
activity of feudalism determined that commercial leaders would become
the next ruling class and the new system would be an intensified form of
commodity production. No other kind of economic activity and ruling
class could have found the resources to sustain themselves at that historical moment.

Agency is cultural because it is cultivated by social experience. Rich social experience seems to be indispensable for producing original work. Fowler arrived at this conclusion in his study of 25 great mathematicians (18 men and 7 women): "The early lives of great mathematicians were richly stimulated in symbol modes that generated semiautonomous cognitive systems capable of acquiring, processing, and originating vast complexities of abstract mathematical concepts. Rich early experiences may be a necessary condition for the full development of competence potentials" (Fowler, 1986, p. 87; see also Howe, 1999a,b). Mozart's extraordinary musical talent was definitely fostered by an unusually stimulating social and musical environment. While Mozart transcended his formative experience and raised musical creativity to a level far above his teachers', his transcendence depended on extraordinary experience. Mozart built upon what he had been exposed to; he did not build something out of nothing (Halliwell, 1998, pp. 23–24, 43–44).

To understand genius, one should "suspend the charismatic ideology of 'creation' which ... undoubtedly constitutes the principal obstacle to a rigorous science of the production of the value of cultural goods. It is this charismatic ideology which directs the gaze towards the apparent producer—painter, composer, writer— ... thereby avoiding any inquiry beyond the artist and the artist's own activity into the conditions of this demiurgic capability" (Bourdieu, 1996, p. 167; White, 1949, pp. 233–281).[10]

ADVANTAGES OF ACTIVITY THEORY FOR CULTURAL PSYCHOLOGY

Activity theory possesses several advantages over other theoretical approaches for understanding and improving the cultural character of psychology. It provides:

1. A specific and comprehensive definition of cultural psychology that is built on a rigorous definition of culture. Culture is a system of social activities, artifacts, cultural concepts, and psychological phenomena. These are organized in clusters that comprise cultural fields (see Fig. 1.2). The discipline of cultural psychology studies the content, mode of operation, and interrelationships of psychological phenomena that originate in, are formed by, embody, perpetuate, and modify activities, artifacts, and concepts.

2. A unifying and clarifying direction to the field of cultural psychology. Activity theory directs cultural psychologists to investigate the interrelationships of social activities, artifacts, concepts, and psychology. This focus defines the field of cultural psychology. It sets the parameters of

what qualifies as cultural psychology. It provides cultural psychologists with a common ground and language. Science requires well-defined basic concepts that are coherently related to each other, and that comprehensively and incisively account for real phenomena (Ratner, 2000a).

3. A conceptual foundation for the science of cultural psychology. Science is possible only if phenomena have regular characteristics and interact in regular ways. Haphazard features that change randomly are not amenable to scientific investigation. Activity theory conceptualizes cultural psychology in a way that is amenable to scientific investigation. It links psychological phenomena to a system of cultural factors that interact according to definite principles.

Activity theory recognizes order in culture beneath the dizzying diversity of cultural factors and experiences. Activity theory organizes a vast number of cultural elements—such as television, newspapers, books, parental socialization practices, peer interactions, school rules, traffic rules, dress codes, church services, clothing styles, building architecture, the myriad of attitudes that people hold, and the infrastructure of roads, shopping centers, and residences in a community—into a system of activities, artifacts, and concepts. Research on particular items partakes of and contributes to knowledge of these three factors.

Conceptualizing culture and psychology as organized into patterns of factors rather than as a dizzying diversity of haphazard, individual elements, enables cultural psychology to follow the analytical thinking that all sciences use. All science penetrates beneath the ostensible appearance of things to comprehend essential patterns and explanatory factors. Just as Newton discovered that seemingly disparate events such as apples falling and planets revolving are really forms of an essential factor, gravity, so cultural psychologists shall discover that the modern concept of self, the notion of developmental stages that parents apply to their children's behavior, modern women's assertiveness, women's desire to make decisions about abortion, the demand for tolerance of diverse life styles, and the emotion of romantic love are all forms of individualism that originates in unregulated, privately controlled, free-market economic activity.

Activity theory leads to construing cultural psychological phenomena in the shape of a funnel: diverse phenomena (e.g., romantic love, modern self-concept, women's aggressiveness) are construed as points on the large circular head of a funnel, and they are unified by a common stem in the form of a cultural concept or activity—such as economic individualism.

4. An enriched description and explanation of psychological phenomena. Linking psychological phenomena to cultural activities, artifacts, and concepts enhances the description of their features by casting them in specific cultural terms. It also explains their reasons for existing. A con-

textual analysis of psychological phenomena enriches our understanding in the same manner that understanding the rules of baseball is necessary to understand a "strike" in that game, and understanding capitalist economic relationships is necessary to understand a labor strike against management. These advantages of a cultural analysis can be seen in Southall's (1973, p. 66) linking of courtly romantic love to the social activities, relationships, and conditions in which it occurred:

> An important characteristic of courtly love wherever it was found was that it was aristocratic. It grew up in a feudal society and the love of a troubadour was thought of in terms of feudal relations. The lover devoted himself to the service of his mistress, who became his liege lady. He was her baillie and had to render her the submission of a vassal ... Such a conception of the relations between a lady and her lover would be likely to grow up in a typical Provencal castle in which there were very few women of rank but many landless knights, squires, and pages, who were feudally inferior to the lady of the castle. This relationship helps to explain the extreme humility which is one of the characteristics of courtly love. Another result of the association between courtly love and feudalism was that knightly qualities, especially courtesy and loyalty, which would in any case be desirable in a lover, came to be especially valued.

While courtesy, humility, yearning, and adoration in courtly love can be noticed without a cultural analysis, these qualities are concretized and explained by situating them in the feudal social relationships where they occurred. Our knowledge of social relationships leads us to recognize their specific characteristics in psychological phenomena.

5. A recognition that all facets of culture are constructed by human agency. None of them is reified, natural, or permanent. All of them are changeable via agency.

6. A general conceptual structure for comprehending the cultural aspects of all psychological phenomena in all societies. Activity theory provides a general conceptual basis for understanding the particular, variable cultural aspects of psychological phenomena. In other words, if one seeks to understand the cultural specificity and variability of psychological phenomena, one should follow the tenets of activity theory and link psychology to the particular social organization of activities, artifacts, and concepts. If one fails to follow these general guidelines, the specific, variable cultural character of psychology will be overlooked.

Of course, activities, artifacts, and concepts take on specific characteristics in particular societies. As such they are the basis of psychological specificity and variability. The point is that all the psychological specificity of all people throughout the world is a function of their social activities, artifacts, and cultural concepts.

7. A recognition that change in any of the constituents of culture requires change in others as well. Change in activities requires that

cultural concepts and psychological phenomena (perception, reasoning, emotions, motives, imagination, problem solving) change. Change in psychology, artifacts, and concepts, in turn, requires transformations in underlying activities. This is an important connective to mainstream psychology which seeks to improve psychological functioning on an individual level. For example, educational success is supposed to be enhanced, and antisocial behavior reduced, by parents and teachers praising children to augment their self esteem. Drug and alcohol abuse is supposed to be mitigated by telling adolescents to "say no to drugs." School violence will supposedly cease if parents spend more time with their children. In the traditional model, content-free interpersonal experiences (spending more time, praising) are seen as enhancing content-free psychological phenomena (self-esteem) that will improve social life (reduce violence and drug abuse). Social life is improved from the bottom up through new individual experience and psychological phenomena.

This model of psychological change and social improvement is naïve. It fails to directly confront the social organization of activities, the artifacts, and cultural concepts that foster psychological dysfunction (see White, 1949, pp. 125–136).

This failure is exemplified in discourse analysis. Discourse analysts reduce society and social life to forms of discourse. Discourse is the paramount social influence on individual psychology. Consequently, psychology can best be improved by altering discourses. Social institutions, activities, roles, class, and conditions are exempt from analysis and change. For example, Gee's discourse analysis in education interprets educational problems as problems in discourse and his solution is to improve students' discursive capability by apprenticing them to rich environments and traditions of Discourse (Gee, 1992, pp. 124–127). Gee states that even this limited solution is not feasible for many minority and lower socioeconomic students because 'mainstream' Discourses, often conflict seriously (in values, attitudes, ways of acting, thinking, and talking) with their own home- and community-based Discourses (ibid., p. 117). Gee's advice for these students is to lower their sights, get help editing written material, and try to "psych out" interviewers who are gatekeepers to educational and occupational advancement (ibid., pp. 118–119).

Gee never indicates that the discourse problems of poor students are rooted in activities, conditions, resources, and opportunities. Consequently, he never considers changing these aspects of poor students' lives.

In contrast, activity theory would trace the students' discourse problems to their position in economic, political, and educational activities. Their position deprives them of the resources and opportunities necessary to adopt fulfilling life styles, including discourses. *The structure of these economic, political, and educational activities needs to be transformed*—toward greater democracy, equality, cooperation, and human fulfillment—if poor students are to adapt fulfilling norms of discourse (including thinking, talking, and acting). This insight is one of the practical values of activity theory.

NOTES

1. Of course, individuals do many things outside of socially organized activities. They engage in personal pursuits such as hobbies, friendships, and enjoying nature. However, we shall see that even personal pursuits are structured by their position in the interstices of socially organized activities.
2. Although workers and entrepreneurs are legally free, they are constrained by social pressures. Competitive pressures of supply and demand from other individuals determine whether individual decisions are successful. The free market does not eliminate social influences on the individual. It simply leaves it up to him to fathom these influences and cope with them. Actually, competitive market forces are extremely coercive because they operate impersonally and unpredictably. Economic agents do not directly organize their behavior together. Each acts independently and imposes his action on others (lowering prices, introducing a new product, finding a new job). Others feel the brunt of the action *ex post facto*.
3. The character of many roles/activities has been radically transformed by the inexorable expansion of capitalist economic activity. Business leaders and their political representatives have been remarkably successful in commodifying most aspects of professional sports, entertainment, news gathering and reporting, book publishing, health care, and even politics, law, child care, and education (see Noble, 1998; Sklair, 1998; Spring, 1998 for documentation of the commercial influence on education worldwide; Swartz, 1997, Chap. 8 for a discussion of how education reproduces economic activities from the perspective of Bourdieu).

   The commercialization of news can be gleaned in one sentence from a recent report: "As entertainment costs went up, news became a comparatively stronger profit generator for station managers, who with the help of consultants devised stunts and gimmicks to draw viewers" (*The New York Times*, July 3, 2000, p. C7). In other words, station managers became interested in promoting news programs because they were cheaper to produce and hence could generate greater profits. They were not interested in news because of its informational value, only for its exchange value. If news were more expensive to produce these managers would be less interested in it. Furthermore, the managers sought to attract more viewers to watch the news by providing stunts and gimmicks! They made the news sensationalistic, increased the "chatty" comments, and hired famous personalities to comment on the news. Again, the managers did not enhance the newsworthiness of the news. Nor did they appeal to or cultivate people's interest in news. Rather than improve the "product" they simply surrounded it with misleading images—much like manufacturers of cigarettes and junk food do—to entice people to consume a cheap product (see Exoo, 1994 for a thorough documentation of the effect of commercialization on the news and entertainment).

   Commercial pressures are increasingly eroding the autonomy of the natural sciences as well. Corporations are expanding their funding of scientific research—they currently fund 25% of research—and they are placing restrictions of this research. They tend to fund projects that have the greatest commercial applications rather than the greatest intrinsic scientific value. Moreover, they appropriate the results of the research and prevent its dissemination throughout the scientific community. Corporations demand nondisclosure agreements, worldwide patent rights, royalties, and intellectual property rights. These restrictions lead to publication delays of the findings or nonpublication altogether. An official of the American Association of The Advancement of Science recently stated that "The commercialization of science has resulted in a new regime of secrecy which is very concerning to the scientific community" (*The New York Times*, April 6, 1999, p. D3). Medical research is particularly prone to commercial corruption. Many medical scientists receive monetary remuneration from drug companies and this biases their research in favor of drugs that the companies are trying to market. An analysis of 70 studies on the safety of a heart drug found that 96% of authors who had drug company ties found the drugs to be safe, while among experts with no drug company connections, only 37% said the drugs were safe. When drug companies pay for research into the effectiveness of their own pain relievers, 100% find their drug superior to a competitor's. An analysis of company-funded studies published in peer-reviewed journals found that results of the studies favored the company's products 98% of the time. Drug companies often have their employees write research studies and then pay a prominent researcher to be named as the author even though he contributed nothing to the research except his name (*San Francisco Chronicle*, Aug. 16, 2000, p. A3).

4. Eckert (1989, p. 7) makes the important point that most analysts of these two diverse adolescent styles attribute them to either personal choices or to family dynamics. Jocks are either more mature than Burnouts, or, according to some, Burnout parents simply do not spend enough time preparing their children for a successful life. These analyses share a common preoccupation with individual processes to the exclusion of social class pressures—standard of living (housing, nutrition, clothing, transportation, and cultural resources), educational background, work pressures, discrimination, and neighborhood—that structure interpersonal and psychological processes.

5. However, Kulick arrives at a different conclusion. He claims that changes in cosmology, or meaning, were the most significant cause of linguistic shift. He goes so far as to state that "Gapun might be held up as a case in which the macrosociological changes that are occuring can be said not to have caused language shift, but rather, to have been *caused by* shift: in attitudes, perceptions of self, and ideas about language" (p. 260). This is an odd conclusion considering that Kulick extensively documented changes in social activities that were instrumental in the shift in meanings and language. Kulick's attributing the language shift primarily to a new cosmology grants them an autonomous status ungrounded in activities. This leaves those ideological changes unexplained. It also minimizes the importance of social activities when their importance is obvious. Kulick's explanation does not do justice to his data and is unwarranted by that data.

6. Findings in social psychology concerning conformity, social cognition (e.g., the self-serving bias), attribution theory (e.g., the attribution error), and attitude change all express broad cultural values and activities despite the fact that they are presumed to be universal (Hogan & Emler, 1978). The same is true for findings in other fields of psychology such as developmental research (Cushman, 1991; see also Ci, 1999a,b; Ratner, 1997a, pp. 231–240 for additional discussion of political concepts that are embedded in psychological concepts).

7. The content of compensatory behavior is not determined by frustration, deprivation, and trauma. These can make individuals hypersensitive and rigid, and they may lower one's level of aspiration; however, they do not mandate that one will become a janitor; love a particular person; be abusive, competitive, conservative, racist; or prefer math 1A to English 1A in high school. The content of these choices is cultural. Low self-esteem individuals can be

kind, peaceful, and cooperative, just as high self-esteem individuals can be competitive, calculating, and aggressive. Once a certain course of action is charted—based on social models—a person's psychological deprivation may lead to using it as a protective shield against emptiness. However, the deprivation, per se, does not determine which course of action the deprived individual will adopt. These details are a function of social experience and can be altered only by altering the social organization of life. Crime will not be eradicated, nor will world peace be achieved, through "boosting" people's self-esteem. Individuals who use antisocial behavior as a defense against low self-esteem will be reluctant to renounce it, and they require help to enhance their self-esteem in order to entertain the possibility of pro-social behavior. However, this psychological work will lead to pro-social behavior only if it is fostered by a cooperative social milieu. Raising self-esteem in a competitive, individualistic society will not generate pro-social behavior. Psychological change must be part of social reform but it cannot replace it. Subjectivity does not conjure up life styles by itself. Its activity is circumscribed and organized by social activities, artifacts, and concepts.

Freud erred in attributing content to the psyche itself. He postulated biological origins of love and sex that built in particular content to them, for example, a biological urge for the male child to have an exclusive psychological and sexual relationship with his mother that led to hating his father. He also believed that natural biopsychological mechanisms such as reaction formation determine that a repressed desire would be transformed into a desire with an opposite content. Thus, the psychological mechanism determined the content of the new desire. Freud's attributing content to psychic mechanisms led him to overlook the role of social experience in this regard.

8. Cooley's "looking glass self," Mead's "taking the role of the generalized other," plus social referencing, attachment, joint attention, and imitation all express this human social intentionality. Social intentionality (rather than egocentrism) seems to be a basic characteristic of humans. At 8 months, babies follow the pointing of other people and observe whether others have followed their pointing (see Bruner, March 9, 2000; Ratner, 1991, Chap. 4; Tomasello, 1999.)

Unfortunately, most authors restrict social intentionality to interpersonal interactions with individuals and they ignore organized social life.

9. Brison (1998, p. 381) put it well when she said that "All groups within society do not seem to have equal capacity to innovate on cultural scripts." Certain groups are better prepared by their background and current social position to innovate than others. The Kwangas, for example, support men who innovate; however, they criticize women who do so. This social difference makes it far easier for men to be creative compared with women.

10. More ordinary feats of overcoming adversity to achieve normal development also depend on extraordinary social experiences. Werner (1989) investigated children who were at risk for developmental deficiencies. Two thirds of the at-risk children who grew up in poor families developed serious learning or behavior problems by the age of 10. However, one third of these poor children grew up adequately. Interestingly, these latter children succeeded because of special treatment from caretakers. In certain cases the caretakers developed a protective relationship with the poor children because they cherished certain physical or psychological traits in the latter. In these cases, the resiliency of the children was due to the way that their traits attracted the care of adults, not to some intrinsic capability to succeed on one's own (Werner, p. 108D).

Sameroff and Fiese (1992) replicated Werner's analysis of individuals who seemed to transcend their impoverished social background. The authors found 20% of their subjects performed better than peers from similar backgrounds. Their explanation is as follows: "When we searched among our measures to find the factors that permitted these children to do better than their peers, we found differences in the attitudes and practices of their parents ... The parents had constructed a safe family environment in which their children could develop in the midst of the social chaos that typified their neighbors. The environment was modified to foster development rather than hinder it" (p. 352). Thus, even individual exceptions to social trends are prepared by social factors rather then individual ones.

Garbarino, Kostelny, and Barry (1997, p. 318) arrive at the same conclusion: "In analyzing how some children grow up as competent adults despite negative surroundings and considerable adversity, researchers have identified three crucial factors: (a) a warm and affectionate relationship with an adult who cares for and supports the child; (b) an environment that includes high expectations for the child and faith in the child's ability; and (c) opportunities for the child to participate in the life and work going on around him or her."

Groups of people similarly succeed or fail depending on the social conditions in which they live. Ogbu (1987, pp. 152–153; Ogbu and Stern, 2001). shows that a people's ability to resist the oppressive effects of exploitive culture depends little on personal attributes and primarily upon their social–historical position in it. "Autonomous minorities" such as Jews and Mormons succeed in America and overcame initial estrangement, discrimination, and inferior status because they came to the United States with a distinctive and intact cultural identity, and because they were allowed to enter certain educational and occupational positions in the middle and higher regions of the cultural hierarchy. In contrast, "castelike minorities" such as American Indians and black Americans experienced the most difficulty in overcoming discrimination and inferior status because they were subjugated and deprived of their cultural identity, and they were denied opportunities for true assimilation.

INDIVIDUALISTIC APPROACHES TO AGENCY: A CRITIQUE

In recent decades, many cultural psychologists have endorsed a very individualistic conception of agency. They regard agency as producing individual, personal acts and attitudes. According to this conception, individuals negotiate their life styles in interpersonal dialogues, or they construct their psychological "life spaces" individually, independent of even interpersonal, linguistic interactions. In neither case are broader social constraints on these constructions acknowledged. Culture is merely the sum of individual acts (Bhaskar, 1989, p. 27). This individualistic view of agency is prevalent throughout the social sciences, especially in anthropology and cultural psychology. Although this viewpoint repudiates the cultural aspects of agency discussed in Chapter 1, ironically it is presented as cultural psychology by scholars who are reputed to be cultural psychologists. This trojan horse threatens to subvert the cultural thrust of cultural psychology. I therefore feel it necessary to critique it here.

THE INDIVIDUALISTIC CONCEPTION OF AGENCY AND CULTURE

Among the cultural psychologists who advocate the individualistic approach to agency, Jerome Bruner, Sylvia Scribner, Jaan Valsiner, and Dorothy Holland are prominent figures whose work warrants evaluation. Although much of their work has explored ways in which psychological phenomena are cultural, they endorse a decidedly noncultural view of agency. It is their articulation of agency, not the entirety of their work, that I address here.

Bruner believes that culture comprises symbolic meanings that are interpersonally negotiated through linguistic discourse. This interpersonal semiotic negotiation of meanings is the way agency actively constructs culture: "If one is arguing about social 'realities' like democracy or equity or even the gross national product, the reality is not in the thing, not in the head, but in the act of arguing and negotiating about such concepts. *Social realities are not bricks that we trip over or bruise ourselves on when we kick at them, but the meanings that we achieve by the sharing of human cognitions* (Bruner, 1982, p. 837, emphasis added). In Bruner's world, we do not encounter and are not bruised by armies, wars, inequality, abuse, exploitation, pollution, global warming, power, poverty, wealth, disease, the world bank, congress, the CIA, immigration quotas, emigration restrictions, or prisons. These are not real things "out there in the world" that directly affect us. They are simply meanings that are negotiated through interpersonal communication. We can easily change these concepts by simply renegotiating them with our colleagues.

Bruner espouses this conception of culture because it provides room for individuals to actively participate in cultural construction. If culture consists of negotiated meanings then all individuals are cultural agents because everyone daily expresses his or her opinions about cultural things to other people: "It is the forum aspect of a culture [in which meanings are negotiated and re-negotiated] that gives its participants a role in constantly making and remaking the culture—their *active* role as participants rather than as performing spectators who play out canonical roles according to rule when the appropriate cues occur" (ibid., p. 839).[1]

For Bruner agency conducts face-to-face conversations among individuals. Bruner does not consider negotiations about meanings to occur in organized groups where group processes/dynamics transcend individual behavior (à la Durkheim). He never considers negotiations about meanings to occur in administered institutions (à la Weber). Nor does he consider negotiations about meanings to arise in practical activities such as work, education, politics, law, religion, medicine, book and magazine publishing, entertainment, and news industries which are organized in definite roles that carry differential power, opportunities, and rewards (à la Marx). For Bruner nothing outside the interpersonal negotiation of meanings affects that process. He explicitly denies the existence of social conditions, institutions, bureaucracy, wealth, power, physical force, technology, the physical environment, and even customary, normative actions, because these are all transformed into mental significations. With things, social life, people, and even behavior reduced to mental significations, there are no real societal influences on the individual (i.e., psychology) that need to be understood or challenged. In this sense Bruner's agency operates outside society.[2]

In a later piece entitled "On the Dialectic of Culture" (Bruner & Amsterdam, 2000, pp. 217–245), Bruner acknowledges that institutions and social rules do affect psychology. However, he minimizes their impact and in the end espouses his earlier position exalting the mental freedom of individuals. For Bruner, the dialectic of culture consists in the tension between established canons of action, institutionalized and administered in organizations, and the human tendency to create alternatives to them. Bruner recognizes that the status quo includes social roles that orient people to think and act in particular ways, for example, "We behave and think 'post-office' in the post office." He also speaks of social change including actions to alter social institutions and normative actions. However, these acknowledgments of social conditions and forces turn out to be largely nominal. They are constantly shot through with assertions that individuals are ultimately free of social bonds because they can exercise their imagination and exercise in dialogue about their creative ideas.

Bruner negates the power of social institutions in a number of propositions. First, social institutions are not too constraining because they themselves are products of negotiation. Moreover, in Bruner's view, compliance with social norms is purely voluntary. Institutions don't compel particular behaviors; it's just easier and more effective to act according to social norms. For instance, in New York City "You don't *have to* deal with municipal functionaries as a New Yorker would. But it's easier, and maybe even more effective" (p. 235). Social influence is therefore easily avoided if one tolerates some inefficiency and discomfort. Rather than culture penetrating into an individual's psychology and organizing it, it is more akin to a set of aids for making life easier that a person can accept or reject.

Social influence is attenuated further because individuals always have many opportunities to develop alternative ideas: "Cultures ... institutionalize 'sites' to aid us in possible-world construction, such as theater, fiction, and partisan politics" (p. 235). These alcoves exist because of the "human mental capacity that *compels* us to project our imaginations beyond the ordinary, the expectable, the legitimate" (p. 235). The continual striving to project our imagination beyond the given cannot be squelched. It is respected by leaders and managers of society who institutionalize sites where people can escape from social norms and devise new ideas and actions. Administrators of the status quo may disapprove of dissidents, but "they [dissidents] are *always* left some elbow room to do their thing" (p. 237, emphasis added). Individuals are always free to reconstruct their lives.

The most important element in such reconstruction is imagination. Bruner insists that the "orthodoxies of a culture are always in a dialectical relationship with contrarian myths, dissenting fictions, and (*most important of all*) *the restless powers of the human imagination*" (p. 232, emphasis added). "The dialectic between the canonical and the imagined is not only inherent in human culture, but gives culture its dynamism, and in some unfathomable way, its unpredictability—its freedom" (p. 232).

Freedom for Bruner consists in exercising the imagination. He doesn't emphasize that action, especially action to alter social systems, is vital for people to be free. Nor is it even necessary that imagination have a certain content that could lead to certain action. Freedom is not imagination of a more democratic, peaceful, cooperative, egalitarian, environmentally sensitive social system. Nor does freedom consist in action that implements thoughts in practice. Freedom is merely any mental exercise of imagination that conjures up new thoughts.

If freedom is defined as exercising imagination, then we are all free right now because we can use our imaginations at any moment. Alienation, oppression, and conformity are wiped away at a stroke by defining freedom as the imagination that lies within us. Freewheeling individual mentation and interpersonal discourse remain the cornerstones of Bruner's agency.

Another variant of the individualistic conception of agency is Scribner's work. She regards agency as improvising creative acts in the course of social routines. As people engage in social practices they invent idiosyncratic thoughts and behaviors that testify to their activity. Scribner agrees with Bruner that individuals do more than play out canonical roles according to rules. They also bend the rules in small ways because they are active agents.

For instance, a group of dairy workers was given the task of filling empty cases with milk bottles. Each case held 16 quart bottles. One task was to put 22 bottles in cases. The instructions were written as 1 (case) + 6 (bottles). The standard, literal solution would be to find an empty case, fill it with 16 bottles, then find another empty case and fill it with 6 bottles. Another task required cases to be filled with 10 bottles. The instructions were written as $1-6$. The standard, literal solution would be to find a full case and remove 6 bottles. Scribner found that many of the workers bypassed literal solutions and improvised more efficient ones. To arrive at 10 bottles, many workers found partially filled cases (e.g., containing 13 bottles) and removed a few bottles to reach the required 10. A 13-bottle case required removing 3 bottles instead of 6. In certain instances, workers found a case with 8 bottles and added 2 to reach 10. In these cases, they transformed a subtraction problem into an addition problem (Scribner, 1983/1997, p. 302).

Scribner exults over the workers' creativity in improvising strategies (ibid., p. 307). She says that the shortcuts were more efficient ("optimal," "optimizing") than the literal solutions (ibid., pp. 302–303, 307). The mental shortcuts bypassed formal mathematical thinking and employed intuitive visualization instead. Scribner also claims that the shortcuts were idio-syncratic responses that introduced variability into the work routine (ibid., pp. 304, 306). In her words, literal "algorithms describe how computers solve problems. Variability and flexibility describe how skilled workers solve problems. Here we have a basic structural difference between formal, academic thinking and practical thinking at work" (ibid., p. 307). Scribner is saying that formal, socially structured, shared thinking that uses algorithms is mechanical, stereotyped, inhuman, and inefficient. In contrast, informal strategies are visual and intuitive, creative, variable, and human. Informal strategies constitute freedom for the workers: "With domain-specific knowledge, expert workers have greater opportunity to free themselves from rules, and to invent flexible strategies" (ibid., p. 307).

Scribner locates agency in individual, idiosyncratic improvised responses that are independent of established cognitive conventions, rule-governed behavior, and social institutions and conditions.

Holland endorses a similarly individualistic view of agency. She professes interest in the formative influence of social practice, social interac-tions, or "figured worlds" on psychological phenomena (Holland et al., 1998, pp. 39–41). However, she focuses more on the fact that people interpret a social world than on the cultural content of the interpretations. One of her studies investigated the ways in which college girls experience romantic love (ibid., Chap. 5). She reports that some girls pursue romantic love enthu-siastically while others are either ambivalent or reject it. One girl, Sandy, sought romantic love but had trouble establishing the kind of relationships she wanted with men. She also learned that a potential boyfriend from back home was involved with someone else. So she took a stronger interest in friendships and developed a special friendship with one person (ibid., p. 106). Another girl, Karen, tried to make herself more attractive by sug-gesting to her boyfriend that she had many other suitors. Holland explained these strategies as based on personal decision-making processes that the subjects employed: "These strategies were ones the women themselves had improvised or decided to use ..." (ibid., p. 112). Holland explains the sub-jects' approaches to love as stemming from personal traits such as their iden-tification of themselves as romantically inclined and skillful (ibid., p. 116).

Holland clearly believes that agency is an individual phenomenon that constructs a personal "life space." She does not mention any cultural influences that may have motivated or constrained the girls' personal decisions. Nor does she mention any ways in which the decisions may have reflected and reinforced cultural influences.

One of the most radical views of agency as an individual phenomenon is Valsiner's. Formerly an advocate of Vygotsky's sociohistorical psychology, he now asserts that culture is a set of "suggestions" that individuals can freely accept, reject, or modify as they wish. Valsiner replaces sociohistor-ical psychology with a new formulation called "co-constructionism." In contrast to sociohistorical psychology, which construes the individual as profoundly affected by culture, co-constructionism grants primacy to the individual's decision about how to deal with culture. Acknowledging that his new position is a wholesale rejection of sociocultural psychol-ogy, Valsiner states, "The logic of the argument supporting the relevance of the social environment in human development is *reversed* in the co-constructionist paradigm" (Branco & Valsiner, 1997, p. 37, emphasis added). According to the new paragidm, "Most of human development takes place through *active ignoring and neutralization of most of the social suggestions* to which the person is subjected in everyday life" (Valsiner, 1998, p. 393, emphasis in original).

Valsiner believes that psychological distancing from society enables the individual to construct a personal world of meanings that can "tran-scend the complex state of any collective culture" (ibid., p. 116). Individuals do much more than selectively synthesize elements from social life. They create meanings that transcend and change it (ibid., p. 114). Culture is continually being changed by ordinary individuals constructing and externalizing new meanings.

Valsiner even contends that infants construct their own personal goals. They utilize culture as an instrumental means for achieving their own goals; they do not adapt themselves to established culture as social scientists formerly believed: "Children create what is necessary for reach-ing their personal goals through social mediation in their interpersonal relations with peers" (Vasconcellos & Valsiner, 1998, p. 86). "The child ... utilizes the collective culturally meaningful surroundings to build his or her personal understanding of the world. The ways in which the latter is constructed are *the child's own*—each child creates a unique personal world" (ibid., p. 87, emphasis added).

Valsiner's antagonism between individual agency and culturally con-structed, shared activities rests on a belief that culture is toxic to individ-ual autonomy and fulfillment. Social influences are regarded as "collective cultural viruses" that are "affect-laden meanings [symbolic concepts] meant to infect or penetrate personal belief systems (systems of personal sense). Their success, however, depends on whether the individual's per-sonal culture in its present state is susceptible to such influence, or whether it contains psychological 'antibodies' or conflicting beliefs (that had emerged during previous experiences), that block or neutralize the 'attack'" (Lightfoot & Valsiner, 1992, p. 396). In other words, individual processes determine the effect that social life has on a particular person. Social life affects someone only to the extent that he or she lets it.

With culture construed as toxic, individuals must protect and insulate themselves from it:

> In order to guarantee relative stability of the personality system, it has to be well buffered against immediate social suggestions. The latter may be filled with dramatisms, hurtful efforts, or declarations of love or hate (or both), yet the likelihood of such single episodes having "long-term effects" of any direct kind need not be taken for granted. Hence, what is usually viewed as "socialization efforts" (by social institutions or parents) [is] necessarily counteracted by the active recipients of such efforts who can neutralize or ignore a large number of such episodes, aside from single particularly dramatic ones. (Valsiner, 1998, p. 393)

Valsiner's preoccupation with individual activity in opposition to culture is evident in his analysis of the way in which a woman, Jenny, uses language to present herself to people. She is portrayed as having various personal desires and using cultural symbols to express them. Cultural symbols are external to her desires and are freely selected and discarded as needed. In Valsiner's analysis, Jenny uses cultural meanings of words to express her personal feelings toward marriage and to present herself to others (Valsiner, 1998, p. 333). Valsiner never discusses ways in which Jenny's feelings are themselves influenced by cultural activities and values.

Valsiner's insistence that individuals create their own personal meanings in opposition to society contradicts his view that individuals "co-construct" their meanings (and psychologies) in conjunction with cultural processes. Valsiner's actual psychological explanations, descriptions, and analyses disregard any serious impact of culture on psychology.

In summary, the individualistic view of agency in relation to culture proposes:

1. Agency initiates individual acts of personal significance. These individual acts can be negotiated among several people. Acts of agency operate independently of broad, macroscopic activities. Bruner prioritizes the individual formation and negotiation of symbols over their collective form. In his 1982 article, he does not consider collective ideologies, propaganda, and doctrines that influence peoples' psychology. Nor does Bruner consider the role of administered social organizations such as the Vatican, the Chinese communist party, the American State Department, American news companies, and corporations in promulgating particular symbolic meanings of things. Bruner considers only local, small-scale, interpersonally negotiated meanings.

2. Individual constructions are more creative, profound, interesting, efficient, and effective than objectified, socially organized acts and artifacts. Scribner expresses this view in her contention that

informal, nonliteral, solutions—which spontaneously visualize and feel a situation rather than cognize it—are optimizing in comparison with literal, cognitive solutions that utilize academically taught formal algorithms. Valsiner and Holland similarly believe that personal meanings and acts are more creative than normative collective behavior.

3. Society is composed of individual behaviors. In Bruner's view, society is a forum for individuals to negotiate meanings in face-to-face interactions. In Valsiner's view, society is the sum of personal meanings devised by individuals.

Society changes as individuals change their personal behavior. Individualistic cultural psychologists never consider agency as working in social movements to alter social institutions, conditions, systems, or ideologies that are represented by vested interests who resist change.

4. Cultural influences are negligible. They are merely "suggestions" that are readily ignored, circumvented, and negated by individuals. They have no power to affect us unless we allow them to.

CRITIQUE OF THE INDIVIDUALISTIC VIEW

Individualistic cultural psychologists manifest a palpable antipathy to broad culture beyond the individual. Their cultural phobia subverts a serious analysis of psychology as a cultural phenomenon.

The assumptions of individualistic cultural psychologists are unsupported by empirical data. These authors never demonstrate the extent to which individuals actually ignore, circumvent, or negate society. This would require rigorous procedures for making detailed comparisons of personal constructions with social practices and concepts to ascertain whether the former are really unique and creative. The authors never perform this kind of empirical analysis to substantiate their claim. They simply present a behavior and cavalierly declare it to be a personal meaning with no justification whatsoever. Nor do these authors demonstrate that personal constructions are more creative and efficient in general than socially constructed activities and concepts. Nor do they provide any examples of societies being formed and transformed by individual behavior.

In fact, existing theoretical and empirical research contradict individualistic tenets, specifically with regard to the following.

1. A great deal of empirical and theoretical research from sociohistorical psychology, sociology, anthropology, history, biology, and political

philosophy demonstrates that agency is socially formed. That is, agency is oriented toward, depends on, and is constrained by social activities, institutions, conditions, and movements (see Tomasello, 1994). Individualistic psychologists simply dismiss this research and replace it with the notion that agency is a personal capability. Individualistic cultural psychologists commit what social psychologists call "the fundamental attribution error"—the tendency to attribute behavior to personal dispositions rather than situational influences (Norenzayan & Nisbett, 2000).[3]

2. Agency is structured by social institutions, structures, behaviors, and dynamics. They structure psychology by imposing rules of behavior, benefits, and punishments. Institutions and structures are not simply suggestions or meanings that can be ignored with impunity. Moreover, they are largely controlled by an elite minority of individuals while the majority of people are disenfranchised from negotiating the rules of behavior.

Bruner (1982, p. 840) himself notes that educational institutions have traditionally been authoritarian. Likewise, corporate decisions to terminate thousands of jobs at a stroke are not negotiated with employees, nor are they merely mental significations, nor are they ignored by the workers who suffer from them. The university administrator who reduces expenses by crowding 300 students into a lecture hall and hires a teaching assistant to teach the course does not negotiate with the students, yet her action directly affects their experience. Corporate domination of entertainment, sports, government, medicine, and news imposes social relationships and concepts on people and impedes the ability of citizens to negotiate their life styles. Discrimination in loaning money, selling houses, and offering jobs is another kind of real action that directly affects behavior without negotiation. The mother who watches television during dinner and does not communicate with her child similarly affects the child's psychology without linguistic negotiation. Valsiner himself incongruously acknowledges that sexuality is culturally canalized: "Sambia male 'temporary homosexuality' is part of the cultural canalization of young boys to strict heterosexual orientation, social identity as warriors, and bonding with their age sets" (Valsiner, 1998, pp. 379–380).

Agency is also structured by narratives. Narratives do not simply express personal or interpersonal meanings, as individualists assume. Narratives are social formulations whose cultural content structures an individual's identity. Individuals use social narratives to describe their own experiences, and in so doing their own experiences take on a socially shared form. Thus, individuals use religious narratives or corporate narratives to describe and understand their own experiences. They see themselves through (in terms of) the narrative (Linde, 2001). They do not transform every social narrative into projections of their own experience.

3. Agency actively strives to conform to social conventions. It does not necessarily seek to insulate itself in a world of personal meanings. Individuals desperately seek to purchase popular consumer products, cultivate an acceptable body, live in fashionable neighborhoods with acceptable addresses, and have socially desirable boyfriends and girl-friends. Failing to conform to these social standards makes people miser-able and even mentally ill. A disturbing example of this social intention-ality is the widespread desire among black Jamaicans to admire and cultivate the physical features of Caucasians. Although more than 90% of Jamaicans are dark-skinned descendants of Africans, and only 0.2% of the population are white-skinned descendants of Europeans, blacks admire and adopt Caucasian features. Black parents and teachers routinely favor light-skinned children. Dark-skinned adolescents are dissatisfied with their bodies and yearn for light skin, straight hair, blue eyes, and straight noses. They bleach their skin and take animal hormones to lighten it (Leo-Rhynie, 1997). Clearly, the agency of black Jamaicans is striving to emulate a foreign ideal of other people rather than create unique personal meanings.

4. Most of the choices that people believe they freely make unwit-tingly incorporate cultural concepts, activities, and artifacts. This can be seen in the basic act of forming a personal identity. "Although individu-als are highly active in the process of self-making, the materials available for writing one's own story are a function of our public and shared notions of personhood. American accounts of the self, for example, involve a set of culture-confirming ideas and images of success, compe-tence, ability, and the need to 'feel good'" (Oyserman & Markus, 1998, p. 123). "The public representations of selfhood that characterize a given sociocultural niche function as common denominators—they provide the primary structure of the selves of those who live within these contexts. These shared ideas produce necessary, although often unseen, common-alities in the selves of people within a given context" (ibid., p. 109). "Although making a self appears to be an individual and individualizing pursuit, it is also a collective and collectivizing one" (ibid., p. 107). Identify-formation must be a collective and collectivizing process because, "From a societal perspective, self-construction is too important to be left as a personal project. Social integration and the social order require that individuals of a given group have reasonably similar answers to the 'who am I' and 'where do I belong' questions" (ibid., p. 107).

Blumer (1969) provides another vivid example of how individual agency is subsumed within general activities and concepts. He studied the behavior of dress designers and buyers in the Paris fashion industry. At a seasonal opening of a major Parisian fashion house a hundred or more designs of women's evening wear may be presented before an audience of from one to two hundred buyers. The buyers are "a highly competitive and secretive lot" who decide which designs to purchase independently of each other, without knowledge of each other's selections. One might expect such competitive and independent buyers to select widely different designs. In fact, the more than 100 buyers purchase only seven styles all together. Their individual agencies uncannily act within a very small range of behaviors although theoretically they have the freedom to act in very disparate ways. Blumer explains this commonality as stemming from their common participation in the women's fashion industry: "By virtue of their intense immersion in this [activity] the buyers came to develop common sensitivities and similar appreciations. To use an old but valuable psychological term, they developed a common 'apperception mass' which sharpened and directed their feelings of discrimination, which guided and sensitizes their perceptions, and which channeled their judgments and choices" (ibid., p. 279). For the same reasons, dress designers create remarkably similar designs despite the fact that they work independently of each other and are also competitive and secretive (ibid., p. 280).

Wertsch similarly found that college students who independently wrote essays about the origins of the United States employed a common cultural explanatory concept. All the students believed that the founding events in American history were motivated by a quest for freedom. Wertsch's conclusion is worth quoting because it emphasizes the shared perspective that results from appropriating common cultural concepts ("narrative tools"):

> One of the most striking facts about the texts is that *all of them were fundamentally grounded in the quest-for-freedom* narrative tool [i.e., ideology]. No matter how much or how little the subjects seemed to accept and agree with this narrative tool, they all used it in one way or another ... [Even] subjects [who] conveyed that they were resisting the quest-for-freedom narrative, in the end still employed it. In fact no student even attempted to employ another narrative tool in any extended way ... In such cases, individuals may try to resist the ways in which such cultural tools shape their actions, but they are often highly constrained in the forms that such resistance can take. (Wertsch, 1998, pp. 107–108)[4]

These examples demonstrate that "It is in each agent, and therefore in the individuated state, that there exist supra-individual dispositions capable of functioning in an orchestrated or, one could say, collective way" (Bourdieu, 2000, p. 156). The dispositions among disparate individuals are shared because they occupy similar social positions, which results in similar experiences. Common experience with similar conditions leads to acquiring shared dispositions even without interpersonal communication or agreement among the individuals (ibid., pp. 145–146).

Another telling example is the manner in which parents choose schools for their children. When parents are given monetary vouchers to use for tuition at the school of their choice, their choices do not reflect an idiosyncratic, personal decision. Their choices replicate their social class standing, with upper-class parents sending their children to better schools than lower class parents do. As Howard Gardner concluded in an incisive review of a school system that expanded parents' choice,

> Choice turns out to be a positive benefit for parents who are educated, knowledgeable, and able to make use of their power within the system. However choice does not really exist for everyone. Those with low incomes simply cannot choose where to live, drive their children to distant schools, or find the money to cover the higher costs, fees, and perquisites that are expected at tonier schools. Far from become more egalitarian, the school system has become increasingly stratified as families segregate themselves by ethnic group and by socioeconomic status. Moreover, those with options desert the less effective schools, thereby abandoning them to those with the fewest options. (Gardner, 2000, p. 48)

Gardner's words are aptly chosen when he states that "Families segregate themselves by ethnic group and by socioeconomic status." Families make choices; however, they are structured by social class and ethnic group. The result of these socially structured choices is a socially stratified pattern of education, not a random or egalitarian one. Movements to expand personal choice (e.g., by privatizing social services) really serve to solidify the existing class structure of society (see Saltman, 2000). "Individual choice" is a smokescreen for social determinism. The only way to overcome social determinism and expand choices for people is for the majority of the population to directly and deliberately control social processes.

The fact that ostensibly free choices uncannily assimilate and perpetuate prevalent social practices and values can be seen in the cases that individualistic cultural psychologists present. In one of Valsiner's cases, a woman was entering a church and encountered a beggar asking for alms at the entrance. She refused his request on the grounds that he was only pretending to be poor and didn't really need the money. Valsiner (1998, p. 120) proclaims that in this refusal the woman "distanced herself (ignored or negated) from a social demand" and engaged in an act of personal construction/agency. However, her refusal reflects a widely held repugnance toward begging. She distanced herself from the immediate social demand of the beggar by invoking a different social concept of begging. The woman simply selected one social value and behavior over others. She did not creatively construct a unique personal meaning that transcended and modified culture.

In another case, Valsiner believed that a 1 1/2-year-old baby girl playing with a doll was engaged in "constructing her understanding of the symbolic aspects of her own actions" (Vasconcellos & Valsiner, 1998, p. 96). It is impossible to determine whether the baby was constructing personal understandings and meanings. The authors never stipulated any criteria for identifying them nor did they interview the baby to ascertain what she was thinking. Most of the behaviors that the authors report ostensibly seem to qualify as social conformity rather than active construction of personal meaning. After one boy hit the baby, other boys started imitating this action rather than opposing it. Later, in scene 6C, a small boy tried to get into the box where she was playing but she hit him and kept him away. In this act, she was evidently protecting herself from a boy who, based on previous experience, appeared threatening to her. This behavior is simply a common form of self-protection and shows no indication of being a unique personal invention.

Another of Valsiner's studies revealed more obvious instances of social conformity. Branco & Valsiner (1997) studied 3-year-olds in the hope of demonstrating the individual processes that persons generate (p. 55) to continuously reorganize the constraining social system (p. 49) and introduce novelties into it (p. 61). The authors' observational analysis of interpersonal interactions found a quite different pattern of behavior: the children conformed to adult social demands and were not creative agents. An adult facilitator encouraged cooperation among the children (p. 56) and the initially rebellious and self-centered William quickly (in 2 minutes) complied with the adult's exhortations to help others (p. 57).[5]

Holland's examples of personal agency, which purportedly transcend social norms of love, are similarly unconvincing. The author provides no detailed information about her subjects' thinking that would substantiate her claim. The descriptions that are provided indicate more social conformity than personal creativity. For example, Karen's strategy of enhancing her attractiveness by exaggerating her appeal to numerous men bears striking resemblance to a principle of free market economics—namely, that increased demand drives up the value of a commodity. Businessmen often exaggerate the demand for a product to enhance its attractiveness and increase its price. Employees often exaggerate the number of job offers they have, or could have, to raise the value of their salaries. From Holland's brief description, Karen evidently imported this common business practice into her personal world of romantic love.

Scrutiny of Scribner's workers indicates that they too adopted prevalent social strategies in their ways of minimizing labor. The mental shortcuts they devised enabled them to work more quickly and efficiently, which is exactly what corporate managers demand. Far from escaping the controls of management, the workers accepted the capitalist principle of economy of effort (Scribner, 1997, p. 307). The specific cognitive shortcuts that the workers improvised may have been spontaneous; however, the impetus for devising them and the effect they produced clearly recapitulated a prevalent principle of the capitalist organization of work.

In addition, the workers' improvisations were simple and minor recalculations that required little intelligence or ingenuity. Visually recasting a problem from $16 - 6$ (bottles) to $6 + 4$ may be an improvisation; however, it is hardly a brilliant reconceptualization that deserves awe and admiration. Even apes engage in visually recasting problems and improvising solutions, as Kohler's classic demonstrations prove.

Scribner greatly exaggerates the creativity of mundane thoughts, as do all the cultural psychologists we have been examining. They take any glimmer of individual action as a sign of great individual initiative and creativity that transcends cultural customs. However, most acts of individual agency are quite uncreative variations in existing cultural practices and concepts. They do not liberate people from social constraints as our cultural psychologists claim.

5. Personal psychological constructions are not more creative than socially constructed, formalized, institutionalized ones. Higher formal mathematics that is developed and taught in educational institutions is infinitely more creative, imaginative, accurate, and useful than impressionistic visualizations and arithmetical improvisations.

6. Agency does not become more creative, fulfilling, and empowering by constructing or negotiating personal meanings, as individualistic cultural psychologists suppose. Genuine individual agency, in the sense of being creative, insightful, and fulfilling, develops only when the individual is cognizant of essential features of the world beyond himself. The most profoundly creative achievements in human history—by geniuses such as Shakespeare, Galileo, Michelangelo, Rembrandt, Mozart, Einstein, Darwin, Marx—have comprehended essential features of the world that are inspirational to millions of other people. In no way are they personal meanings that are significant only for the individual inventor. As Hegel said in the introduction to his *Philosophy of Fine Art*, "the productive imagination of the artist is the imagination of a great mind and heart, the apprehension and creation of ideas and of shapes, and, indeed, the exhibition of the profoundest and most universal human interests in the definite sensuous mold of pictorial representation" (Hegel, 1970, p. 69).

7. Social reality is not reducible to semiotic meanings and meanings are not reducible to interpersonal decisions (Hacking, 1999, p. 24; see also Mayfield & Thorne, 1992, for a critique of the linguistic turn in history; Roseberry, 1982, for a critique of it in anthropology; Bergesen, 1993, for

a critique of it in sociology). Symbolic meanings are inspired and constrained by socially organized activities. Moreover, symbolic meanings are collective, emergent representations that are promulgated and shared by many members of a subculture (Flick, 1998).

8. Individualists believe that freedom can be found outside social systems in individual minds and actions. They accept social unfreedom but believe that this is inconsequential for personal freedom, which can blossom in many ways. Individualists espouse the existential view of freedom as personal thoughts and acts. In this view, personal freedom can supercede social life. However, personal freedom is contingent on social freedom and democracy. It cannot blossom as long as social relationships are coercive, oppressive, mystified, and dehumanizing.

9. The notion that individuals effect substantial changes in their lives overlooks the fact that psychology is organized by cultural processes and that substantial psychological change requires major alterations in these formative social relationships, conditions, and institutions. A good example is the recent attempt of parents in a small suburban community in Minnesota to spend more time with their children. Their children had been devoting most of their free time to extracurricular activities such as sports, plays, ballet, and music practice at school, churches, and in youth groups. Parents requested that these organizations reduce the time that children were required to spend so that they could have more time at home with family members. Although many children and team leaders agreed with the ideal, they resisted the change because they feared that it would lead to a decline in their performance and ultimately to losing in competition with teams from other communities that would practice more than they did. One parent said, "Less competitive programs can hurt your chance for a college scholarship" (*The New York Times*, June 13, 2000, p. A14). Thus, competitive pressures from the broader society constrained the behavior of a local community despite the desire by many to change.

Even the individual's imagination is socially organized to operate in certain directions. What we imagine is socially constrained. Thus, the mere exercise of imagination does not necessarily produce ideas that contradict the status quo, as Bruner and others erroneously believe. Contradicting the status quo requires extensive information about, and critical evaluation of, the principles and processes of the social system. And particular social conditions are necessary for fostering such a critical imagination. Individualistic cultural psychologists such as Bruner never raise questions about which social conditions and concepts provide the best social basis of fostering a definite kind of imagination that will be critical of society. They fail to recognize that, like all psychological phenomena, imagination has a social basis, and that the social basis must be transformed for imagination to be liberating.

Martin-Baro (1994, p. 27) described the failure of psychologists to recognize this point: "Psychology has always been clear about the necessity for personal liberation; that is, people's need to gain control over their own existence ... Nevertheless, psychology has for the most part not been very clear about the intimate relationship between an unalienated personal existence and unalienated social existence, between individual control and collective power, between the liberation of each person and the liberation of a whole people."

10. Social institutions, conditions, systems, artifacts, and ideologies do not change through piecemeal changes in personal thinking and behavior. On the contrary, they change via organized social groups—from medical associations to business councils to labor unions to feminist organizations to anti-abortion groups—engaging in systematic, massive campaigns to reorganize obdurate, objectified social entities. Social change involves legal, political, social, economic, and often military campaigns to overcome the enormous resistance of the establishment to qualitative change (see Ratner, 1993a, 1997a,b, 1999; White, 1949, pp. 121–145, for further critiques of the individualistic approach to cultural psychology). While these campaigns are envisioned by creative acts of the imagination, the latter are not the most important contributors to freedom. True freedom requires real transformations in the social organization of activities, artifacts, and cultural concepts. Without these, imaginative propositions are merely imaginary.

Of course, social change is initiated by a few individuals. They develop initial insights and programs that introduce new ways of thinking and acting. However, these individual changes need to be sustained and amplified in social movements if they are to have any significant effect on the culture. The advances that women have made in the past 50 years with regard to increased participation in athletics, business, politics, and education have resulted from organized movements that mounted legal, political, and social challenges to prior discrimination. These advances have not been the result of individuals quietly and personally changing their own life styles.

Individuals actively deal with conditions of alienation. This is the grain of truth in the individualistic view of agency. However, this view is wrong in its perception of the content and function of agency in alienated conditions. Individualists believe that agency distances itself from all social conditions and produces freedom, creativity, and fulfillment everywhere, even under alienation. In reality, the agency of most people under alienation adapts to it and internalizes it (internalizing oppression). Alienated agency does not escape from alienated social relations. It only contains the *potential* for liberation. It must realize this potential by engaging in social action to humanize the social organization of activities and concepts.

11. Individualists mistakenly equate a cultural view of psychology with the denial of agency and individual processes. They assume that the social formation, function, and characteristics of psychology means that social and psychological phenomena are reified, inevitable, and permanent, and that people are passive byproducts of nonhuman processes. Individualists believe that social life stifles agency and that agency flourishes only among individuals outside society. They dichotomize individual agency and social life.

This argument is fallacious. It fails to recognize the dialectical relation of self and society. The cultural view I have elaborated posits a dialectical relationship between self and society. It recognizes that the self is dependent on and constrained by social institutions, conditions, etc.; however, the self is a distinctive entity within this system. The self is active as a social agent, not as an asocial agent. Being social, the self is, or at least can become, sensitive to contradictions in society. People can see that the American political system claims to be democratic, yet is controlled by a wealthy elite through lobbying. They can see that the ideology of hard work bringing material gains does not apply to everyone. They can see that the ideology of the free market is contradicted by monopolies and exclusive marketing agreements that prevent certain products being sold. The social self can then figure out social solutions to these contradictions. These solutions are not personal, idiosyncratic novelties; they are fashioned from social trends and possibilities. For instance, Marx argued that one of the trends of capitalist society is enormous vertical and horizontal integration of enterprises. He argued that the planning and organization of these enterprises could constitute the basis of a new collective society run by the majority of people instead of only the wealthy. Thus the existing society contains the seeds of new social forms. The social self realizes this and works to develop the new out of the old. Social change is thus perfectly compatible with the social self that operates within a social framework. In fact, social change is possible *only* in these terms.

12. Most personal meanings are minor variations within cultural patterns. They do not transcend normative cultural patterns (Bourdieu, 1990b, p. 60). They spring from idiosyncratic experiences with particular people and situations. Bourdieu correctly explained that:

> Since the history of the individual is never anything other than a certain specification of the collective history of his group or class, each individual system of dispositions may be seen as a structural variant of all the other group or class habitus, expressing the difference between trajectories and positions

inside or outside the class. "Personal" style, the particular stamp marking all the products of the same habitus, whether practices or works, is never more than a deviation in relation to the style of a period or class so that it relates back to the common style ... (Bourdieu, 1977, p. 86)

In the field of journalism, for example,

"The journalist" is an abstract entity that doesn't exist. What exists are journalists who differ by sex, age, level of education, affiliation, and "medium". The journalistic world is a divided one, full of conflict, competition, and rivalries. That said, journalistic products are much more alike than is generally thought. The most obvious differences, notably the political tendencies of the newspapers—which, in any case, it has to be said, are becoming less and less evident—hide the profound similarities. These are traceable to the pressures imposed by sources and by a whole series of mechanisms, the most important of which is competition ... If X talks about a book in Liberation, Y will have to talk about it in Le Monde even if he considers it worthless or unimportant (Bourdieu, 1998a, pp. 23–24).

Vygotsky also recognized that "Each person's individual experience is conditioned by the role he plays in his environment" (Vygotsky, 1997a, p. 212).

Shared social experience and meanings dominate idiosyncratic experiences and meanings. For instance, adolescents have idiosyncratic experiences with unique sets of friends and parents; however, their experiences, senses, and meanings are nevertheless extremely similar. The vast majority of adolescents react to their unique parents with a common, limited range of emotional, cognitive, and perceptual phenomena. In the United States, most adolescents rebel against their parents, and become secretive and egocentric—which the vast majority of parents attest to with shared patterns of dismay and despair. This common experience dominates individuals of diverse personal backgrounds and attributes who are interacting with different parents. This commonality is the result of the common social role that adolescents occupy in society (namely, being in a transition period from childhood dependence to adult independence) and a common stock of constructs that they use to understand and react to their different parents.

An individual will have a far greater awareness of his cultural experience if he understands its social composition than if he understands the personal identities and actions of the participants. An adolescent will have a deeper understanding of being an adolescent if he comprehends the social position of adolescence than if he merely reflects on the individual actions of himself and his parents. Emphasizing personal, idiosyncratic aspects of experience impedes comprehending the cultural character of psychological phenomena (White, 1949, pp. 121–145).

13. Certain personal meanings and idiosyncratic traits seem to originate in idiosyncratic experiences with particular individuals and do not seem to be related to broader cultural processes and factors. For example, Peter married a dominant woman who resembles his mother in her dominant personality, and he is submissive to her just as he was to his mother. Sally's parents stopped having sex when they were in their late 40s and Sally stopped having sex with her husband when she was 45 years old. John's mother periodically slashed her wrists in front of him; now he suspects that people are trying to manipulate him and he distrusts them. Fred's mother didn't allow Fred to go out at night, and now he is afraid to do so. Sara's father was very disorganized and he rarely finished what he started; Sara has the same personality. These uncanny and persistent family patterns, brilliantly elucidated by psychodynamic psychologists, seem to be entirely interpersonal phenomena with no connection to the broader culture. They are not variations around an essential core of normative cultural activities or concepts; in many cases they oppose culturally shared and sanctioned traits.

We may say that such idiosyncratic traits and meanings coexist with cultural traits that are shared by numerous individuals and families (e.g., individualistic self-concept, eating disorders in women, domestic violence among lower class men, high rates of pregnancy among lower class teenage girls). Any individual has certain idiosyncratic traits and certain cultural traits, which are roughly depicted in Fig. 2.1.

Although unique family and individual traits are evidently noncultural in origin and distribution, their existence is supported by the structure of contemporary society. The differentiation of family from public activities creates a family enclave in which interactions can occur that are discontinuous with public life. This situation is similar to the position that the natural sciences occupy in contemporary society (see Chapter 1).

The family would not be free to develop idiosyncratic behaviors in other social systems. For example, where all the men live together in a

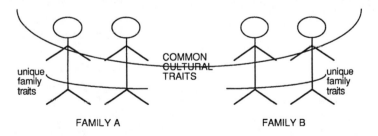

FIGURE 2.1. Shared cultural traits and unique traits in families.

long house they would acquire shared personality traits and they would transmit these, rather than idiosyncratic personal traits to their children. Actually, present trends in capitalist society may be working to reduce the autonomy of the family and promote uniform experiences and meanings. Public activities, artifacts, and concepts increasingly intrude into the family and structure the experiences and ideas of family members in common ways.

If individual psychology contains cultural and idiosyncratic aspects, then understanding an individual requires understanding both aspects. Focusing on uniqueness overlooks important cultural aspects of an individual's psychology. Because individuals are not entirely individual, an individual analysis is incomplete, as cross-cultural therapists have begun to realize (see Seeley, 2000, esp. pp. 149–165 for excellent examples).

In fact, before clinical psychologists analyze and treat a particular psychological problem, they need to determine that it is idiosyncratic to a patient and his family, and is not a cultural problem. They must undertake a cultural analysis before they embark on an individual analysis. If shyness among girls, for example, is a cultural trait then it is not appropriate to look for idiosyncratic family dynamics to explain a girl's shyness. It would be more helpful and accurate to identify the cultural sources of this trait and work to alter them. Similarly, if domestic violence is primarily a cultural problem of lower class men, then treating it as a personal problem would be misguided and ineffective. Such a treatment would neglect the cultural basis and expression of the problem. The problem could be understood and solved only by tracing it to the patient's class position and the cultural forces that bear on him.

Clinical psychologists should appreciate cultural psychology because individuals with unique personal traits often draw on cultural activities, artifacts, and concepts to express or mitigate personal traits. For example, a young woman who felt lonely and unappreciated because her parents excluded her engaged in various forms of self-gratification such as shopping. She invoked a prevalent social behavior to derive some sense of fulfillment while acting alone because she did not have the social skills to develop friendships with other people. Although her psychological problem was based on family dynamics, her attempted resolution of that problem invoked public cultural means.

The reader may ask whether the existence of unique family psychological functions contradicts my earlier critique of personal meanings. I do not believe there is a contradiction because the idiosyncratic functions I have acknowledged are quite different from the personal meanings I criticized. Although unique family psychological functions operate outside of broad social influences, they are not free personal constructs or interpersonally negotiated. They are fostered over generations by family dynamics that individuals rarely understand, much less control, repudiate, or alter. It is only with the help of well-trained psychodynamic therapists that individuals can understand and begin to alter these ingrained habits. In addition, unique traits do not comprise macrosystem activities, concepts, and artifacts as individualists claim. Unique family traits have virtually no impact on the broader society. Social activities, concepts, and artifacts are emergent social phenomena that have a different basis from these individual reactions. Nor do unique family traits repudiate or transform social activities, concepts, and artifacts. On the contrary, social experiences tend to overpower idiosyncratic meanings and attributes. For example, in his famous study of inhibited and uninhibited babies, Kagan discovered that 40% of extremely inhibited infants became less timid by 5.5 years, which Kagan attributed to the extraverted emphasis in American society. This emphasis also encouraged most extremely uninhibited infants to remain that way—fewer than 10% became more timid (Ratner, 1991, pp. 153–154). The power of social experience to bend contrary personality attributes is also reflected in changes over generations in the personalities of immigrant groups. First generation immigrants typically display personalities that veer sharply from the traditional traits of their parents. Second-generation immigrants are even more fully acculturated and typically lose virtually all of the traditional traits. If daily social interactions do not obliterate contrary personality traits, social authorities (legislators, agencies, police, newspaper and magazine managers) will initiate action to suppress them. In addition, unique family traits are not more creative or liberating than social activities, concepts, and artifacts. Finally, idiosyncratic meanings are a small part of an individual's psychology. The bulk of it is cultural in nature. Thus, acknowledging idiosyncratic family traits does not support the individualistic notion of personal meanings.

The Scientific and Political Value of Conceptions of Agency

If agency is a cultural phenomenon and the individualistic account of agency is wrong, then what accounts for the popularity of this misconception? The answer is that the individualistic account reflects certain aspects of agency as it exists in contemporary capitalist society. It reflects the personal choices that people have—the legal right to change jobs and residences, travel freely, choose a spouse, read whatever one wishes, buy and sell property, and vote for government officials. The emphasis that individualistic cultural psychologists place on personal choices corresponds to the emphasis that people in everyday life place on their personal choices. This is what makes the individualistic account plausible.

However, this account is only partially accurate. It misconstrues many aspects of agency in contemporary society. The individualistic account also misconstrues itself—its own origins, point of view, limits, and social implications. I shall examine these two misconceptions in order.

Oxymoronically, individualistic cultural psychologists have no interest in or comprehension of the cultural character of agency. Ironically, their perspective is so dominated by the privatized form agency takes in contemporary society that it overlooks social aspects of agency. The social ignorance of individualism is akin to believing that the exchanges that take place in a market economy are freely decided and have nothing to do with background conditions such as the amount of capital one has at one's disposal and competitive pressures from others' actions.

Individualistic cultural psychology ignores the specific organization of social life that imparts the existing form to agency. For instance, it ignores the capitalistic organization of work, education, politics, law, and the family which limits the agency of most people to personal acts and precludes control over social relationships, institutions, conditions, and dynamics. Individualistic cultural psychologists presume that the focus of agency on personal acts is natural and universal. They never acknowledge cultural variations in ways that agency acts on cultural phenomena and is influenced by them. Like most naturalistic theories of psychology, individualistic cultural psychology fails to recognize that the characteristics of agency that it touts as natural are actually current cultural characteristics (see Cushman, 1991 for a related analysis of ideological bias in individualistic psychological theory).

The individualistic view is so fascinated by the personal decision-making of contemporary agency that it overlooks the alienation inherent in this form of agency. It fails to see that the personal, mundane acts that it glorifies as freedom and creativity are stultified, conformist, alienated, isolated, self-centered acts. It fails to see that "Our great modern world is all too often a world in which men and women do not exist for others; in which, although there are no public censors, there can also be no public goods; in which monolithic social ends are prudently outlawed by imprudently proscribing all social ends; in which altruistic behavior is discouraged in the name of bargaining efficiency and utility accounting" (Barber, 1984, p. 71).

Defining agency as constructing personal meanings further mystifies social reality because it creates a false sense of equality, democracy, and fulfillment. All people appear to be equally fulfilled and active because they construct and negotiate personal meanings. A loader of milk bottles is as agentive in this sense as a president. The notion of personal agency erases social inequalities in power. Society also appears to be democratic and fulfilling because it allows its citizens to be agents. Bruner believes that because people negotiate meanings, society is a democratic forum. He even claims that cultural establishments always promote alternatives to themselves and negotiate compromises with the opposition (Bruner & Amsterdam, 2000, p. 231). Strangely, Bruner fails to recognize the massive efforts by establishments such as the Federal Bureau of Investigation, Catholic Church, Chinese Communist Party, and so forth to control, coopt, and stifle true alternatives.

The individualistic notion of agency exempts society from criticism because it presumes that each individual is responsible for his own problems. Because each individual can deal with social events any way he wishes, any difficulties he may suffer are attributable to his style of dealing with events, not to the events themselves. People who suffer under poverty, war, discrimination, and autocratic leadership could disabuse themselves of any problems by simply learning to ignore, circumvent, or negate them. If they don't, it's their fault. There is no need to criticize or alter the social system.

Lacking a cultural analysis and unwittingly endorsing alienated agency as normal and natural precludes the possibility that agency and society could have different forms. Peoples' agency could be much more meaningful, insightful, creative, and fulfilling if it directed social activities as well as individual acts. However, individualistic cultural psychologists never entertain this possibility because they mistakenly believe that agency is already realized in making personal choices in the existing society. Utilizing an alienated, individualistic view of agency and culture prevents cultural psychologists from seeing beyond it. Seeing things through this view prevents "seeing through" it.

The individualistic conception of agency not only misconstrues its object (agency in the real world), it also fails to understand itself—its origins, standpoint, limits, and social implications. The individualistic viewpoint touts itself as scientifically comprehending the true, essential nature of agency. Actually, it comprehends nothing of the true, essential social nature of agency. The individualistic view is therefore not at all scientific. It only has the limited perspective of laypersons whose impressions of social life do not comprehend it. Individualistic cultural psychologists lack the scientific sophistication that comes from critically understanding the origins, character, development, and functions of phenomena. The individualistic standpoint unknowingly reflects cultural features of agency instead of reflecting on their origins, development, and functions. The individualistic conception of agency in culture is ethnocentric because it touts limited, limiting notions of agency and culture as scientific concepts that represent the full, true, natural, universal character of these phenomena. In Bourdieu's terse words, "Personalism is the main obstacle to the construction of a scientific vision of the human being" (Bourdieu, 2000, p. 132).

The individualistic view of agency and culture is a form of "scholasticism" that ignores "the demands of the situation, the constraints of economic and social necessity, and the urgencies it imposes or the ends it proposes" (Bourdieu, 2000, p. 12). Bourdieu points out that scholastics (and individualists in particular) are not only ignorant of social constraints on individual behavior; they are also unaware of their ignorance of the social basis of behavior; and they are unaware that their ignorance has a social basis (Bourdieu, p. 15). The individualistic view is a product of modern society: "It was only with the Renaissance that man's essential aloneness came to be construed as a liberation rather than a purgatory" (Barber, 1984, p. 69). Norenzayan and Nisbett (2000) similarly point out that the individualistically based fundamental attribution error is characteristic of Western society but not of Asian countries, where people explain behavior as determined by demands of the situation rather than individual dispositions. One feature of modern society that promotes individualism is the private ownership and exchange of economic resources, including labor power. Another structural contribution to the individualistic standpoint, according to Bourdieu, is the large degree of autonomy that academics have in their work, along with the specialization of academic work apart from other activities. These characteristics of academic activity lead many academics to disregard political, economic, and familial influences on individuals (see Ratner, 1994 for a cultural psychological analysis of the unconscious).

In contrast to the individualistic approach, a truly cultural psychological view of agency emphasizes the dependence that agency has on social relationships. It emphasizes the fact that agency forms social relationships and has a social form that is rooted in the way activities are socially organized. A cultural psychological view elucidates the concrete social character of agency, critiques it, and suggests improvements. It critiques the particular historical organization of social life that fosters the social character of agency. And it encourages collective movements to humanize social activities as the key to promoting psychological well-being.[6]

A cultural psychological view of agency applies a cultural analysis to its own standpoint. It recognizes that its conception of agency rests on

cultural values and has cultural implications. The notion that agency is socially intentional rests on the value that humans depend on each other and need to establish harmonious social relationships. The critique of existing forms of agency rests on the value that existing social life (i.e., social activities) has deleterious features that can be made more humane and democratic. The cultural implications of this position are that social change is necessary and possible. Cultural psychology maintains that the cultural values that underlie its analysis of agency strengthen its analysis and make it more accurate and useful. Contrary to popular opinion that regards cultural values as biasing objectivity and utility, cultural psychology argues that certain cultural values aid the understanding of particular issues. The spectacular progress of the natural sciences was certainly abetted by cultural values of capitalism—which is why the natural sciences are so much more advanced in capitalist countries. In the same way, the cultural perspective that I have utilized herin helps to deepen an understanding of agency and other psychological phenomena.[7]

A truly cultural psychology links individual psychological understanding and improvement to social understanding and improvement. It directs people toward understanding the social bases and characteristics of their individual psychology, circumventing deleterious social activities and concepts where possible, and collectively uniting with other people to transform deleterious social activities and concepts into humane ones. In these ways cultural psychology can use its scientific analysis to help people develop their agency. People's potential will become actual when the existing social actual is recognized to be the potential for a better, new social actuality.

NOTES

1. Discourse analysts similarly assume that when individuals engage in dialogues, discourses, or narratives they are being active agents by creating meanings (Matsuki, 2001, p. 542). This is true even when they talk to themselves. For instance, Matsuki analyzed a wartime narrative of one Japanese woman. The woman described a setting in which a Japanese policeman criticized her mother. The mother concluded with the statement, "So much for people with power." Matsuki claims that this thought was a rebellious one that emanated from her inner self (ibid., pp. 543–544): "Her rebellious voice was never uttered outwardly, but it was certainly there, representing her agentive self, which always existed ... " (ibid., p. 545). Matsuki presents no evidence for her contention. Moreover, the narrator's single sentence is too fragmentary to know what meaning she intended. Consequently, it is impossible to determine how active, agentive, or rebellious she was being. "So much for people in power" could mean they are sometimes pompous, sometimes err, they are always corrupt, they should be controlled or eliminated. If the first two meanings were intended, there is certainly nothing rebellious or active about the subject's thought. Matasuki is grasping at straws to establish the agency of individuals. She

construes an ambiguous thought that is not verbalized to others as a significant act of independence.

2. Harre (1984) incisively explains the individualistic nature of interpersonal formulations such as Bruner's. Harre points out that the idea of social plurality can take several forms. It can be a distributive plurality (or an "aggregate group," or "taxonomic group") in which a group is the sum of individual traits. Or it can be a collective plurality (a "structured group") that emerges from a social process that transcends particular individuals. Bruner's collectivity, like Moscovici's and Tajfel's, is a distributive one that is in the last analysis a version of individualism. Only structured or collective groups are real social entities. There the properties of individuals are a function of the group organization into roles and relationships. Only collective groups grant a decisive role to social processes. In aggregate groups social processes are purely the result of (derived from) individual acts.

3. This individualistic viewpoint also exists in sociology—espoused by Goffman and his followers (see Giddens, 1987, pp. 109–139)—and in philosophy—espoused by Winch and Wittgenstein (see King, 2000). Goffman proclaimed his work to be microsociological because it studied face-to-face social interactions. These he defined as "that which uniquely transpires in social situations, that is, environments in which two or more individuals are physically in one another's response presence" (cited in Giddens, 1987, p. 111). His work is not about "the organization of society ... I make no claim whatsoever to be talking about the core matters of sociology—social organization and social structure" (cited in ibid., p. 111). Giddens aptly explained that "Goffman's main concern throughout his writings involves individuals directly attending to what each other are saying and doing for a particular segment of time." Therefore, "Goffman is above all the theorist of co-presence, not of small groups" (ibid., p. 115). Even when individuals are group members, their interactions are to be understood in terms of an immediate interpersonal encounter, not in terms of their membership of the group (ibid., p. 116). Goffman "is not interested in ... for example, the role of a doctor in relation to the wider medical community" (ibid., p. 116). Goffman's focus on face-to-face encounters leads him to concentrate on such interpersonal dynamics as mutual eye contact, body space, and details ("moves") of the conversation act such as turn taking (timing), silences, and volume of speaking. This conversation analysis lacks a relation to the existence of social institutions (ibid., pp. 133, 138):

> Although Goffman often notes that there are formalized settings in which institutionally sanctioned power is exercised—such as the court room—he rarely analyses such circumstances in the detail accorded to other settings of the interaction. Nor does he often analyse the interaction of the powerful—at least, in circumstances in which that power is being exercised. Decisions and policies having consequences for very large numbers of people are as often formulated in circumstances of co-presence as are the more mundane forms of interaction upon which Goffman usually concentrates. (ibid., p. 134)

All of these features of Goffman's microsociology are recapitulated in individualistic cultural psychology. They all lead to a common error of overlooking the ways that personal interactions embody characteristics of social activities (ibid., p. 135).

4. Wertsch recognized the dominance of common cultural concepts in individual thinking although it contradicts his belief that individuals create novel, disparate personal meanings in their transactions with information (Wertsch, 1998, pp. 112–119).

5. These findings did not alter Valsiner's notion of a primordial nonsocial person who circumvents society. Valsiner focused on the minute divergences and convergences of

personal goals during the interactions and he disregarded the social relationships that were embedded in them.

6. A cultural approach to promoting psychological functioning reduces the need for personal psychotherapy. The acceptance and support that are currently primarily available from individual therapists will become prevalent features of humanized social relationships and social influences.

7. This argument, that culturally based subjectivity can comprehend reality, has been propounded by Popper under the name of critical realism, by Campbell under the name of fallible realism, and by Bhaskar under the name of critical naturalism (see Ratner, 1997a, pp. 191–201; Bourdieu, 2000, pp. 109–122 for discussion of this point).

Part 2

METHOD

3

IMPLICATIONS OF ACTIVITY THEORY FOR CULTURAL PSYCHOLOGICAL RESEARCH

Evidence in Chapter 1 points to the conclusion that human psychology is cultural because it originates in, is formed by, reflects, and perpetuates cultural activities, concepts, and artifacts. These factors and processes are the object of cultural psychological research. Specifically, cultural psychological research should:

1. Explore the manner in which activities, artifacts, and concepts penetrate psychological phenomena and constitute their cultural features. As stated in the introduction, cultural psychology investigates the manner in which culture is in psychology, not simply the psychology of people in a culture. Cultural psychology thus studies the internal relationship between activities, artifacts, and concepts and psychological phenomena. This internal relationship is exemplified in the homology between the dichotomized schizophrenic self and bourgeois individualism; in the homology between capitalist commercial relationships and personality traits; and in the homology between ancient Korean shame and Taoist concepts about self, human nature, and the world. The internal relationship between activities, artifacts, concepts, and psychological phenomena is also exemplified in the homology between (a) the subordinate domestic position of Victorian upper middle class women; (b) prevalent cultural concepts that women were frail, submissive, beautiful, restrained, clean, pure, and spiritual; (c) the covering of furniture legs with doilees to prevent women from encountering physical features that resembled human limbs; (d) Victorian women's personality traits (docile, patient, dependent); emotions (fearful, guilty, expressive), concern for beautiful slim appearance; and (e) hysteria (the symptoms of which reflected and created a physically incapacitated, dependent individual) (see Ratner,

1991, pp. 264–277, 1994, 1997a, pp. 100–101, 104–108, 2000b for additional examples).

Cultural psychology is not content with merely ascertaining
correlations between activities, artifacts, concepts, and psychology (e.g.,
depression is more prevalent in the United States than in Zimbabwe). Such
correlations overlook the manner in which psychological phenomena *depend
on, embody, and resemble* activities, artifacts, and concepts (e.g., how the specific quality of American depression depends on, embodies, and resembles
the features of specific American activities, artifacts, and concepts).

Explaining the internal relationship between psychology and activities, artifacts, and concepts requires a profound study of a single society.
Cultural psychology is thus more the study of a single society than it is
comparing psychological characteristics in different societies. The weakness of comparative cross-cultural psychological research is that it is
merely descriptive, in the sense that it is fascinated by the characteristics
of psychological phenomena (e.g., "American self-concept is more individualistic whereas Korean self-concept is more collective."). While such
differences may indeed be fascinating, they need to be grounded in activities, artifacts, and concepts.

2. Compare the cultural origins, formation, characteristics, and
functions of psychological phenomena in diverse societies. It is not sufficient to simply compare characteristics of psychological phenomena in
different societies. Rather, cultural psychology relates the characteristics
of psychological phenomena to cultural activities, artifacts, and concepts.
This cultural constitution of psychological phenomena in different societies is compared. Thus, we might analyze the cultural characteristics, origins, formation, and functions of shame in two societies. This would be a
much more complete picture of the cultural nature of shame than simply
comparing the qualities of shame apart from their grounding in cultural
activities, artifacts, and concepts.

Cross-cultural psychological comparisons must be based on mono-
cultural research that illuminates the internal relationship of psychology
and other cultural factors. Of course, a researcher may first engage in
research that compares characteristics of a psychological phenomenon
(such as love, shame, mental illness, color perception, perception of optical illusions) in different societies. This kind of research is undoubtedly
fascinating. However, at some point the psychological characteristics
need to be grounded in the cultural factors that constitute them.

Comparing the cultural origins, formation, characteristics, and functions of psychological phenomena in different societies can yield a variety
of conclusions. An emotion that initially seems to be identical in two

populations, for example, shame with the same characteristics in two populations—may (a) prove to be identical in the two groups; (b) on detailed comparison, turn out to be different forms of that emotion, for example, shame in ancient Korea is infused with Taoist concepts while shame in contemporary Korea is infused with modern concepts of self-blame over a failure; or (c) the phenomenon may turn out to be different emotions altogether, for example, a kind of shame versus anger.

Comparing psychological phenomena in two populations requires recognizing general and specific features. Taoist and contemporary shame can be compared only if they have some general features in common that make them forms of *shame*. Their differences are variations in the general form of shame.

Similarly, we can decide whether two instances of behavior are similar or different forms of mental illness, or mental illness at all, only if we acknowledge general features of mental illness to serve as a criterion. The same holds for emotions, intelligence, and other psychological phenomena. We must have a general conceptual definition of intelligence to determine whether different acts in different domains (intellectual, artistic, mechanical) are intelligent (see Ratner, 1997a, pp. 57–59).

Transcultural definitions and features of psychological phenomena coexist with cultural differences in those phenomena. The general, transcultural features do not negate specific cultural differences, nor do specific cultural differences negate general, transcultural features. Both coexist at different levels of generality.

3. Investigate the psychology of individuals to ascertain the presence of various activities, artifacts, and concepts in the formation, function, and character of psychological phenomena. Conclusions about the psychology of groups (ethnicity, gender, class, and age) are derived from investigations on individual members of groups. This ensures that conclusions about groups are grounded in the reality of the individuals who compose them. It helps guard against overgeneralizing about the cultural psychology of group members. Proceeding from individuals enables us to identify contradictions among group members. It also enables us to identify aspects of their cultural psychology that contradict their social position and may be utilized to change it.

Studying individuals to identify cultural aspects of psychology is a methodological strategy that in no way recapitulates the process by which an individual's psychology is culturally formed. An individual's psychology is formed through social processes and reflects them. However, the study of cultural psychology of individuals proceeds in reverse fashion—it investigates the outcome of the formative process as it exists in the individual's psyche and then traces this outcome back to its cultural origins and social distribution.

Studying individuals from the perspective of activity theory has nothing in common with the microsociologies (such as Goffman's sociology of interaction rituals, Collins' interaction ritual chains, ethnomethodology, and conversation analysis) that study individual interactions *instead* of socially organized activities, conditions, artifacts, and concepts (see footnote 3, Chap. 2).

4. Predict trends in the qualities of psychological phenomena from trends in activities, artifacts, and concepts.

5. Identify aspects of psychological phenomena that contradict normative activities and concepts. The origins of these psychological phenomena should be explained—perhaps in contradictions among cultural activities, concepts, and artifacts that agency exploits.

6. Investigate the cultural formation of psychological phenomena. This includes the social processes of negotiation and/or domination that adults use when they construct psychological phenomena. It also includes the socialization processes that parents use to shape the psychology of their children.

Cultural psychological research requires special knowledge, skills, and procedures.

The Researcher Must Possess a Comprehensive, Detailed, Profound Understanding of Social Activities, Artifacts, and Concepts to Relate Them to Psychological Phenomena

He or she must be a scholar of history, sociology, anthropology, and related disciplines in the social sciences (economics, political science). This knowledge must comprehend diverse patterns of activities and concepts. No activity or concept is monolithic. Each is organized in a variety of ways (especially in modern societies). The cultural psychologist must know that economic activity in the United States is sometimes organized very autocratically and impersonally while sometimes it is organized more democratically. The frequency of each pattern should be calculated in order to comprehend the full nature of economic activity in this country and its effects on psychology. The cultural psychologist should have similar information about concepts, for example, of women, the individual, and the family. Each of these cultural concepts is variegated into several forms. The relative frequency of each should be noted and related to psychological phenomena.

This cultural knowledge will guide:

- The formulation of hypotheses about the cultural features of psychological phenomena. A hypothesis-guided study can proceed from theoretical speculation or an observation. One might theorize that as countries around the world modernize by adopting Western socioeconomic–political activities, eating disorders among women will become more prevalent, people's self-concept will become more individualistic, and friendships will become more utilitarian and less committed. Based on cultural knowledge of Buddhism, one might seek to test a hypothesis that sadness is ennobling to many Sri Lankans. Based on knowledge of an oppressive social system one might hypothesize that particular factors therein lead individuals to become fatalistic and passive. Based on knowledge that news and entertainment media are becoming increasingly commercialized and their products increasingly trivialized, the cultural psychologist may hypothesize that these trends will lead people's cognitive processes to become less analytical.

- Detecting cultural features of psychological phenomena in exploratory studies without a hypothesis. We may seek to identify cultural concepts that underlie moral reasoning of children, or ethnotheories that parents have about disciplining their children. Or, we may seek to determine ways in which Confucian ethical principles are incorporated into modern Chinese thinking and behavior. In these cases no specific hypotheses are advanced. The researcher must be knowledgeable about potentially relevant activities and concepts such as the position of women, mothers, children, and the family in society, as well as Confucian ethical principles. This knowledge will guide inquiry about these activities and concepts that may bear on psychological issues.

- The definition of psychological issues in cultural terms. For example, if one seeks to investigate the quality of marriage in Puerto Rico among the poor, one faces the question: What are the important issues in marriages among these people that can be used as criteria of good or poor marriages? It would be ethnocentric to assume that marriages of Puerto Rican subjects can be defined in terms of Western criteria such as decision-making processes, for example, the equity or inequity of decision-making power among spouses. The concept of decision making presupposes a situation of choice, with each spouse bidding for his or her preference among numerous possible actions. Very poor citizens of Puerto Rico do not inhabit this kind of situation. Their margin of choice is very slim because they are faced with a continual struggle for basic necessities. Thus, decision-making is not a criterion of quality of marriage. A more relevant factor is the harmony with which the division of labor of tasks was carried out between spouses (Rogler, 1989, p. 297).

Cultural psychological research on attachment would similarly need to define it in culturally appropriate terms. Rothbaum, Weisz, Pott, Miyake, and Morelli (2000) correctly observed that "core tenets of attachment theory are deeply rooted in Western thought and require fundamental change when applied to other cultures or minority groups" (p. 1094). For example, Bowlby's definition of secure attachment stipulates that such babies manifest autonomy, high self-esteem, persistence in meeting their needs, resilience, emotional openness, and adventurous exploration of their environments. This kind of secure attachment is promoted, according to the theory, by sensitive parents who provide a tolerant environment that allows children to express themselves in opposition to their parents. However, attachment in Japan needs to be defined differently according to Japanese values and life styles. Securely attached infants would manifest dependency on their parents because this is highly desirable in Japan. They would look to parents for guidance rather than striking out on their own to explore the environment. They would restrain emotional expression, especially of feelings such as hostility that jeopardize social harmony. They would be self-effacing rather than assertive. Sensitive parents would similarly be defined as keeping their children physically and emotionally close to them, even dependent on them. They do not encourage autonomy, free exploration, or self-expression.

Research on psychological phenomena must be framed in terms of their cultural qualities. Imposing Western definitions of attachment on other societies leads to overlooking indigenous qualities of attachment. It also leads to misconstruing indigenous qualities as inferior or pathogenic; for example, Japanese attachment is regarded as an insecurity and deficiency when viewed from Western standards.

This point needs to be reconciled with the point made earlier that transcultural definitions of psychological phenomena must exist if two populations are to be compared. Transcultural definitions consist of general features while indigenous cultural forms consist of specific features. Attachment must have certain general features that apply to Japanese and Americans in order to denote it in both societies. However, the specific form attachment takes in the two societies must be acknowledged.

- Investigative procedures—for example, whether interviews or questionnaires are more appropriate to particular kinds of people; the topics, questions, and statements that are presented to subjects; the categories of subjects that may be addressed about certain kinds of topics; and the kinds of social relationships which need to be cultivated with subjects (see Briggs, 1983).

- Analytical methods, for example, how to interpret and code statements/behavior. Is a smile an expression of happiness or sadness? Is an unusual behavior mental illness or a religious ritual? Were human sacrifices in Aztec civilizations violent acts of murder? Are Sambian rites of passage for young men—in which they are required to perform oral sex on older men—instances of homosexuality? Is female circumcision in Africa a kind of sexism? Is shame among contemporary Koreans the same as shame experienced by ancient Taoists? Knowledge of social activities and concepts clarifies the cultural psychological significance of an expression. Without cultural knowledge, the observer may be easily misled by superficial similarities or differences in psychological expressions.

- Ascertaining the accuracy of subjects' knowledge about the cultural origins, characteristics, formation, and functions of their psychology. The culturally informed researcher will detect when subjects' responses about cultural issues are fragmentary, superficial, inconsistent, and distorted. He will also be able to encourage subjects to think about these issues more deeply to resolve these problems (Merton & Kendall, 1946, p. 541).

One must have knowledge about the research topic and subjects *before* commencing the research to obtain accurate and relevant information. It is a well known paradox of research that one must possess some prior understanding of the subject matter to investigate it properly.

Bringing cultural knowledge to bear on all facets of research makes research culturally sensitive. Rogler explains this in the following eloquent statement:

> Research is made culturally sensitive through a continuing and open-ended series of substantive and methodological insertions and adaptations designed to mesh the process of inquiry with the cultural characteristics of the group being studied. Considerations pertinent to the culture become an organic part of the process, every bit as important to the success of the research as are the more formal research procedures codified in epidemiology and clinical research

textbooks. The insertions [of cultural issues] and adaptations [of research to cultural issues] span the entire research process, from the pretesting and planning of the study, to the collection of data and translation of instruments, to the instrumentation of measure, and to the anlysis and interpretation of the data. Research, therefore, is made culturally sensitive through an incessant, basic, and active preoccupation with the culture of the group being studied throughout the process of research. (Rogler, 1989, p. 296)

To Elucidate the Specific Cultural Character of Psychological Phenomena the Researcher Must Construe Them in Concrete Rather than Abstract Terms

Psychologists typically construe memory, schizophrenia, group processes, and moral and cognitive development as content-less general processes. They regard memory as a general, universal process of recalling information. Even when phases of memory are distinguished, such as short and long term, or episodic, semantic, and procedural, these are regarded as invariant, culture-free processes. Moral and cognitive development are regarded as traversing universal, content-free stages. Schizophrenia is similarly construed as content-free mental processes such as delusions, hallucinations, and flat affect. Group processes and communication are defined abstractly as taking turns, offering advice, solving problems, asking questions, and managing conflict and stress. Socialization of children is construed as forming an attachment, providing varying amounts of stimulation, and maintaining social interactions through pointing, paying attention, and taking turns. Emotions are regarded as dependent on how much attention one pays to something, and how predictable and pleasant it is (Ratner, 1997a, pp. 109, 120–121, 129).

Comprehending the cultural character of these phenomena requires attending to the schizophrenic individual's specific misunderstandings, anxieties, uncertainties, and thoughts about self and others (Fabrega, 1989). It requires comprehending the specific ways that communicators take turns (e.g., do people of certain ages and genders speak first or frequently?), give advice about certain kinds of issues, and manage certain kinds of conflicts. It requires comprehending the specific ways that individuals in particular groups recall particular kinds of information. It requires knowing the specific behaviors and values that caregivers encourage in specific situations with infants. It requires knowing the particular conceptions that people have about ethical ways of dealing with particular things. It also requires knowing what people find pleasant and unpleasant about various situations that elicits various emotions in them (ibid., pp. 108, 129–132).

The practical import of this point of view is brought out by Goldhagen in his study of the Holocaust. Goldhagen (1996, pp. 379–413) emphasizes that the killing of Jews rested on concrete cultural concepts such as fanatical anti-Semitism. It cannot be understood in terms of abstract, universal social psychological processes such as conformity, obedience to authority, fear of punishment, self-centeredness, authoritarianism, or diffusion of responsibility. None of these processes accounts for the specific actions involved in killing Jews, or the cultural identify of the victims or the perpetrators. As Goldhagen eloquently explains, abstract, ahistorical explanations imply that

> The task of explaining (1) the willingness of Germans (2) to slaughter (3) the entire Jewish people is no different from the task of explaining how (1) any person can be brought (2) to do anything that he does not want to do (3) to any object, whether that object is a person or a thing. The conventional explanations do not account for the historic specificity of the perpetrators themselves and of the society that nurtured them, for the explicit, extraordinary character of the perpetrators' actions, or for the identity of the victims. The structure of the conventional explanations is such that they deem all of these features of the Holocaust, including that it was genocide, to have been epiphenomenal and therefore irrelevant to its explanation … Coercion, obedience to authority, social psychological pressure, self-interest, and displacement of responsibility onto others are explanations, according to their own logic, that are applicable equally and as unproblematically to the perpetrators of the Holocaust as they are to explaining, say, why bureaucrats today would help to implement a policy regarding air quality that they think might be misguided. (ibid., p. 392)

In contrast, a cultural–psychological analysis of the perpetrators of the Holocaust identifies specific cultural factors and factors that account for the specificity of the killers' actions and identities, and the identities of the victims. It was Germans who killed Jews in a maniacal, genocidal fashion because they had specific cultural beliefs about Jews, which were different from their beliefs about the Danes, and which rendered the Jews, unlike the Danish people, fit and necessary to annihilate (ibid., p. 394). A cultural–psychological analysis is the only one that renders the genocidal behavior of the perpetrators intelligible. It is also the only one that can fruitfully guide efforts to prevent such behavior from recurring.

THE CULTURAL FEATURES OF PSYCHOLOGICAL PHENOMENA MUST BE GLEANED FROM INVESTIGATING THE PHENOMENA THEMSELVES

The manner in which psychological phenomena are organized by and reflect activities, artifacts, and concepts must be gleaned by investigating the features of psychological phenomena. Knowledge of social institutions, conditions, concepts, and artifacts does not predict the actual ways that these organize human psychology. The reason is that they do not automatically determine mental functioning like computer chips implanted in the psyche. Individuals fashion psychological phenomena from activities and concepts, and the former are never duplicates, or clones, of the latter. Social activities and concepts comprise the parameters within which psychological organization takes form. However, the actual form which psychological phenomena take is constructed from these parameters by individuals. It cannot be reduced to social events; it is a unique form of them. Leontiev expressed this well when he said:

> Social conditions carry in themselves motives and goals of his activity, his means and methods; in a word, society produces the activity of the individuals forming it. Of course, this does not mean at all that their [individual] activity only personifies the relationships of society and its culture. There are complex transformations and transitions that connect them so that no direct information of one to the other is possible. For a psychology that is limited by the concept "socialization" of the psyche of the individual without its further analysis, these transformations remain a genuine secret. This psychological secret is revealed only in the investigations of the genesis of [individual] human activity and its internal structure. (Leontiev, 1978, Chap. 3)

Agency makes a cultural analysis of psychology demanding because it forces us to ascertain the manner in which activities and concepts have been appropriated by people to form psychological phenomena. Agency does not disregard culture as individualistic psychologists believe. On the contrary, agency brings culture to bear on psychological phenomena. Agency is like a crystal that refracts culture. Since agency is part of cultural processes, its state reveals the relative strength of these processes; it is a barometer of culture. If agency recapitulates economic principles in psychological phenomena, then we know that economic principles are a strong cultural influence on psychology. If agency recapitulates religious principles in psychology then we know that these are a strong cultural factor. As Sartre (1963, p. 152) perceptively said, "It is the work or the act of the individual which reveals to us the secret of his conditioning."

Investigating psychological phenomena can lead to surprising discoveries about their cultural characteristics. For instance, Lystra (1989) studied love letters at the turn of the 20th century. She discovered cultural complexities that had escaped less phenomenologically oriented researchers. Other social scientists had evidently "read off" emotional experience from the socioeconomic division of labor between the sexes. They had assumed that the division of labor that left middle-class women at home while their husbands worked in business cleaved emotional and sexual experience along the same lines. Men were assumed to be much less emotional than women, especially in feeling and expressing love. However, subjective reports demonstrate that men felt and expressed romantic love quite passionately. The reason is evidently that romantic love was associated with the private world of family and personal life that was compartmentalized from and opposed to public life of work and politics. Consequently, emotional rules that governed love did not reflect the norms of public life. They reflected the feminine domestic arena where emotions of love were encouraged in both sexes. Men's emotionality was culturally organized in its expression and content; however, its cultural characteristics and origins were discovered only through investigating individuals' psychology.

A similar demonstration of this point is Daly's (2001) study on how individuals experience family time. Through interviews, Daly found that this experience was culturally shaped in unexpected ways. Parents' experience of time spent with family members fell far short of the cultural ideal of intimacy, relaxation, and spontaneity. Most parents reported that family time was insufficient and marred by conflict and burdensome demands. Many parents were tired from their outside responsibilities and consequently were irritable in dealing with their families. Much of their family time was occupied trying to make their children happy and there was little time to spend enjoying their spouses. Even time with children was not fulfilling because it was rushed to fit in other responsibilities that were always hanging over it. Parents routinely felt guilty for their inability to have closer relations with their family. Daly's research on individuals reveals the manner in which modern demands of work and other social relationships affect one's sense of family time. This cultural shaping of psychology would be difficult to know without investigating the experience of family members.

Although the experience of family time was discovered in individual accounts, and although the experience of individuals departs from the cultural ideal of family time, *the experience of individuals is usually not an individual experience.* It is usually not unique to an individual, nor is it personally constructed by an autonomous individual. On the contrary, the experiences that individuals have are usually common to many people, and are usually shaped by widespread cultural factors. These include socially organized activities such as work and cultural concepts such as the goal of helping children to be happy. The experiences that individuals have are usually social in origin. Consequently, *studying individuals can inform us about culture if we comprehend the common features of individuals experience and the cultural factors that shape it.*

EXPERIMENTAL PROCEDURES ARE POWERFUL TOOLS FOR INDICATING THE ASSOCIATION BETWEEN PSYCHOLOGY, ACTIVITIES, ARTIFACTS, AND CONCEPTS

Experimental procedures are powerful tools for differentiating cultural factors and identifying their relative influence on each other (see Ratner, 1997a, pp. 123–127, 215–217, 225–228 for an explanation of these techniques). Experiments allow one factor to vary while holding other factors constant. This control unambiguously demonstrates whether variation in the single factor has an effect. Of course in real-life complex interactions, any relationship between a few factors is modified and modulated by many others. However, experiments nevertheless demonstrate that a relationship between particular factors tends to exist. Complex real-life interactions can be elucidated by experiments conducted in natural settings, or by naturally occurring experiments such as when social factors change without being manipulated by a social scientist. (The political division of Germany after World War II constitutes an exemplary natural experiment. Here, a single people with a common culture was divided into different socioeconomic–political systems, and within several decades profound cognitive and personality differences emerged among the separated populations.)

Several interesting natural experiments exist in the area of personality attributes. Certain hermaphrodites are reared according to a gender that contradicts their biological sex. Since both biological and social factors coexist in the same subject, the gender identity that a young adult hermaphrodite develops indicates which factor is dominant. Virtually all such subjects (whose socialized gender contradicts their biological sex) develop a gender identity that corresponds to their socialized gender rather than their biological sex (Ratner, 1991, pp. 214–217).

Another natural experiment confirmed this result. This experiment occurred among the Luo people of Kenya. The Luo occasionally assign young boys to engage in female work activities such as pottery making, basket weaving, cleaning house, cooking, and tending children. When a boy occupies a feminine role, he dresses in women's clothing; uses women's mannerisms, speech patterns, and tone of voice; and even takes on female sexual behaviors. (This event is similar to the *berdache* in early American Indian societies.) What makes this event an experiment is the fact that the boys are assigned to female roles on the basis of family need, not on the basis of their personalities (Ratner, 1997a, pp. 104–105). If the boys were assigned to cross-gender roles because of their personalities or skills, then their adult feminine personalities may simply be a continuation of their earlier femininity rather than an effect of occupying the work role of women. That situation would be a quasi-experiment rather than a true experiment. Two factors would vary—the boys' early personalities and their assignment to women's work—and this would prevent knowing that gender role is responsible for the boys' later personalities. A conclusion that gender role affects personality is valid only if gender role is the only factor that varies. Individuals must be otherwise indistinguishable. This was the case in the Luo situation and it allows us to conclude that gender role influences personality.

An example of a natural experiment is the rise of romantic love among the middle class in 18th century Europe and the 19th century United States. Historical evidence indicates that this romantic love was historically unique. It is a passionate/sensuous, visceral, spontaneous, disorienting feeling that is quickly aroused by the personal and physical attributes of another person. It is a euphoric feeling of intimate psychological bonding with another individual. As such, it was quite different from the romantic love initiated by the aristocracy in the 12th century, and it was different from the Puritanical love among the early American colonists (Ratner, 2000b, pp. 12–16). The isolated appearance of modern romantic love among the middle class at a particular historical time demonstrates that it depends on a particular life style. Of course, the life style of the middle class is so complex that it does not immediately reveal what the important elements were that fostered modern romantic love. However, at least this naturalistic experiment reveals that modern romantic love is fostered by a middle-class life style. At least it convinces us that romantic love is not natural, universal, or accidental. It directs us to investigate what specific factors of the middle class were responsible for the rise of romantic love.

Natural experiments also reveal that middle-class life fosters particular kinds of psychological distress among women. Middle-class women develop different psychological phenomena from men within the middle class and also from women in other classes. Agoraphobia and hysteria were widespread maladies among white middle-class women during the Victorian period, yet they were much rarer among middle-class men and also lower class women. Middle-class women's role is thus isolated as a social factor that can be seen to foster agoraphobia and hysteria— although the particular aspects of this role that affected psychology must be investigated.

Scribner and Cole discovered a natural experimental situation in which a very specific cultural factor was isolated in relation to cognitive processes. They found a society in which members had comparable levels of formal education and social status but differed in literacy. The authors found that literacy had no independent effect on cognitive skills such as memory, logical reasoning, and categorizing information (see Ratner, 1997a, p. 215).

Nadel (1952) utilized a natural experimental situation to ascertain the social basis of witchcraft. He isolated a social activity that accounted for different belief systems concerning witchcraft. The Nupe of Northern Nigeria believe that witches are always women—mostly older, dominating females who attack a younger man. Men are never accused of witchcraft. Males fight to cleanse villages of witchcraft by organizing secret societies that threaten and attack witches. A neighboring people, the Gwari, believe that witches and their victims can be male or female. Witchcraft is diminished by an annual cleansing ritual that embraces the whole community, irrespective of gender. Witchcraft for the Nupe involves gender antagonisms that are absent in Gwari witchcraft.

Nadel sought to isolate social activities that generated these different belief systems. He found that the two societies were similar in most factors and only differed in one or two. One of these naturally isolated factors was linked to the differences in witchcraft (see Ratner, 1997a, p. 215). The two societies are neighbors in an identical environment; they speak closely related languages and have an identical kinship system. Political organization and the regulation of male adolescence are similar; so is their economy, religion, the conception of the body (possessed of a double soul), reincarnation, and life and death. One crucial difference stands out from these resemblances. It is the economic position of wives. Nupe wives are generally successful traders. They are usually wealthier than their peasant husbands. Although men are nominally the head of the family, husbands are often heavily in debt to their wives, and the latter assume many of the financial responsibilities that traditionally belong to husbands. Wives pay for the children's education, bear expenses for family feasts, and find a bride-price for the sons. This reversal of traditional roles is openly resented by the men, who are, however, helpless to redress the situation. Men also resent the fact that women greatly limit the number of children they bear—by abortion and contraception—to be able to work. In contrast, Gwari wives occupy a domestic position in the family and economy that does not threaten Gwari men.

The positions of men and women in familial and the economic activities clearly generate the Nupe's and Gwari's different conceptions of witchcraft. The natural experiment allows this factor to be isolated as pivotal. Since gender differences are the primary way in which the two societies differ, they must be pivotal to differences in belief systems (and associated emotions and other psychological phenomena). In addition, the content of Nupe witchcraft is homologous with the content of Nupe gender antagonisms. Female domination of men is reflected in the concept of what a witch is—namely, an older, dominating woman who threatens younger, weaker men—and the fearful manner in which witchcraft is opposed—by secret male organizations that would be crushed if they were public. The more traditional gender roles among the Gwari and the absence of gender conflict, generate a gender-neutral notion of witches as equally male and female. In addition, men and women cooperate in combating witchcraft openly.

Sherif's natural experiment (cited in Chapter 1, pp. 19–20) on the psychological effects of competition and cooperation artificially manipulated theses social relationships to demonstrate their impact. His experiment is a brilliant and rare example of artificially manipulating social factors in natural settings.

Yet another kind of experimental technique that is useful for cultural psychology is a statistical analysis of data to control for social factors. Brooks Gunn (cited in Chapter 1, pp. 22) employed a statistical analysis to experimentally demonstrate the effect of poverty on antisocial behavior and IQ. She statistically controlled poverty rates for blacks and whites (by selecting black and white subjects from the same income levels) and discovered that this eliminated differences in IQ scores between the groups.

Belek (2000) performed a similar kind of statistical analysis to disentangle the effects of social class, income, education, and area of residence on psychological distress. Belek defined social class in Marxist terms as one's position in the mode of production. Class is distinct from income and education because a schoolteacher, semiskilled factory worker, and a small shopkeeper may earn the same income; however, one is a salaried employee, the other is paid hourly, and the third is self-employed. They are thus treated differently and have different rights, responsibilities, rewards, and opportunities. Similarly, a carpenter can be a worker, a manager, or a self-employed "petty-bourgeois" businessman, and these different class positions/social relationships structure the carpenter's psychology in different ways. Belek calculated mental health scores of subjects residing in a slum area and the city center of Antalya, Turkey. He calculated the variation in these scores in relation to the subjects' income, education, area of residence, and social class. The results demonstrated that when individuals are equated on the first three factors, their mental health scores varied according to their social class (categorized as blue-collar, unqualified, self-employed, white collar, highly qualified, and bourgeoisie). The lower the class, the greater the psychological distress for individuals of similar income, education, and residence. These latter three factors yielded little variation in mental health scores, either individually or together. Thus, "social class is a stronger predictor of health status than income, education, and area of residence" (ibid., p. 98).

It is imperative to be aware of experimental principles in order to avoid confounding factors and drawing erroneous conclusions. For instance, since it is normally impossible to randomly assign people to live in particular social activities, use particular artifacts, and attend to particular cultural concepts, most cultural psychological research must sample individuals from existing groups. Experiments under these conditions are quasi-experiments. Knowing the strengths and weaknesses of quasi-experiments is critical in order to draw appropriate conclusions from them and to identify inappropriate conclusions. Since subjects in quasi-experiments are selected from naturally formed groups, rather than being randomly assigned to those groups, the association of group membership with some psychological process may be the spurious result of other factors that led subjects to join their groups in the first place. If students from two schools with different programs achieve different scores on IQ tests, this result cannot be attributed to the school programs because students from different social classes or family backgrounds may attend the different schools and these factors may be responsible for the IQ differences.

Leventhal and Brooks-Gunn (2000, p. 331) caution that most research on the psychological effects of neighborhood utilizes quasi-experimental designs and is susceptible to the confound that individuals and families with particular psychological characteristics inhabit particular neighborhoods, or move from them. If highly educated or motivated individuals live in affluent neighborhoods and poorly educated or motivated individuals live in poor areas, then we cannot know whether a particular psychological/behavioral outcome is due to the neighborhood or the individual's characteristics. Therefore we must control for individual and family factors. In other words, individuals and families must be matched (equated) on relevant factors so that only social factors vary. One way to control for individual and family factors is to randomly assign residents to neighborhoods and housing projects. This can be done through government housing programs. Random assignment to conditions eliminates any selection bias from individual factors.

While experimental research is a powerful tool for indicating an association between psychology, activities, artifacts, and concepts, it has a number of weaknesses. One is that real life is not amenable to precisely isolating circumscribed factors. We have seen that even a relatively specific social factor such as gender role contains a number of elements that are difficult to isolate and control. Typically, natural experiments are left with broad factors that limit the precision with which social influences on psychology can be identified. In addition, experiments fail to illuminate how cultural factors penetrate into the psyche of individuals and affect their perceptions, motivation, emotions, reasoning, memory, development, imagination, personality, and mental illness. Thus, experiments can demonstrate that poverty fosters low IQ and particular forms and rates of mental illness; however, the manner in which poverty affects these phenomena remains mysterious. In other words, the manner in which poverty forms IQ and mental illness is not disclosed by experiments. We may say that experiments identify the external relation of psychological phenomena and activities, artifacts, and concepts—or the fact that there is a causal relationship—but experiments fail to disclose the internal relation between psychological phenomena and activities, artifacts, and concepts. Another way of expressing this point is to say that experiments illuminate psychology in culture—for example, IQ in poverty—however, they fail to illuminate culture in psychology, for example, how poverty permeates psychological phenomena (Ratner, 1997a, pp. 217–220).

The limitations of experiments can be ameliorated. The best corrective is to employ qualitative methodology in conjunction with experiments to elucidate the cultural features within psychological phenomena (see ibid., pp. 220–228). Nadel's research on witchcraft is a good model of this. We saw that in addition to employing the experimental method of differences, Nadel also identified congruences in the content of witchcraft and gender roles. The experimental situation identified gender roles as the necessary reason for different concepts of witchcraft (because gender roles were the primary social difference between the Nupe and the Gwari); a qualitative resemblance between gender roles and witchcraft indicates the actual penetration of gender roles into the conception of witchcraft. It is important to discuss this kind of qualitative analysis in detail.

Qualitative Methods are Necessary for Discerning the Cultural Character of Psychological Phenomena

Qualitative methodology analyzes the content and mode of operation of psychological phenomena. For example, qualitative methodology discloses that the "the self" is experienced as autonomous or as socially embedded, that "happiness" is experienced as wild excitement (as when one wins a championship basketball game in the last second to play) or a profound calm (which occurs when watching a beautiful sunset or a sculpture such as Michelangelo's *David*), that shame is experienced as an avoidable personal failure to succeed or an unavoidable fate of mankind to renounce its ego, and that memory recalls information out of context ("free recall") or contextually.

Qualitative methodology assumes that the nature of a psychological phenomenon is complex, subtle, variable, and difficult to recognize in behavior because any act may represent a number of psychological phenomena and a number of psychological phenomenon may be expressed by a single act. Conceptualizing and investigating the specific form and content of psychology is therefore a priority for qualitative methodology. The extent (degree) to which a phenomenon exists in a particular individual or group is a secondary question that can be addressed only after the quality has been established.

Qualitative analysis infers and deduces the nature of psychological phenomena from behaviors and statements. This process of interpretation is called "the hermeneutic circle" (Ratner, 1997a, pp. 133–142, 213–228).[1] If a mother slaps her child in the context of: the child has just run out into the street without looking to see cars speeding by, the mother explains that it is dangerous to act this way, the mother says "I hope that this spanking will help you to remember to carefully look next time," the mother apologizes to the child later and explains that she didn't want to hurt him, the mother tells her husband that she was worried their son would get hurt running into the street, then we are justified in inferring that psychologically she loves her son and is concerned for his safety. If a mother slaps her child in a context of: he does not say hello to her after coming home from school, she never explains her action or apologizes for it, and slaps him this way in many other situations, then we are justified in inferring that psychologically she is behaving cruelly and irrationally. We postulate specific psychological qualities (about the mother) that are logically congruent with the pattern of relevant behaviors.

In a situation in which subjects are presented items to solve, or agree or disagree with, qualitative methodology would analyze what the items mean to the subject, what kinds of items she favors and disfavors, and what strategies she uses to solve problems. The researcher would infer from these the form and content of a psychological motive, emotion, perception, or cognitive process. In contrast, positivistic methodology simply counts the number of items that a subject favors or disfavors, or solves, and concludes that she is high or low on the dimension that is ostensibly measured.

A qualitative analysis can compare specific psychological qualities to the quality of cultural activities, artifacts, and concepts. This procedure discovered the homologies we noted in Chap. 1—between the dichotomized schizophrenic self and bourgeois individualism; between capitalist commercial relationships and personality traits; between ancient Korean shame and Taoist concepts about self, human nature, and the world; and between the subordinate domestic position of Victorian upper middle class women, prevalent cultural concepts that women were frail, submissive, beautiful, restrained, clean, pure, and spiritual, and Victorian women's personality traits (docile, patient, dependent), emotions (fearful, guilty, expressive), and hysteria (whose symptoms reflected and created a physically incapacitated, dependent individual).

To understand the cultural organization of psychological phenomena, qualitative methodology must be employed in two stages. The first encourages subjects to fully express themselves in statements and behavior. A hermeneutic interpretation then infers and deduces the qualities of psychological phenomena that underlie extended patterns of behavior (see Ratner, 1997a, Chap. 2 for an explanation of the ontological, epistemological, and methodological principles of hermeneutic interpretation).

Once qualitative methods have helped to identify the quality of a psychological phenomenon, a further act of interpretation compares it with the form and content of activities, artifacts, and concepts. Such comparison of the concordances and discrepancies among these factors reveals the manner in which activities, artifacts, and concepts organize psychological phenomena. This kind of cultural–historical interpretation of psychology was the crux of 19th century German hermeneutics. Advocates such as Dilthey maintained that "the interpretation of meaning belongs to the larger sciences of history ... To understand means 'to understand historically'" (Ermarth, 1981, p. 179).

Rather than expand on the principles of a qualitative cultural psychological methodology (which I have done in Ratner, 1997a, Chaps. 4, 5), I will illustrate them with an example from research. A remarkably clear and skillful application of qualitative methodology to cultural psychology is Goldhagen's (1996) research on the psychology of the Holocaust.

The research explains cultural factors that motivated ordinary Germans to murder Jews during the Holocaust. It traces the murderous behavior to psychological motives, emotions, perceptions, and reasoning which are shaped by cultural values. Goldhagen argues that many ordinary Germans enthusiastically searched out Jews, and humiliated, tortured, and wantonly killed them because they had adopted the cultural concept of anti-Semitism. The perpetrators on the Holocaust were animated by a particular cultural psychology that disposed them to commit atrocities. The perpetrators did not posses the same "basic instincts" of compassion and helpfulness toward Jews that all people are supposed to have toward other humans. Consequently, the perpetrators did not need to be forced to circumvent these humane instincts in order to slaughter Jews (Goldhagen, 1996, pp. 23, 385, 408–409). On the contrary, their cultural psychology predisposed them toward such behavior.

Goldhagen illuminates the psychological processes involved in genocide by utilizing the methodology of hermeneutics. Hermeneutics advocates comprehending the psychological significance of an act by grasping its relationship with related acts. Goldhagen vividly describes a range of auxiliary acts that collectively illuminate the motives, emotions, perceptions, and reasoning of German killers of Jews. The killers often humiliated their victims before they killed them. They kicked and beat them as they marched them to gas chambers and shooting sites. They took photos of themselves dominating their victims before killing them. They enthusiastically hunted out the Jews from hiding places when they could have searched less diligently and allowed the Jews to remain hidden. The soldiers walked into hospitals and shot sick Jews in their beds. They killed 2-year-old children by picking them up by their hair, shooting them through the back of their heads, and throwing them into a grave. The perpetrators searched out and killed Jews who had renounced their Jewishness and converted to Christianity. The killers joked with each other as they shot their victims. They forced Jews to lie on top of corpses and shot them. Many perpetrators each shot hundreds of Jews in a day and then resumed slaughtering hundreds more the next day. During time away from the killings, the perpetrators enjoyed life and were undisturbed by having slaughtered hundreds and thousands of victims. The killers often walked next to their victims, shepherding them to execution sites and then shooting them at point blank range. They did all this to defenseless individuals who posed no physical threat to the killers.

The interrelated web of auxiliary acts allows us to infer and deduce that the perpetrators enthusiastically desired to kill, derived pleasure from killing, felt no remorse, felt no compassion for their victims, hated the Jews, perceived them as evil, wanted to eliminate them from the earth, and perceived them as subhumans who deserved to die an excruciating death. We can infer from the diligence in searching out Jews (even Christianized Jews) and their systematic, large-scale slaughter that the perpetrators were motivated by the desire to exterminate Jews.

The manner in which the genocide was carried out—the details of the murderous acts—can be explained only by acknowledging these psychological phenomena. Goldhagen postulates psychological states that are not directly observable but that are necessary to generate to genocidal behavior. Absent the motives, emotions, perceptions, and reasoning processes, the specific atrocities of the Holocaust would not have occurred.[2]

Goldhagen does not stop at a psychological explanation of the Holocaust. He takes another audacious intellectual step and seeks to explain the perpetrators' psychology in terms of cultural values or concepts. Goldhagen employs his powerful analytic skills to sift through the myriad cultural factors of Nazi society and identify anti-Semitism as a cornerstone of the perpetrators' psychology.

A rabid anti-Semitism was rampant in Germany in the years preceding the Holocaust. Four hundred years before Hitler, Luther denigrated Jews (Goldhagen, 1996, p. 284). In the early 19th century Germans deeply felt that Jews should be eliminated (ibid., p. 375). The Nazis fanned anti-Semitic sentiments so that Germans in the 1930s regarded Jews as demons whose very existence threatened to pollute humanity. Jews were regarded as cunning, cruel, evil incarnate, the cause of turmoil; they were a plague that needed to be exterminated (ibid., p. 398). Death was not sufficient punishment for such subhuman creatures. They must be brutalized and made to suffer. They were construed as devoid of human feelings and therefore fair game for subhuman treatment (ibid., pp. 397–398).

Goldhagen argues that anti-Semitism was a cultural concept that formed the core of the perpetrators' psychology and behavior (ibid., p. 399). It generated the form and content of the Germans' motives, perceptions, emotions, reasoning, and treatment of the Jewish people (p. 402). Anti-Semitism is what Bourdieu calls a *habitus*: a socially structured structure of beliefs that structures a person's psychological structure. Anti-Semitism imparted consistency to the Germans' psychological phenomena and behavior. Of course, governmental policies and institutions were necessary to unleash anti-Semitic ideas and allow them to culminate in genocide. However, anti-Semitism provided the ideational orientation to commit genocide (ibid., pp. 416–419).

Goldhagen identifies anti-Semitism as the cultural core of the perpetrators' psychology by employing a powerful logical analysis. This includes pinpointing the logical coherence between the belief system of anti-Semitism and each of the psychological phenomena and behaviors (ibid., p. 399).

Anti-Semitism made Hitler's genocidal plans and policies understandable and acceptable to millions of Germans, whereas such plans and policies would have evoked outrage in other countries (ibid., pp. 403, 418). It led Germans to accept the most irrational Nazi claims—that Jewish children in Poland had to be killed in retaliation for the British bombing of German cities (ibid., p. 404). It lifted the ethical and emotional restraints that normally inhibit people from murdering masses of other humans (ibid., 414). It accounts for the Germans' continued slaughter for Jews at the end of the war in defiance of Himmler's orders (ibid., p. 403). It accounts for soldiers killing Jews even when their commanders offered to release them from this duty (ibid., 405). It accounts for the joy and pride the soldiers took in killing Jews. It accounts for the Germans' debasing, Jews and shooting mothers holding their babies at point blank range. It accounts for the geographic scope of the Germans' exterminationist drive against the Jews throughout Europe. It accounts for the comprehensiveness of the drive to kill every last Jewish child and even Jews who had assimilated into German culture and identified with it (ibid., pp. 412–414). It also explains the more lenient treatment that German soldiers meted out to other enemies. Finally, the widespread anti-Semitic view of Jews unified the psychology and behavior of millions of Germans:

> Animated by common views of Jews and thus by a common guide to action, it is no wonder that so many Germans from different walks of life, from different social backgrounds, under different institutional arrangements and with different opportunity structures, in vastly different settings—in totally organized camps, in the partly routinized, partly wild roundups and shooting operations, in the relatively unsupervised "Jew-hunts" requiring initiative, and in the virtually autonomous conditions of the death marches—engaged in the actions specified here as having been common to the perpetrators … The genocidal devotion that antisemitism imbued in ordinary Germans gave so may people—who, it might have been thought, were by dint of background and training not unusually fit to become genocidal killers—the resolve to persist in the task despite its evident horror and the visceral revulsion that many felt upon their initiation into it. (ibid., p. 400)

Goldhagen employs qualitative methods to analyze behavioral data, discern a particular psychology, and identify cultural characteristics and constituents of that psychology. His conclusions are convincing because they logically mesh with the data. They account for all the data and make it intelligible. (In the next section we shall see that his conclusions are the only ones that account for all the data. Competing explanations are inconsistent with at least some of the data.)

Only qualitative methodology could substantiate the existence of a particular cultural psychology that generates complex, irrational, unusual, mind-boggling behavior such as the Holocaust. Only qualitative methodology can capture the congruence between macro-level concepts about Jews and micro-level individual atrocities by soldiers against Jews. Qualitative methods are scientific procedures for investigating cultural psychological phenomena. Qualitative methods are not prescientific techniques which are useful only for exploratory phases of research before "truly scientific" positivistic procedures are invoked.

When it is done well, explicating qualitative resemblances between psychology and activities, artifacts, and concepts has the same power and legitimacy as scientific explanations about the origins of the planet Earth, the extinction of dinosaurs, and the evolution of *Homo sapiens* from other primates. All of these explanations rest on logical relationships between explanandum and explanans. Natural scientists know that dinosaurs required certain ecologies, they know that at a certain time the ecology of Earth changed and that simultaneously dinosaurs became extinct—these facts were themselves inferred and deduced from physical materials; they were not directly apprehended by the sense organs. Scientists can logically conclude that the changed ecology was inhospitable to the biological requirements of dinosaurs and caused their extinction. The argument is persuasive because it elucidates the internal, logical relationship between the ecology and the biological needs of dinosaurs. Although there is no experimental proof or direct observation of the relationship, the logic of the argument is so compelling that it has been accepted as a scientific fact. This logical explanation, based upon a conceptual understanding of the internal relationship between ecology and biological requirements of dinosaurs, is far more convincing than a statistical finding that changes in ecology immediately preceded the disappearance of dinosaurs. Such a statistical finding fails to explain the relationships that make up the conjunction of events.

Explanation by qualitative resemblance in cultural psychology is as valid as it is in natural science. Moreover, it is superior to statistical comparisons of overt, physical, quantitative properties that are extolled by positivists.[3]

Some interesting work in the area of discourse analysis employs qualitative resemblance to identify cultural concepts and activities in discourse about marriage. In a discourse analyzed by Gee (1999), a woman discusses why she would not leave her marriage. She says, "Why in the world would you want to stop and not get the use out of all the years you've already spent together?" Gee observes: "The phrase 'time spent' here, then triggers the well-known metaphor in our culture: 'time = money,' so that time spent in marriage is being treated as an 'investment' of time (like an investment of money). In terms of the investment metaphor, if we invest money/time, we are entitled to a 'return.' So according to this model, it is silly not to wait long enough, having made an investment, to see it 'pay off' and be able to 'get the use out of' the time/money that has been invested" (ibid., p. 69). In this case, Gee goes beyond the woman's statement and recognizes that it embodies a "master cultural model" that derives from commercial economic activity. The woman did not state that marriage was an investment, however her words express this concept.

Identifying the concept (model) of an investment draws out important implications of the woman's thinking that would be fruitful to explore in further interviews. The investment model opens up a line of questioning about whether the woman remains married because she fears losing the time she has invested in her relationship; whether she values the investment of time more than her husband; whether she might have left if she had less time invested; and what kind of return would justify the investment of time she has put in. By categorizing the statement as denoting an investment, the features of that category can be brought to enrich the investigation of the particular statement, just as identifying an organism as a virus, or disease symptoms as tuberculosis, allows the categorical understanding to enrich the understanding of the particular case.

Going beyond the individual to a broader category enhances the under-standing of the individual.

Gee's exemplary linking of individual attitudes to cultural concepts and activities is unfortunately atypical. Most work in discourse analysis, for example, focuses on the linguistic (semiotic) properties of statements and ignores cultural concepts and activities that are embodied in the statement's content (see Ci, 1999b; Ratner, 1993a,b, 2000a). Edwards' (1999) "discursive psychology," which derives from discourse analysis and ordinary language philosophy, exemplifies this shortcoming. In one case study, Edwards col-lected statements following the death of Princess Diana. One extract stated that, "She indulged in 'infantile' temper tantrums and forced the rest of the Royal family to 'put up with her childlike self-centeredness.'" Edwards' analysis consists of reminding us that, according to the extract, "the 'tantrums' were plural, and they stemmed from character ('her child-like self-centeredness') rather than situation. The Royals apparently did not, by their actions, provoke such tantrums, but were 'forced' to 'put up with' them" (ibid., p. 287). The analysis adds nothing to what the statement said. There is no attempt at analyzing cultural values that may be reflect-ed in the notion that tantrums are infantile personal traits rather than provoked by a situation. Nor is there any interest in assessing the truth value of the statement that Diana was self-centered. We may say that Edwards' approach is too "experience near" to what the subjects say and adds nothing to their words.[4]

Most of Gee's work on discourse analysis also falls short of the fore-going exemplary analysis. It concentrates on paraphrasing the words that subjects use. In one of his analyses, he investigates cultural concepts regarding child development in the discourses of middle-class and work-ing class parents. Middle-class parents state that their children pass through developmental stages, so Gee says they employ a cultural model of developmental stages. Working class parents say their children need to be socialized to care about the family, so Gee says they employ a cultural model that emphasizes socialization and caring about the family. If parents talk about success, then they are using a "success model;" if they talk about supporting their family, they are using a "breadwinner model" (Gee, 1999, pp. 122–123). In these cases, Gee's cultural models are nothing more than the subjects' own words. Gee becomes mired in the same "reiteration com-pulsion" that plagues Edwards—he simply reiterates what the subjects have said (see Bourdieu, 2000, pp. 147, 174).

Gee's analysis would have been greatly strengthened if he had eluci-dated elements of cultural activities, artifacts, and concepts that were implied by the parents' words but that go beyond them. He might then have concluded that the cultural model evidenced in the parents' discourse about developmental stages is an individualistic view of children: stages of development are an unfolding of individual capabilities with minimal interference from parents and positive support for the child's natural tendencies (see Cushman, 1991 for this kind of analysis). Identifying this individualistic cultural model would bring out important implications of the parents' thinking. These include the prediction that parents will patiently wait for children to manifest behaviors rather than try to teach them, that parents will accept what their children do as being intrinsic to their character, that parents will minimize restrictions on behavior because this would stifle a natural inclination, and that parents will generally cater to the child rather than expect her to meet adult standards. Understanding the individualism that underlies the notion of developmental stages would enrich our understanding of parents' thinking just as categorical analyses generally enrich the understanding of particular cases.

A deeper concern with culture would also lead Gee to elucidate the social source of people's discourses. In most of his examples, Gee simply identifies the group of people who adopt various discourses and cultural models—for example, middle-class parents adopt developmental stages, working class parents emphasize socialization, and professors use academic terminology. However, Gee scarcely mentions the social organization of economic, educational, and family activities of middle- and working class parents, or of professors and middle school teachers. Doing so would explain why the different groups adopt different cultural models.

THE QUALITATIVE METHOD THAT INVESTIGATE CULTURAL FACETS
OF PSYCHOLOGICAL PHENOMENA MUST BE RIGOROUS AND
SYSTEMATIC IN ORDER TO DRAW WARRANTED CONCLUSIONS

To know what is being investigated, and to draw accurate, useful conclusions about a topic, qualitative procedures must be rigorous. They must provide specific, clear definitions of terms. They must also demonstrate the logical connection between psychological phenomena and behavior, as well as between psychological phenomena, activities, artifacts, and concepts.

Rather than discuss general principles for enhancing objectivity in qualitative cultural psychological research (which I have done in Ratner, 1997a, pp. 67–68, Chaps. 4, 5), I would like to present illustrative examples from Goldhagen's study of the Holocaust. In the previous section I reviewed his cultural hermeneutic analysis to justify two conclusions: the perpetrators of the Holocaust possessed a particular psychology, and anti-Semitism was a cultural factor that generated this psychology. The conclusions are justified because the explanatory concepts are logically consistent with the soldier's genocidal behavior. Moreover, the explanatory concepts account for a wide range of data, and are not contradicted by any of it. These logical relationships are solid grounds for believing that the genocidal behavior was inspired and directed by a psychological system of motives, perceptions, emotions, and reasoning processes, and that this psychological system was generated by the cultural concept on anti-Semitism.

Goldhagen buttresses his argument by rebutting competing explanations (Goldhagen, 1996, pp. 9, 379–385, 399, 408, 417). One explanation is that the German soldiers, like the populace at large, were obedient people who passively followed orders to kill Jews. However, this claim is refuted by the fact that Germans defied a number of state policies around the time of the Holocaust. Ironically, some of the killing of Jews occurred in direct defiance of commands to cease this behavior: Near the end of the war, Himmler issued an order to stop murdering Jews, yet many German soldiers disobeyed this order and continued the slaughter (Goldhagen, 1996, pp. 382–383). This fact refutes the notion that the perpetrators of the Holocaust were acting out of blind obedience to authority.

Another explanation for participating in the Holocaust is that the soldiers were forced to by the threat of punishment. However, this is refuted by the fact that no Germans were punished for refusing to kill Jews. Germans killed in the absence of coercion. In many cases, commanders explicitly told soldiers that they did not have to kill and would be excused if they declined. Himmler even issued an order to this effect. Some soldiers did publicly decline and were not punished. "It can be said with certitude that never in the history of the Holocaust was a German, SS man or otherwise, killed, sent to a concentration camp, jailed, or punished in any serious way for refusing to kill Jews" (ibid., p. 379). The soldiers who participated in the killings were aware that they could have avoided it if they had so desired (ibid., pp. 213–216, 252–253).

A milder form of coercion—namely, group pressure—is refuted by the fact that many military units did not unanimously endorse or participate in the killing of Jews. Therefore unanimous group pressure, which social psychologists tout as necessary to produce high rates of conformity, was not necessarily present. Nor did the size of the group affect soldiers' rate of participation in the killings (ibid., p. 275).

Another competing explanation—that the perpetrators of the Holocaust acted so abominably because they had received intense indoctrination in Nazi ideology—is also rebutted by Goldhagen's deft marshalling of evidence. If this hypothesis were true, then soldiers who had not been so indoctrinated would have acted more humanely toward the Jews. To test this deduction, Goldhagen sampled soldiers who were not

Nazi party members and who had little ideological and military training. These were soldiers in police battalions who were reservists, outside the Nazified military system, and were mature men families and children. Yet they participated willfully, ruthlessly, and shamelessly in slaughtering Jews (ibid., p. 277). This fact refutes the notion that the perpetrators were extreme individuals who had received intense Nazi indoctrination. It indicates that quite ordinary Germans engaged in genocidal behavior and that ordinary—that is, widespread, commonplace—cultural factors were responsible (ibid., p. 464).

In addition to being falsified by empirical evidence, competing explanations fail to explain the culturally specific details of the perpetrators' genocidal behavior, their identify, and the identify of their victims. The competing explanations fail to explain why it was Germans who slaughtered Jews in the particularly ghoulish manner that defines the Holocaust.

In contrast, Goldhagen's cultural–psychological analysis of the perpetrators of the Holocaust identifies specific cultural factors and factors that account for the specificity of the killers' actions and identity, and the identity of the victims. Germans killed Jews in a maniacal, genocidal fashion because they had specific cultural beliefs about Jews, which were different from their beliefs about the Danes, and which rendered the Jews, unlike the Danish people, fit and necessary to annihilate (ibid., p. 394).

Goldhagen's conclusions meet all the scientific standards for objectivity. They illuminate important features of the data, they are consistent with all the data, no other conclusions are as successful in these regards, and his conclusions are consistent with other theoretical and empirical knowledge about culture, psychology, and behavior that is described in Chap. 1.

The fact that Goldhagen's analysis is a rigorous, objective qualitative study of cultural psychology does not mean that every one of his conclusions is necessarily true. He may have overlooked certain important data that would lead to different conclusions. However, this would not invalidate his methodological stance. It would only point up an incompleteness in his data collection. All science is factually incomplete in the sense that there are always facts that escape the attention of the scientist—either because they are not known or else they are known but are thought to be irrelevant to a particular issue. The factual incompleteness of science does not impugn its overall methodological approach. Physics, chemistry, biology, astronomy, and geology are all objective sciences with solid methodologies even though they are constantly discovering new facts that falsify particular conclusions. A particular methodology can be objective—in the sense of elucidating the nature of the object under investigation—without being entirely accurate. Similarly, some of Goldhagen's facts and conclusions may be incomplete or even false without diminishing the importance of his methodological approach. We can learn from him the way to investigate a specific cultural psychology, the process of inferring psychological phenomena from behavior, and the process of identifying cultural factors that organize psychological phenomena and behavior.

Unfortunately, many qualitative researchers pay little attention to objectivity. They employ weak methodologies and draw unwarranted conclusions. For instance, Vasconcellos and Valsiner (1998) sought to illustrate how 18-month-old babies are active agents who "co-construct" social situations rather than conform to them. The authors sought to empirically confirm Valsiner's individualistic perspective that "children create what is necessary for reaching their personal goals through social mediation in their interpersonal relations with peers" (ibid., p. 86). "The child ... utilizes the collective culturally meaningful surroundings to build his or her personal understanding of the world. The ways in which the latter is constructed are the child's own—each child creates a unique personal world" (ibid., p. 87).

To substantiate this hypothesis, the authors first need to conceptually define "personal world," "personal goals," and "personal understanding." It is incumbent on Valsiner to present conceptual criteria for knowing whether a baby's behavior or thought is an actively created unique one or whether it merely recapitulates social events. Valsiner also needs to carefully probe and analyze actions and statements of babies to discern whether they are active personal constructions or not.

Unfortunately, Valsiner made no effort to consider any of these elementary methodological principles. He simply observed babies interacting and impressionistically concluded that active co-construction occurred. One observation noted that "Pamela is quietly playing by herself inside her box with her small doll." The authors concluded that "Now she can be involved with the construction of her understanding of the symbolic aspects of her own actions" (ibid., p. 96). It is impossible to determine whether Pamela is constructing personal understandings and meanings because the authors never stipulate any conceptual criteria for identifying them, nor do they probe the psychological significance of Pamela's behavior to know whether she has constructed them. Simply playing by oneself is insufficient evidence for drawing any conclusions about what might be transpiring in the mind.

Impressionistic qualitative research is encouraged by a belief in postmodernism and neo-Kantianism. In repudiating positivism, many qualitative researchers have embraced postmodernism and neo-Kantianism as alternatives. These two doctrines privilege individual subjectivity over everything else. They reject reality beyond the individual and reduce reality to the individual's meanings. They are anti-realist doctrines that regard worldly phenomena as unknowable, ephemeral, intangible, indefinite, and hazy. Things are analogous to Rorschach ink blots: they are opportunities for individuals to define and redefine according to their own subjective meanings. Being is only the way that being is signified; there is nothing substantive beyond the subject's signification; therefore knowledge and psychology are not influenced by real phenomena. Rather, the individual produces reality through definitions and communication about it (Brandist, 2000).[5]

Denying reality independent of the observer denies any notion of objective methodology that reflects this reality. If a world beyond the observer is unknowable because it is always clouded and constructed by one's own values, there is no point in systematically studying it. Vague impressions about other people's psychology are sufficient because no more definite, accurate understanding of their psychological world is possible. Cocooned in a private world of meanings, the observer is more concerned with her own values than the reality of other people. She is not only insulated from apprehending other peoples' reality, but she is also prevented from agreeing with other observers about reality because everyone sees things differently. Postmodernists celebrate diversity of opinion and disagreement because these testify to the exercise of individual subjectivity.

Postmodernism underlies Valsiner's impressionistic methodology as well as his notion of agency (described in Chap. 2). Bruner espouses a similar inclination toward postmodernism and neo-Kantianism (identified in Chap. 2) and it also leads him to devalue rigorous social science methodology, as Phillips (2000, pp. 63–64, 71–72) points out.

One of the most explicit proponents of postmodernism in qualitative research is Steiner Kvale. He denies any cultural–psychological reality independent of the observer that can be objectively known. He therefore repudiates a realist reading of interview accounts that searches for the native's point of view and the text's essence and truth. He says that the question "How do you know what the person really means?" naively assumes a "fictitious entity" (Kvale, 1996, p. 225). "The search for real meaning nuggets leads to a reification of the subjective rather than to … an enrichment of the subjective" (p. 226). Kvale counterposes a postmodernist approach that solicits a range of diverse interpretations. Rather than seeking intersubjective agreement about the subject's meaning (psychological reality), "the goal is to proliferate, juxtapose, and create disjunctions among different ways of reading" (ibid., p. 226). Kvale insists that instead of a subject's psychological reality that can be known by an observer, there is only an inchoate flux that is linguistically defined by the observer. Moreover, any observer's linguistic construction (production) of a subject's meaning is acceptable because there is nothing beyond the construction to verify. Reality is whatever anyone makes it to be.

Postmodernists and neo-Kantians distort the hermeneutic approach to social science. Contrary to their opinion, the founders of hermeneutics acknowledged a social–psychological reality that is independent of the researcher and they insisted that the researcher must comprehend this reality objectively. Hermeneutics originated as a way of ascertaining the true meaning of biblical texts to settle religious controversies. It did not advocate solipsistic notions that there are no definite meanings, that the observer constitutes reality, and that all interpretations are equally interesting and useful.

Dilthey, the great systematizer of hermeneutics, strongly insisted that hermeneutic interpretations be rigorous and objective (Harrington, 2000; Ratner, 1997a, pp. 60–62, 183–202). He argued that the social and natural sciences share these general goals. Of course, the two branches of science require different specific procedures to comprehend their vastly different subject matter. However, they do, can, and must share general goals of precision, clarity, and objective comprehension of real qualities if both are to qualify as science. Ermarth (1981) observes that the whole current of 19th century German hermeneutic thought—ranging from Herder, Humboldt, and Schleiermacher through Droysen and Dilthey—was concerned with the justification of interpretive understanding as knowledge or science. Hermeneutics strives to accurately understand the meaning behind (or within) expressions. Although interpretation of a person's mental processes is conducted from the observer's vantage point, that does not preclude a valid, objective interpretation (ibid., p. 181). A defining characteristic of human beings is their ability to understand the thoughts, motives, intentions, and other mental processes of others. This intersubjectivity (which includes empathy, sympathy, joint attention) is the basis of communication, social planning, cooperation, and regulation (see Tomasello, 1998, 1999, 2000). If ordinary people can understand and cooperate with each other, surely skilled social scientists can accurately interpret the subjective processes of their subjects.

Many rationalist critics of postmodernism have pointed out that postmodernist philosophy is self-defeating (cf. Merton, 1972; Phillips, 2000). If statements about anything are only expressions of the observer's own values, and are uninformative about things themselves, then postmodernist statements about epistemology must be construed as personal opinions of the speaker rather than valid claims about epistemology per se. But then there is no reason for anyone to listen or agree with them. Why should anyone be interested in a personal fabrication that has no information value, truth value, or use value? In fact, people should *not* agree with postmodernism because they would be abandoning their own personal viewpoint which comprises their unique humanity. Thus, post-modernists must hope that nobody listens to them or agrees with them! Because they do not actually hold this hope, and instead vociferously argue to convince people that postmodernism is *true* and should be accepted, they contradict their own solipsism and demonstrate that is untenable.

The only tenable position for social scientists to take is that people do have culturally organized perceptions, emotions, cognitive processes, motivation, imagination, personality, and mental illness. These are real and they exist independently of the researcher. The cultural psychologist should describe and explain the real cultural psychology of people as objectively as possible. This will be scientifically interesting as well as socially useful—whereas emphasizing the researcher's personal value system is neither. It goes without saying that objective research is never absolutely and finally true. It always approximates a grand reality that is never completely known; and objective research is always open to refine-ment as new information is accumulated. These qualifications do not negate the importance and possibility of conducting objective research that is oriented toward understanding the cultural psychological reality of people and that increasingly approaches this goal. It also goes without saying that all researchers base their research on certain values. However, these only have value if they facilitate understanding the cultural psychological world of the people.

It requires active, creative cognitive skills to comprehend the com-plex, dynamic, socially constructed psychology of people. The researcher must accumulate a great deal of information about cultural activities, artifacts, and concepts. She must also possess sophisticated abilities to analyze and synthesize socially constructed psychological processes. And she must empathically elicit information from subjects. Kvale and post-modernists are thus dead wrong in asserting that objective research reifies the subject and depersonalizes the researcher.

Cultural Features of Psychology Must be Discerned by the Cultural Psychologist Through Skillful, Probing Analysis Because People Are Ordinarily Not Aware of Them

Cultural aspects of experience are unwittingly played out in the same uncanny way that childhood habits and unresolved needs are played out in one's marriage. Just as it requires a trained observer (e.g., therapist) to detect the homology between personal relationships in childhood and in marriage, so it requires a trained cultural psychologist to detect the homology between activities, concepts, and psychology. Durkheim emphasized this point in a statement that sounds remarkably like Marx: "Social life must be explained, not by the conception of it held by those who participate in it, but by profound causes which escape consciousness; and we also think that these causes must be sought chiefly in the way in which the associated individuals are grouped (cited in Harre, 1984, p. 933).

Dilthey similarly distinguished between "elementary forms of understanding" that the layperson has of social life and "higher forms of understanding" that are reflective, scientific analyses of the relationship between expressions and their social context (Harrington, 2000). Individuals are normally unaware of the historical character of their actions. Only sophisticated social scientists grasp the historical, cultural character of mundane acts. They transform *Geschafte* into *Geschichte*. A historical hermeneutical understanding of meaning, and mental processes in general, reconstructs the consciousness of the subject by the cultural–historical consciousness of the interpreter (Ermarth, 1981, pp. 178–180). Dilthey employed the concept *Besserverstehen* to denote the fact that an observer can have a better understanding of a subject's cultural–psychological consciousness than she might have (Bourdieu, 1996, pp. 93, 207–208; Ratner, 1997a, pp. 61–62).

Nisbett and Wilson (1977) report many experimental demonstrations of people being unaware of influences that affect their responses. The typical design of these experiments is to manipulate some feature of the experimental situation, detect the effect of this feature on a response, and then ask subjects if they are aware that their responses have been affected and what factor might have been at play. In most instances in which experimental manipulation did affect responses, subjects were not aware that their actions had changed. They were certainly not aware that any particular factor had influenced behavioral change. For example, when experimental manipulations affected subjects' attitudes, they did not realize that their attitudes had changed, nor did they realize that any change in conditions was responsible for this change. In verbal conditioning experiments, the introduction of certain cue words affects the subjects' response words. Yet when asked why they mentioned the response words the subjects did not attribute their verbal behavior to the cue words. Similarly, manipulating the description of an individual's personality affects how attractive he appears to others; yet subjects are not aware that the attractiveness score that they give to the target person are influenced by the description of his personality. In the same vein, a prose selection was altered and several versions were presented to subjects. The different versions had no impact on subjects' emotional responses; however, subjects believed that their emotional responses had been influenced by the different passages.

Nisbett and Wilson (p. 248 ff.) propose that peoples' perception of causality depend on implicit concepts of causality. Individuals adopt theories about which causal relationships are plausible. This belief leads people to perceive and remember one thing causing another even when it does not. Conversely, when people do not believe that one thing causes another, the two will not be perceived and recalled as standing in a causal relationship even when they really do.

Nisbett and Wilson's account is a powerful explanation of people's inability to perceive social influences on their psychology. If individuals live in a society in which the activities and predominant ideology obscure social influences on psychology, they will not perceive these influences. Only individuals whose activities and ideology render a social analysis of psychology plausible will perceive this causal relationship when it exists. Perception is not a direct replica of reality; it is mediated by culturally derived concepts. These concepts may in turn obfuscate the social reality that generated them.

Because social concepts may blind people to social reality, the impact of the latter on psychology must be elucidated by the researcher. He can encourage subjects to reflect on social influences that do not immediately come to mind. Painstaking questions can be asked that challenge subjects' first impressions and prod them to deeper reflection concerning social influences. (Chapter 4 describes ways of doing this.) Interviews can elicit more cultural information than privately written essays because individuals writing privately will not have the stimulation to reflect on social matters that they are unused to considering. Despite skillful probing by the researcher, most subjects will not become fully aware of the cultural origins, formation, characteristics, and function of psychological phenomena. Consequently, the researcher must elucidate the cultural aspects of psychology that remain embedded in subjects' experiences but that remain unknown to them. (Chapter 5 describes ways of doing this.)

Arriving at a cultural–psychological analysis is analogous to a physician arriving at a medical diagnosis: The physician listens to the patient's report of symptoms and then utilizes his medical knowledge to identify what disease the patient has. The doctor's diagnosis surpasses the patient's description of symptoms because the patient does not have the knowledge to know which disease the symptoms express. The physician must base his diagnosis on the reported symptoms; however, he goes beyond the symptoms to understand the disease that the patient does not know. The cultural psychologist proceeds in a similar manner to understand a subject's cultural psychology.

Schutz (1967, p. 6) denotes this process by saying that "The constructs used by the social scientist are, so to speak, constructs of the second degree, namely constructs of the constructs made by the actors on the social scene, whose behavior the social scientist observes and tries to explain in accordance with the procedural rules of science."

Vygotsky (1997b, p. 325) aptly expressed the need for analysis to transcend felt (described) experience. He said, "Not a single science is possible without separating direct experience from knowledge ... If in psychology appearance and being were the same, then everybody would be a scientist-psychologist and science would be impossible."

Vygotsky compared consciousness to reflected light in a mirror: consciousness is a consequence of external objective processes just as reflected light is a result of light sources beyond the mirror. Psychologists should not study consciousness in and of itself any more than they should focus on the light coming from the mirror. The processes that explain, predict, and change consciousness and reflected light are the ultimate goal of science (ibid., p. 327). "Scientific knowledge and immediate perception do not coincide at all. We can neither experience the child's impressions, nor witness the French revolution, but the child who experiences his paradise with all directness and the contemporary who saw the major episodes of the revolution with his own eyes, are, despite that, farther from the scientific knowledge of these facts than we are" (ibid., p. 271; see Ratner, 1991, p. 320).

THE FOREGOING PRINCIPLES OF CULTURAL PSYCHOLOGICAL RESEARCH ARE APPLICABLE TO STUDYING CULTURAL ASPECTS OF PSYCHOLOGICAL PHENOMENA IN ALL SOCIETIES

Our principles of cultural psychological research are general tenets that can elucidate the cultural aspects of psychological phenomena in all societies. All cultural psychological research must take account of the fact that human psychology is selectively formed from cultural activities, artifacts, and concepts and it must be studied in relation to them. Psychology must also be studied distinctively in its own right as it is expressed by individuals. It must be inferred and deduced from complex behavioral expressions through acts of interpretation, and interpretations about peoples' psychology must be objective. The relationship of psychological phenomena to cultural activities, artifacts, and concepts must be empirically established through experimentation and through rigorous logical analysis. People are not fully aware of their own perceptions, emotions, motives, and personality, nor are they fully aware of cultural aspects of these psychological phenomena; therefore research must probe to elucidate these, and cannot simply accept superficial, immediate responses.

Our general methodological principles are universally useful because they correspond to general aspects of human cultural psychology. (I have consistently argued that general features of human psychology coexist with culturally specific, variable ones.) General features of human cultural psychology allow/demand some universality in the methodology that is employed to study it.

Ironically, our general methodological principles are useful and valid guidelines for elucidating the culturally specific features that psychological phenomena possess in particular societies. Relating psychological phenomena to cultural activities, artifacts, and concepts, plus employing qualitative methods to elicit full cultural–psychological significance reveals concrete cultural–psychology in any society.

Conversely, if a researcher fails to utilize these principles and does not use a social understanding to formulate research questions, devise research instruments, and interpret subjects' responses, and if the researcher fails to probe subjects to clarify ambiguous responses and to reflect further on unfamiliar issues, then she will overlook or misconstrue the specific cultural features of psychological phenomena. She will likely impose ethnocentric assumptions on people's psychology. We have discussed examples of research that has failed to illuminate the cultural specificity and variability of psychology because it failed to employ our tenets. Therefore, our general methodological principles protect and preserve cultural psychology; they do not contradict it.

Any science that seeks to study specific, variable phenomena does so by understanding them as variations of general factors that are studied by common methods. A biologist who seeks to understand anatomical differences in birds and apes employs common research methods (dissection, staining of cells, microscopic examination of cells, chemical analysis) to investigate common fundamental factors and processes (genes, neuronal structures, hormones, etc.) that account for the specificity and variation in the two species. Analogously, our general tenets for studying the general factors and processes of cultural psychology (the relationship of psychology to activities, etc.) ultimately reveal the specific cultural–psychological differences among people.

When "the general" and "the specific" are correctly understood as dialectically related, there is no contradiction or opposition between them. Each is real and plays a role in the other. There are generalities in specific features and there are specific variations in general features. We only encounter conundra when we try to expunge one or reduce it to the other—for example, when we insist only on general, universal aspects of emotions or psychopathology and deny or minimize specific differences in them, when we overgeneralize one characteristic and assume its universality, or when we overemphasize individual differences to the neglect of commonalities (see Ratner, 1991, pp. 113–146).

NOTES

1. Detecting qualitative homologies requires a methodology that is different from conventional positivism. Postivists eschew any alternative methodologies as unscientific. However, science is not defined by a particular methodology. The entire history of science demonstrates that methodologies are designed to investigate particular phenomena. New phenomena demand new methodologies. Insisting on one methodology regardless of the phenomenon that is being studied is dogmatism. Making a particular method into an idolatry ("methodolatry") forces the phenomenon into a form that is acceptable to the given methodology and it disregards the concrete nature of the subject matter which may require new methods. If the subject matter is cultural qualities of psychological phenomena, then a methodology must be devised that will illuminate it. One cannot reduce it to forms that are acceptable to positivistic methods if these forms misrepresent the true subject matter. Nor can one dismiss it as an unimportant topic because no adequate methodology exists. Otherwise, scientists would have forsaken the study of atoms, genes, quarks, galaxies, cells, and bacteria because no methods were available to study them at the time they were conceived or discovered.

2. Of course, postulating unobservable phenomena is somewhat hazardous (although direct observation is also, as indicated by optical illusions, misperception of crime perpetrators by victims and eyewitnesses, and everyday miscommunication between couples). However, it is certainly possible to postulate unobservables in a rigorous, objective manner. Natural scientists routinely postulate unobservables. Examples are electrons, germs, magnetic force, DNA, black holes, distant galaxies, the big bang, and the Ice Age. Their specific characteristics were inferred and deduced from observable data with remarkable precision.

   Postulating unobservables is scientifically legitimate and necessary. The unobservable big bang is necessary for understanding the formation of the universe, just as electrons are necessary for understanding properties of matter, and DNA is necessary for understanding cell morphology. Postulating psychological phenomena is just as necessary and legitimate for understanding human behavior such as mass murder. Science—both natural and social—advances by postulating unobservables, not by simply recording overt data. Of course, unobservables in natural science are physical entities expressed in physical units, while unobservables in social science are social and mental phenomena that are not expressed in physical units. However, all science postulates unobservables of some kind (see Ratner, 1997a, Chap. 5 for a discussion of similarities between good social science and good natural science, as well as their differences).

3. Positivistic methods often produce superficial, ambiguous data and arbitrary, misleading conclusions, all of which obfuscate the cultural character of psychological phenomena (Ratner, 1997a, Chap. 1). This can be seen in positivistic questionnaires. Most questionnaires restrict subjects to indicating the degree of amount of a psychological phenomenon (how often it occurs, its strength, or the amount of agreement one feels for an issue). Subjects are usually not allowed to express the way they interpret a statement, reason, feel perceive, or

remember. The quality of their psychological phenomena is thus suppressed. Suppressing psychological quality presumes it is uniform and obvious and not worth investigating; otherwise, neglecting it would be unacceptable. Say we are presented with a statement that "My mother is strong," and we are limited to agreeing or disagreeing along a seven-point scale. This is justified only if we all have the same interpretation of "My mother is strong." If we have different meanings, then the extent of our agreement to statement is meaningless: my agreement would presume that my mother is physically robust, while your agreement to "the same statement" would presume that your mother is psychologically strong. The two agreements would be incomparable. Restricting responses to quantitative forms assumes that statements have a single, universal meaning. Indeed, a psychological variable is defined as something that varies quantitatively but is qualitatively invariant. However, this assumption of invariance is never tested, but is simply built in to the response format. Then the methodology acts as a self-fulfilling prophecy (delusion): With no qualitative meanings in evidence, positivists believe that their assumption of single, universal psychological quality is warranted. This is akin to autocratic leaders forbidding dissent and then deluding themselves into thinking that their subjects agree with their policies (see Mishler, 1986, pp. 26–27). Of course, suppressing the quality of psychological phenomena and arbitarily presuming that a single, universal quality pervalis obfuscates cultural characteristics and constituents of psychological phenomena.

This weakness is exemplified in McCrae's cross-cultural research on personality (McCrae, Yik, Trapnell, Bonn, & Paulhus, 1998). He developed a personality inventory (the Revised NEO Personality Inventory) on which he compared individuals of European and Chinese ancestry. The inventory is comprised of 240 statements with which subjects agree or disagree on five-point Likert scales. The statements were deemed by McCrae to represent 30 personality traits or facets (eight statements for each facet). The 30 facets were then factor analyzed to yield five broad factors or domains (each domain included six facets). For instance, the statement "I try to be courteous to everyone I meet" was categorized by the authors as a component of the trait/facet altruism, and altruism was construed as a component of the domain agreeableness.

The problem is that terms such as "courteous" are loaded with multiple cultural significances and these are obscured by the response format that the authors imposed on the subjects. Acts considered courteous can range from a perfunctory smile of a cashier in a store at a customer because it is a job requirement demanded by her boss, to a genuine helpfulness such as when a long-term resident spends time showing the neighborhood to a newly arrived neighbor, to a minimal interaction that is made out of a desire to avoid contact with someone (as in "at the dinner party she was merely courteous to him"). The response format of the personality inventory does not allow the researcher to know which of these cultural significances is held by the subjects. It restricts subjects to simply agreeing or disagreeing with each statement and it does not allow any articulation of what was being agreed to. The quantitative response (degree of agreement) displaces and obscures the quality of subjects' psychology.

It is impossible to draw conclusions about the cultural psychology of different populations from this kind of quantitative data because psychological themes have been expunged. Populations (and individuals) with the same quantitative score may have widely different psychologies. Groups (and individuals) who all strongly agree that they try to be courteous may mean very different things and act in very different ways. Some groups may be courteous in the perfunctory manner of a sales clerk while others are courteous in a deeper way. For example, when an American teenager brings friends over to her house while one of her parents is home, it is customary for the friends to give the parent a perfunctory greeting and then immediately sequester themselves in another part of the house where they have no further contact with the parent. The adolescents (and even the parent) regard their behavior as being courteous to the parent. In contrast, Chinese teenagers who meet a friend's parent would spend time talking with him. This is their form of courtesy. Both groups would rate themselves as high on courtesy (strongly agreeing to the statement that they try to be courteous) although their behavior is completely different.

The elimination of cultural–psychological qualities from positivistic quantitative responses makes it impossible to know whether subjects who agree with the statement about courtesy are altruistic, hostile, or indifferent to people. McCrae assumes that courteousness is a form, or component, of altruism; however, this is an unwarranted, arbitrary presumption that is not based on empirical evidence in the subjects' responses.

This error is compounded in the next stage in which McCrae categorizes traits/facets within domains. He regards altruism as a form/component of agreeableness; however, the subjects' responses do not indicate this. Again, the positivistic personality inventory restricts subjects to indicating the extent of their agreement with a statement; it prevents them from expressing any meaning or content. Consequently, McCrae cannot know whether endorsing the statement represents agreeableness. If the subjects' endorsement of courteousness signifies attitudes and acts of indifference to people (such as when the store cashier courteously smiles at the customer) or even hostility (as when the hostess is merely courteous to her guest), then the response would not be a component of agreeableness. Designating it as such is another instance of drawing an arbitrary, unilateral, incorrect, subjective conclusion about cultural psychology.

Thus, what McCrae believes to be a study of agreeableness may not involve that trait (domain) at all. He really has no idea of what he is studying because his methodology deprives him of information about people's cultural psychology. His typology of personality types is entirely fictitious with no basis in the subjects' cultural psychology. Ironically, preventing subjects from expressing qualities of their psychology (under the misconception that these are subjectivistic and anathema to empirical scientific investigation) leads positivists to subjectively, arbitrarily, and unempirically invent psychological qualities and attribute them to people.

Positivists such as McCrae counter such objections with the claim that their variables have construct validity because they correlate with other measures of related variables. Thus, scores on the personality trait "agreeableness" correlate positively with measures of friendliness and negatively with measures of "turning against an object." These correlations in predicted directions ostensibly render the foregoing objections about positivism's lack of psychological sensitivity moot: The positivistic measure of agreeableness may be crude in restricting responses to agree/disagree; however, it "works" nevertheless, regardless of hour mysterious and surprising this may be. As one eminent positivist once said to me, "It's all in the numbers."

This reply is flawed. First of all, the correlated variables of friendliness, etc. that are used to validate agreeableness are plagued by the same ambiguity as agreeableness. Friendliness is measured by crude questions and simple, superficial responses just as agreeableness is. Agreement with a small set of statements, or manifesting certain superficial behaviors such as smiling or saying hello can mean anything from trying to have someone like you to hoping they will give you money to feeling that you are their friend. Designating these responses as representing friendliness is arbitrary and subjective and has little psychological reality. The measure of friendliness cannot therefore validate agreeableness because we have no confidence that friendliness is actually being measured. We simply do not know what the measure measures just as we do not know what the measure of agreeableness actually measures.

In addition, the correlations that are taken to validate a measure are typically quite low. McCrae's agreeableness correlates only about 0.2 with friendliness and -0.2 with turning against an object (Costa, McCrae, & Dembroski, 1989, pp. 50–51). It is well known that a correlation of 0.2 accounts for only 0.04 of the variance, leaving 99.06 unexplained by the correlation. Moreover, when pairs of observers rate subjects on agreeableness (as opposed to self-ratings by subjects), their ratings correlate only 0.3 with one another (ibid., p. 53). In other words, raters do not agree whether a subject is agreeable or not, which means that the construct is difficult to identify.

The only reason that positivists accept such psychologically insignificant numbers as meaningful is because they define meaningfulness in statistical, not psychological, terms. A correlation is meaningful to them not because the psychology of agreeableness is coherently related to the psychology of friendliness; it is meaningful only because the *numerical scores* on the measures have a low probability of occurring by chance. Statistical significance is only a probability of obtaining combinations of numbers from a certain sample size; it has nothing to do with psychological issues and relationships (Ratner, 1997a, pp. 34–37).

McCrae's research boils down to behavioristic propositions: subjects express a certain level of agreement with a set of statements (e.g., nos. 1–8); this is different from the level of agreement with another set of statements (e.g., nos. 9–17); therefore, McCrae assumes that 1–8 have some nebulous similarity that we cannot identify because we have not allowed our subjects to tell us, and that 9–17 have some other nebulous similarity that we cannot pinpoint. In the absence of any psychological significance to the responses, we may as well label the first set of responses as X and the second set as Y. Then McCrae finds that X correlates with some other responses (e.g., talking to people) that we can call Z. McCrae labels it as friendliness, but this is arbitrary because we do not know what Z is psychologically any more than we know what X and Y are—that is, we do not know the psychological significance of talking to people (the reasons, motives, emotions, difficulties) so we cannot really call it friendliness. We can predict that a certain number of individuals who score high on X will score high on Z, but, of course, we do not know why since we do not know anything about X and Z. In fact, the reason that we conclude that X and Z have a significant relationship is because statistical tables tell us that the scores on X and Z are not randomly associated (they would occur by chance only 5% of the time). Clearly, these behavioristic propositions amount to numerology (the study of numbers), not psychology (the study of the psyche). The researchers are solely concerned with associations among numbers and they have little interest in, and no information about, psychology.

These behavioristic propositions have the same scientific status as the bare observation that warm weather is associated with plants growing, or that eating foods with a rancid smell is associated with getting sick. In all these cases, there is no knowledge of the nature of the variables or their internal relationship, for example, no knowledge of what a rancid smell means about food (why does food sometimes acquire such a smell), no knowledge about the nature of illness, and no knowledge about why and how rancid smelling food is associated with illness.

A final deficiency of positivistic personality research for cultural psychology is that the entire terminology of the five personality factors/domains militates against elucidating the cultural character of personality. Terms such as agreeableness, openness, and extraversion are exceedingly general and abstract, and they do not denote any specific cultural character. Agreeableness can be a formal politeness, a genuine sharing of views, a genuine desire to please another person, or an instrumental act of concession to get someone to like me and do favors for me. Similarly, friendliness can be long-lasting through adversity or a superficial relationship that is sustained only for brief, easygoing periods. Abstract psychological terms obfuscate such concrete cultural–psychological qualities.

4. This procedure bears a disconcerting resemblance to the notorious *Diagnostic and Statistical Manual* of the American Psychiatric Association. The diagnostic categories of this manual simply paraphrase obvious symptoms and add no information to what is patently observable. If someone is sad for several months he or she is categorized as "depressed;" if he is frightened for several months he is "paranoid;" if he repeats the same behavior for several months he is "compulsive;" if he is afraid to communicate in social situations he has "social phobia;" if he acts out he is "hyperactive."

5. The notion of an individual devoid of any objective connection to the social or physical world and making a private world for himself is not new. Locke, Berkeley, and Hume all espoused this idea that the individual cannot know reality apart from himself and can know only subjective impressions, ideas, and representations. Postmodernism is thus firmly congruent with the subjective individualism of "modernist" thinking that arose with the capitalist economic system centuries ago.

4

Interviewing Techniques for Eliciting Cultural–Psychological Information

Interviews are an excellent means to ascertain the cultural origins, formation, characteristics, and functions of psychological phenomena. The subject can be questioned about cultural activities, artifacts, and concepts that influenced various psychological phenomena. In addition, interviews encourage subjects to describe their experience in detail so that the cultural psychologist can apprehend cultural elements embedded within experience that may escape the attention of the subject.

The pioneering work of American social psychologists and sociologists during the 1930s, 1940s, and 1950s remains invaluable for laying out principles and procedures of interviews that can elucidate cultural aspects of psychological issues. In this chapter I draw on the theoretical and empirical work of Merton (Merton & Kendall, 1946), Likert (1951), Lazersfeld (1934/1972, 1944), Komarovsky (1940/1955), and Katz (Katz & Lazarsfeld, 1955).

The Value of Interviews

The interview is an indispensable tool for conducting cultural psychological research because it allows for the fullest exposition of psychological phenomena and their cultural origins, formation, character, and function. Specifically, interviews facilitate the following objectives.

1. Ascertaining the meaning of words by questioning subjects. Interviews are based on the premise that word meanings are expressed through a network of verbal responses. The phrases, "I love you," "I want my son to do well in life," "Why are you late?" are ambiguous as such and

145

their meaning is expressed only through additional statements. Each phrase can convey a variety of meanings. "Why are you late?" can be a genuine question of concern, or it can be a rhetorical question that expresses annoyance and criticism by the speaker. "I want my son to do well in life" can refer to personal happiness, wealth, or social contribution. "I love you" can connote romantic affection, paternalistic affection, or deep respect. It also can be sarcastic, a joke, or a genuine expression of affection. These meanings are *social meanings* in the sense that they are all known by members of a social group. They are not idiosyncratic meanings. Cultural psychologists use interviews to identify which social meaning an individual has adopted.

Interviews are useful for this purpose because they elicit a verbal context that illuminates the social meaning that the interviewee is expressing. The subject can be directly asked to explain his meaning.

Researchers have traditionally used interviews to clarify or negotiate idiosyncratic meanings of an interviewer and an interviewee (e.g., Mishler, 1986, pp. 64–65). However, interviews can be used to ascertain social meanings as well as individual ones (Ratner, 1997a, Chaps. 4, 5).

Many early social psychologists recognized that interviews elucidate psychological significance better than standardized questionnaires do. Likert admitted that: "On fixed alternative questions, it was discovered that the alternatives often would have different meanings for different respondents ... [Therefore,] Unless the respondent elaborates his answer sufficiently to make clear the meaning he has in mind, the analyst does not know what the respondent means by the approval or disapproval he has voiced" (Likert, 1951, p. 237).

Lazarsfeld expressed the same belief:

> Traditional opinion is that a question should be so worded as always to insure the same reaction on the part of all those interviewed. We advocate a rather loose and liberal handling of a questionnaire by an interviewer. It seems to us much more important that the question be fixed in its *meaning* than in its *wording*. This new emphasis places the responsibility on the interviewer for knowing exactly what he is trying to discover and permits him to vary the wording in accordance with the experience of the respondent. The resulting margin of error would be much greater if a standardized question were to be interpreted in very different ways by different respondents who have their own different experiences in mind. (Lazarsfeld, 1934/1972, p. 193)

A good example of this point is an opinion poll that was conducted in 1943. The question asked, "After the war, would you like to see many changes or reforms made in the United States, or would you rather have the country remain pretty much the way it was before the war?" After the poll was conducted, respondents were encouraged to discuss their interpretation of the question. People had different associations to the word "change." Some believed it denoted a liberal direction such as increases in social security and greater equality for minority groups. Other people took it to mean a change in a conservative direction such as change to a Republican administration, less government control of business, and more control of labor unions. Similarly, some people who answered "remain the same" had in mind conservative aspects of the economy; others giving the same answer wanted to retain liberal aspects such as maintaining high wages. The elaboration of meaning led to substantial changes in results. According to the first restricted answers, 49% of subjects wanted the country to remain the same and 46% wanted changes or reforms. However, after considering what the subjects really meant by their words, 60% wanted changes and reforms while 40% favored remaining the same (Likert, 1951, pp. 238–239). These results confirm Likert's warning that "Direct answers to direct questions cannot be taken at face value" (ibid., p. 243).

Likert's example illustrates how probing is necessary to elucidate the social meaning that subjects express. Each of the notions about "change" and "stay the same" held by Likert's subjects was socially understandable and shared by numbers of individuals. They were not idiosyncratic meanings that expressed purely personal sentiments. Probing was necessary to understand which social meaning a particular subject implied in his use of the phrase.

2. Penetrating beneath immediate, superficial responses to comprehend true motives, perceptions, attitudes, emotions, and personality traits. An example from my research illustrates how inquisitive the researcher must be to comprehend a person's true motives. A Russian colleague and I wanted to determine whether Russians adopt a lazy, fateful attitude or an active, assertive attitude toward remodeling their housing. One question was: "After you formulated your plan for redecorating did you immediately begin to implement it?" One person said, "I waited 2 months because I was busy with other things." The probing question asked, "During that 2 months did you engage in leisure activities such as going to the movies?" The point was to see whether he was really busy or whether he was just procrastinating and lazy. He replied, "Oh yes, I love the movies and went to see several during that 2-month period." Accepting this answer at face value would lead the interviewer to conclude that the man was lazy and passive: after all, he had plenty of free time to see movies so he could have begun his remodeling. The fact that he didn't begin indicates his laziness. However, a further probe revealed more about his personality. "I don't understand why you didn't begin the project if you had free time to go to the movies. It seems you really weren't so busy after all." To which our subject replied, "The remodeling project is a big one and when I work I need large blocks of time. I need to get a complete

sense of what is involved, decide how to organize the task, and make good progress with the remodeling work in order to feel satisfied. I did have an hour or two which is enough to see a movie but it wasn't enough to organize the project. So I had to wait 2 months until I had larger blocks of time to begin the project."

Assuming that the subject was telling the truth, the second probe indicates that he was not lazy despite the fact that he had put off the project and had spent time in recreation. In his mind, all that was justified by his intense work style. It was not due to passivity, laziness, or impulsiveness.

Probing questions yield vital information about the psychological issue that is not obvious in immediate responses. As discussed in Chap. 3, a given behavior may reflect many kinds of psychological states and it is imperative to elicit a wide range of behaviors to accurately interpret the actual state involved.

3. Considering the implications of an opinion that may alter the subjects' responses (Lazarsfeld, 1944, p. 41). If a subject is in favor of cutting taxes, does he know that many government services will have to be reduced? If he is in favor of free speech does he realize that such freedom must also pertain to people who may express opinions that are very distasteful to him?

4. Considering alternate possibilities about issues that may alter the subjects' responses. For example, "You said that mentally ill people should be incarcerated. Are you aware that recently very powerful drugs have become available that effectively control antisocial behavior?"

5. Ascertaining the frame of reference that interviewees use when answering a question. This is important for knowing the situations to which an attitude, emotion, perception, or motive applies. For instance, in my study of moral development, described in Chap. 6, I presented middle-class children with a scenario in which a mother broke her promise. She initially agreed that her adolescent daughter could spend her own money to go to a rock concert. Later she told the daughter that she couldn't go and had to buy school clothes with the money. When I asked the children if the mother acted morally, they said no. From this response it might seem that the subjects believed that keeping a promise is an absolute moral imperative. However, I then modified the scenario by asking: If the family was very poor could the mother break her promise and require the daughter to buy school clothes? The vast majority of subjects said it would be justified by the economic situation of the family—that is, poor families need to spend money on clothing rather than concerts. From this variation in the scenario we can see that the response to the first question had assumed a frame of reference that the family was middle class (as the subjects were) and had money to spare for concerts. In this situation, it

was not deemed reasonable for the mother to break her promise and require the daughter to buy clothes. But in other situations, for example, poverty, it is morally acceptable. The subjects' implicit frame of reference is illuminated only by asking them to consider other situations.

6. Understanding inconsistent responses. The interviewer can inquire about apparent inconsistencies in responses. He can ask the subject to explain whether she regards them as discrepant. This process clarifies the subject's full meaning; it allows the subject to modify her answers to express intended meanings more accurately, or to reflect on and modify her intended meaning altogether. The subject can say, "Oh, I didn't express myself clearly on that second question; what I really meant was ... which is similar to what I meant on the first question. Or, "Well, now that you mention it, my responses were different to the two similar questions. I guess I'm confused/ambivalent about the issue that's being addressed because I haven't thought enough about it. I guess I don't really have a clear opinion about it." Or, "Well, that second question implies ... which is a little different from the first question. My second response reflects that difference in meaning that I perceive."

The fact that interviews allow subjects to review and modify responses makes them an objective tool for capturing subjectivity and psychological phenomena. Interviews are more objective than questionnaires that accept superficial, fragmentary, ambiguous responses as data. One example of the superiority of interviews is their ability to overcome order effects, which are a notorious, unsolvable problem for questionnaires. Order effects are changes in responses to the same questions when they are asked in different orders. Consider two questions: (a) Should the United States allow newspaper reporters from communist countries cover events in the United States and send reports to their home countries? (b) Should communist countries allow American newspaper reporters to cover events in their countries and send reports to American newspapers? When question (a) was asked first, 36% agreed with it; when it was asked second, 73% agreed with it (Ratner, 1997a, pp. 18–20). Questionnaires have no way to resolve the discrepancy of order effects; they cannot determine which order of questions and which corresponding response rate is appropriate.

The reason for order effects is that individuals respond to questions on the basis of a frame of reference. Prior questions form a frame of reference for later questions. Altering the order of questions alters the context in which each one occurs and the significance it has for the subject. The question about whether reporters from communist countries should be admitted to the United States may elicit an initial suspicion about those reporters and a refusal to allow them to work in the United States. However, after subjects agree to Americans working abroad, it appears unjust to deny the same privilege to foreign reporters in the United States. Consequently, the vast majority of subjects agree to question (a) when it follows (b). Order effects are the result of short-term priming by new antecedents that raise new issues for the subject to consider. The diverse order effects are all real. They may not be equally important and long-lasting, however. The initial suspicion about foreign reporters may be a fleeting reaction while the principle of fairness and reciprocity may be more important and a better predictor of future responses.

Interviews resolve order effects by asking subjects to compare their responses to the same questions presented in different orders. In the case of the foregoing two questions, the researcher could ask probing questions such as, "Is it all right for certain countries to restrict foreign reporters but not alright for other countries?" "Should all reporters have the same rights? Why/why not?" These questions would allow the subject to reflect more deeply on her answers and reasons. She could examine her frame of reference. She could reflect on contradictions in her responses. She could revise her frame of reference and responses.

7. Considering the complexity of psychological phenomena. Psychological phenomena are complex and multifaceted. They are not singular and homogeneous. For example, when asked to identify high and low points in a marriage, individuals typically state that a certain period was difficult in certain ways but positive in others. The period was not uniformly difficult or positive. One individual identified a period in which he had financial difficulties; however, he nevertheless managed to pay off a large physician's bill through monthly installments. He turned a low point into a high point. Another interesting complication in identifying high and low points is that the perception of a period as a high or low point might change with time. One woman mentioned as a high point the year her daughter starting dating her future husband. However, she stated that she didn't realize at that time that the daughter would marry the man and so she didn't regard the event as a high point at that time; she perceived it as a high point only in retrospect (Mischler, 1986, pp. 59–65). In these examples, clarification is necessary to illuminate the particular *social* meaning that the periods had for the subjects. The fact that a particular period can be both positive and negative is perfectly understandable to all members of the subject's linguistic community. It simply must be made clear to them that this is the case. Complex meanings are not necessarily idiosyncratic.

8. Ascertaining the intensity (importance) of the issue to the subject. This is not limited to a simple calculation of "not important" or "very important." It includes how much consideration the individual has given to the issue. If someone has thought deeply about something for a long

time, it has a very different significance than if she forms her opinion spontaneously in the interview. The interviewer can ascertain the importance of issues for a person's psychology, in contrast to questionnaires that accept impulsive, impressionistic, perfunctory responses on a par with deeply meaningful ones.

9. Clarifying statistical relationships between "independent" and "dependent" variables. Positivistic research discovers statistical relationships between variables; however, it typically has little empirical data that explains them. As noted in Chap. 3, it is necessary to specify the effective aspect of the situation that led to the response. This is true in experiments as well as naturalistic observations. The question is: "To what did the subjects respond and why did he respond that way?" It is generally impractical if not impossible to experimentally manipulate every aspect of a complex situation to ascertain this. Interviews can probe for this kind of information (Merton & Kendall, 1946, pp. 542–543).

Lazarsfeld (1944, pp. 47–48) presents an interesting historical example of how interviews clarified a statistical relationship. In a famous study, people became panicked after hearing the radio broadcast "Invasion from Mars." People from a lower educational level were most likely to believe in the occurrence of the great catastrophe. Yet some of the less educated people were not frightened at all. The only way to understand the discrepant answers was to interview the individuals. It turned out that many were mechanics or people with mechanical hobbies who were accustomed to check up on the facts of a situation. Their scrutiny of the facts of the broadcast led them to dismiss it.

Without interviews, the absence of panic would have remained a mystery that social scientists speculated about. The interviews solved the mystery of the discrepant cases, and also shed light on the majority response; evidently, listeners became panicked because they didn't scrutinize the actual facts of the broadcast and were swept along by the rhetoric.

Specifying "To what did the subjects respond?" entails specifying their interpretation of the situation. Interviews are the best means for ascertaining this. Another famous case in point is the statistical finding that uncompleted tasks are recalled more frequently than completed ones (the Zeigarnik effect). Interviews determined that that incomplete tasks are regarded as failures that subjects seek to overcome by mentally completing them (Merton & Kendall, 1946, p. 544). This information is an important addition to the statistical relationship because it tells us that subjects who have a different interpretation of uncompleted tasks will not necessarily recall them.

10. Becoming sensitive to the sensitivities of the subject about what kinds of questions are appropriate to ask, when to ask them, how long to

stay on a topic and when to shift topics, whether to probe more deeply, whether the subject understands the intent of the question, and whether to repeat or rephrase the question. The sensitivities of the subject also include the knowledge they have of the topic being studied.

The sensitivities of an individual are cultural as well as personal. They are socially distributed among occupants of various social activities, and they reflect cultural concepts and artifacts.

11. Allowing subjects to reflect on social influences on psychology. Interviewees should be asked whether the media set a model for their self-concept, body image, personality, attitudes, and other psychological phenomena. They should also be asked whether there are social constraints on their behavior and psychology. Probing subjects for insights about social influences on their behavior was a key issue for the pioneers of interviews. They were deeply concerned with influences on work, voting, consumption, and family relationships.

12. Elucidating cultural aspects of psychology by the informed cultural psychologist when individuals are unaware of these aspects. Knowledge is very much a function of one's social activities; people are not intrinsically aware of their environment by virtue of living in it. In Chap. 1 I discussed Marx's concept of ideology as a mystified and mystifying point of view that misconstrues and obfuscates many aspects of society. In modern societies, the ideology of individualism prevails and it overlooks critical social influences on people. Consequently, most people are unaware of many social influences on their behavior and psychology. This is not their fault, nor is it due to any inherent lack of intelligence. It is a function of the social organization of social activities such as the market economy that makes social influences difficult to perceive.

Few people realize that when they regard and treat children as different from adults—including speaking to them in "motherese," dressing them in distinctive clothes, giving them distinctive toys and reading material—this treatment reflects the structural separation of the family from economic activity and the exclusion of children from economic work. Few people realize that providing separate bedrooms for an infant recapitulates and reinforces the separateness and self-reliance of adults in the market economy. And few people realize that their desire for individual privacy reflects their lifelong experience in occupying their own segregated rooms in separated housing structures. The work of Nisbett and Wilson, reported in Chap. 3, demonstrates that individuals are even mistaken about interpersonal influences on their behavior.

Given this *social ignorance*, it is unlikely that interviews will elicit great insights by the subjects about social aspects of psychology. Information about cultural psychology must be obtained by informed,

skillful researchers detecting similarities between psychological phenomena expressed by individuals and social activities, artifacts, and concepts.

This position in no way disrespects or disregards the subject. Quite
the opposite, it stems from a serious recognition of the actual competencies that subjects have. People's competencies are cultural; they are not
natural, universal skills. If people's social knowledge is limited by the
social organization of their activities, this puts more responsibility on the
cultural psychologist to elucidate cultural aspects of psychology. In this
situation, the cultural psychologist must function like a physician who
employs sophisticated medical knowledge to analyze and treat a patient's
symptoms. Just as any good doctor actively listens to a patient before
exercising medical judgment, so the cultural psychologist encourages the
widest and deepest expression of psychological phenomena from his subjects, which he uses as the data to be culturally analyzed. The foregoing
11 points of interviewing are meant to facilitate this process of drawing
the subject out.

Assuming that people naturally possess extensive knowledge about
culture and psychology and that their responses should be accepted without question as accurate insights is an unrealistic glorification of individual experience. It disregards and disrespects the actual consciousness
(subjectivity) that individuals have as a result of their social experience.

Interviews involve two steps. The first is to formulate questions that
encourage the subjects to discuss relevant topics. The second step is to
conduct the interview by engaging in a dialogue with the subjects.

Each of these two steps warrants discussion.

FORMULATING INTERVIEW QUESTIONS

The kinds of questions that one formulates depends on the kind of
interview that one wishes to conduct. There are four kinds of interviews
that require different kinds of questions.

1. *Informal interviewing* is a free-ranging discussion without any
   structure. The interviewer simply explores various topics of
   interest without planning any specific questions or structure to
   the discussion.
2. *The unstructured interview* is a formal interview rather than an
   informal discussion. It is based on a clear plan of target issues
   that the interviewer seeks to understand. This plan is kept constantly in mind and guides the interview. However, the questions

are general to allow the respondent maximum freedom of response. Questions take the form of, "How do you decide where to fish?" "Does your work involve a lot of traveling?"

3. *The semistructured interview* has much of the freewheeling quality of the unstructured interview and allows discretion to probe into related areas. However semistructured interviewing is organized by a specific plan that is formulated in advance. The plan, or *interview guide*, is a written list of questions and topics that need to be covered more or less in a particular order. The plan even includes the kinds of probes that should be initiated after various responses. The interview guide elicits reliable, comparable data because it asks all the subjects the same specific questions.

   The semistructured interview includes two kinds of questions. One type specifies a stimulus (cause) and gives the subject freedom to discuss any effect he desires. An example is, "How did you feel about the argument scene in the movie?" Here, the interviewer fixes the stimulus (the argument scene) but allows the subject to speak about any response he had to it. The other format is to ask a general question and restrict the response, for example, "What about the movie made you feel sad?" In this case, the interviewer specifies the response (sadness) and allows the subject to speak about any aspect of the movie (stimulus) that generates the sadness (Merton & Kendall, 1946, p. 546).

4. *The fully structured interview* is akin to a questionnaire. All the questions are fully prepared in advance, brief answers are solicited, and the respondents are allowed minimal opportunity to elaborate their responses. Examples include pile sorting, triad sorting, and tasks that require informants to rate or rank order a list of things. The respondent may succinctly explain the reason for her behavior, however the explanation takes the form of "because these two can be used together," or "that one is more useful."

Unstructured and semistructured interviews are most appropriate for cultural psychological research. The informal interview is too loose to allow careful exploration of complex, unfamiliar issues that the subject may be unprepared to discuss. Because these issues will not be spontaneously addressed in a meaningful manner, they need to be specifically probed by an interviewer who is prepared to guide the discussion. Another disadvantage of informal interviews is that they are so spontaneous and freewheeling that they typically do not ask the same questions of all subjects. This makes comparing responses and discovering patterns among numerous individuals difficult.

The fully structured interview is nothing more than reading a standardized questionnaire to subjects. It therefore precludes a trusting social relationship between interviewer and interviewee; it precludes clarifying meanings, considering implications and alternate possibilities, and probing for related issues. Merton and Kendall (1946, p. 548) leveled this criticism against structured interviews: "For often the interviewer, equipped with fixed questions dealing with the given topic, does not listen closely or analytically to the subject's comments and thus fails to respond to the cues and implications of these comments, substituting, instead, one of the routine questions from the guide." Instead, the interviewer should "seek to obtain a maximum of *self-revelatory comments concerning how the stimulus material was experienced* ... In these are expressed symbolisms, anxieties, fears, sentiments, as well as cognitive ideas" (ibid., pp. 554–555).

The unstructured interview is appropriate for cultural psychology because it asks general questions that allow the subject to express cultural—psychological issues that are relevant to him or her. They would ask subjects to describe their experience, pleasure, frustration, and personal relationships in certain situations. The interviewer will then use these details as cues for further probes. It is crucial to not begin with restricted, loaded terms that may not be relevant to the subject. We would not initially ask questions such as, "Did you have trouble controlling your feelings?" "Do your feelings intrude into your thoughts?" "Was your sense of autonomy (or personal space) threatened?" "Were you 100% confused?" Such questions presume Western values such as feelings can be controlled, feelings and thoughts are normally distinctive, the self is (or strives to be) autonomous, and confusion (and mental states) can be quantified. Asking such questions forces subjects' responses within a Western framework. Even a negative reply presupposes that they understand the Western values that constitute the question—if one replies, "No, I was not 100% confused" they must accept the notion that confusion can be quantified. Many people may not endorse such values in which case any response is an artificial, coerced, meaningless expression designed to appease the interviewer and conveys no cultural psychological information. In contrast, general questions that ask for descriptions of experience or pleasure are understandable by virtually everyone, moreover they do not presuppose particular cultural issues such as an autonomous self, a distinction between thoughts and emotions, or quantifiable cognitive processes.

The semi-structured interview then pursues these issues. It also inquires about issues that the researcher formulates based upon her knowledge of the society's activities, artifacts, and concepts. Many of these issues would not occur to the subjects without prodding from the researcher.

Interview questions for studying cultural–psychological phenomena should seek to elucidate particular cultural practices and values that are embodied in psychology. This objective holds for exploratory research and for research that is guided by hypotheses. Since exploratory research— for example, what kinds of emotions do the Ifaluk people express, or what is the nature of shame among Koreans?—does not proceed from hypotheses about particular cultural influences on psychology, interview questions would not specifically inquire about these influences. Instead, the questions would keep encouraging subjects to reiterate and explain their responses so that the culturally informed researcher could detect cultural elements in them.

Where research is guided by a particular hypothesis about cultural aspects of psychology, interview questions would specifically inquire about these aspects. We might hypothesize that romantic love is taking on the character of contemporary social relations, or, in other words, the internal and external division of social activities. The specifics of the division of labor would be spelled out in particular subhypotheses that would be translated into interview questions. For example, I have hypothesized (Ratner, 2000b) that romantic love is such an intense feeling because finding intimacy is difficult to find and sustain in a materialistic, self-centered, competitive, alienated society. Individuals desperately strive to find romantic love to compensate for the insecurity, depersonalization, and loneliness of contemporary social life. When people find this love, it is intensified by the fact that it is one of the few sources of personal caring and intimacy in social life. I have also hypothesized that romantic love has an irrational, antisocial quality because it occurs in private, personal relationships outside public life. Love partakes of the division of labor between family and public activities (such as work, politics). Excluded from the cold, calculating world of work and politics, love becomes disinterested in them and is fascinated instead with personal idiosyncrasies that are emotionally felt rather than intellectually analyzed.

Another cultural hypothesis about love is that its quick-forming, intense, sensual passion is stimulated by the quest for quick materialistic gratification which is the goal of capitalist economic production and consumption. In other words, capitalist production and consumption generate a general demand for immediate sensual gratification that extends to romantic love. Modern romantic love develops as a fast, intense sensual pleasure that recapitulates a quick and sizeable augmentation of material wealth in the economic sphere. It also recapitulates the instant gratification of consumerism in which, facilitated by easy credit, customers buy on impulse and immediately enjoy a plethora of sensual stimulation without having to save up money (see Porter, 2000, pp. 258–275 who identifies the novel emergence of passionate romantic love in the Enlightenment with the novel search for continuous sensual pleasure that was associated with the novel mode of capitalist production and consumption). These hypotheses would be reflected in interview questions such as:

1. Were you lonely just before you fell in love, or did you have fulfilling friendships? Can you think of any way in which the kind of relationships you had with others affected your developing a romantic love?
2. Did you feel secure and fulfilled in your work/school just before you fell in love? Can you think of any way in which the level of fulfillment you had in work/school affected your developing a romantic love?
3. Had you experienced difficulty finding romantic love before you met your lover? Did this affect your current falling in love?
4. Were you motivated to seek romantic love by social events around you, such as books, movies, or friends who had lovers? Did your emotional state of romantic love reflect the way you had seen others being in love?
5. What attracted you to your lover?
6. Do your lover's political attitudes affect your love for him or her?
7. Does your lover's job affect your love for him or her?
8. How well did you know your lover before falling in love?
9. How long were you acquainted before falling in love?
10. Did you fall in love through a process of rationally calculating the qualities of your lover or was it a spontaneous, impulsive occurrence?
11. Does romantic attraction seem like a mysterious thing to you?
12. Is there any resemblance between the passionate drive of romantic love and the drive for other forms of sensual gratification in social life? Do other sensual pleasures seem to stimulate the passion of romantic love?

Asking culturally informed questions that are based on hypotheses about cultural aspects of romantic elicits responses that have more cultural content than general questions would elicit. If we simply ask subjects to describe their experience of love, it is unlikely that they would touch on the specific cultural issues that are elicited by culturally informed questions. This is especially true in the area of romantic love, which is construed by prevailing cultural concepts to be personal, spontaneous, and noncultural in essence.

CONDUCTING THE INTERVIEW

Interviewing is a complicated process. At any one time the interviewer may be:

- Listening to what the interviewee is saying, interpreting what she means, and being sensitive to implicit ideas in her statements
- Trying to decide whether what the subject says bears on what the interviewer wants to know
- Refining what the interviewer wants to know
- Formulating an appropriate response to the answer
- Establishing rapport with the interviewee—making her feel comfortable expressing herself, helping her to articulate her opinion
- Thinking of appropriate following questions to clarify a response
- Thinking of appropriate following questions that might extend into new areas
- Attending to the interviewee's demeanor and interpreting it—for example, increased reticence, animation, discomfort, irritability, vagueness, specificity
- Reflecting on previous answers and comparing with present response
- Keeping track of the time
- Taking notes or watching recording devices
- Dealing with distractions such as noises, passersby, phones ringing

Perhaps the most challenging aspect of conducting interviews into cultural psychology is exploring the influence of cultural activities, artifacts, and concepts on psychology that may be obscure to people.

American social psychologists and sociologists of the 1930s, 1940s, and 1950s were especially concerned with this problematic. They developed techniques for helping subjects to sort out social influences. Merton and Kendall (1946) pioneered the "focused interview" to aid informed researchers in probing subjects about their knowledge of social influences.

Interviewees must be carefully guided to reflect on social influences that they normally disregard. Lazarsfeld (1934/1972, 1944, pp. 42–43, 1941/1955; Katz & Lazarsfeld, 1955, pp. 167–174) wrote extensively about this under the rubric "the art of asking why." One reason for directing the attention of subjects is that it is easy for them to lose sight of the question and drift into other topics. For instance, in reply to the question, "What made you change coffee brands?" a woman may speak at great length about the advantages of her new brand of coffee without mentioning the social influence that led her to change brands, for example, that she had learned about it from a household column in the newspaper.

It is also vital to direct subjects' attention to diverse aspects of a behavior that may be influenced by different factors. For example, if we want to investigate the social factors that led someone to purchase a product we need to construe purchasing as including component acts such as:

- Finding out about the particular brand of object
- Finding it attractive
- Wanting to use it
- Buying it instead of a different kind of product, for example, buying sneakers for one's child instead of buying a shirt for the father

The researcher must inquire about each aspect and the influences on it. A single aspect does not comprise the totality of "purchasing." Also, the factor(s) that influence one aspect may not comprise all the factors that influence all the aspects of "purchasing." Posing a general question such as "please identify influences on your purchase of X" would allow individuals to attend to a single aspect—whichever came to mind first—and overlook the other aspects and the influences on them.

It is also necessary to direct subjects to specify the particular manner in which a social factor influenced their behavior. Consider the influence of a newspaper on three women who finish shopping early and desire to see a movie before going home. One woman picks up a newspaper to see what's playing and reads a glowing review of one movie. She decides to see that one. Another woman in the same situation picks up a newspaper to see what's playing, and decides to go to a movie that is playing nearby so that she doesn't have to drive far. The third woman sees the list of movies in the paper and decides to go to one that a friend had raved about. In all three cases, the newspaper was involved in the choice of a particular movie. However, would we say that the paper played the role of an influence in all three decisions? It clearly was an influence on the first woman because it convinced her the movie was worth seeing. In the second and third cases the newspaper played a very different role. It simply informed the women that "their" movie was playing in a particular location. The information it provided did not determine the selection of the particular movie. Consequently, although the newspaper was "a proximal stimulus" in the decision-making processes of all three, it was an influence on the decision only in the first case. Thus, when a subject says,

"I went to the movie after I saw it mentioned in the paper," this does not mean the paper qualifies as an influence on the behavior. It is necessary to know the exact role that the paper played in the decision.

Similarly, Maria may have been told by Hana that a movie is excellent, and that the star is Maria's favorite actor. Maria decides to see the movie because of the actor, not because of Hana's recommendation. Did Hana influence Maria's behavior? According to Lazarsfeld, only marginally. Hana's influence was limited to providing information; she did not actively influence Maria through the force of her personality, reasoning, or aesthetic taste.

Probing to Ascertain Social Influences on Psychological Phenomena

Social psychologists of the 1940s developed powerful analytical techniques for discerning whether an apparent influence on behavior actually qualifies as such. The following examples from Lazarsfeld (1941/1955) illustrate the general approach.

- A respondent says he didn't vote because it rained on election day. That might or might not be an acceptable statement in view of additional information that would be needed. Did he stay home all day because of the rain and not go out to do other things? If he went out to do other things then his answer cannot be accepted as the reason for not voting.
- A housewife uses a brand of soap she has not used before. In an interview she reports that she could not get her usual brand and so bought the one that she found at her dealer's. However, this may be an incomplete answer. If the dealer carried several brands then she still has not explained why she purchased the chosen one. There will probably be an additional reason that she chose that particular one over another one. Perhaps she was familiar with the brand name, or perhaps her choice was limited by price, or perhaps she chose it because it was the nearest one on the counter. Such questions must be asked to ascertain the full, true reason for her purchase.
- A man says he votes for the Democratic party because its candidate is for the common man. But other parties, such as the Greens and the Communists, espouse this cause as well. We therefore need additional information. Does the man know of these other parties? If he does, then we need to question him about why he prefers the Democratic party over these others. Immediately there is more to his voting behavior than his initial response. It is

not simply that the Democrats stand for the common man, but that perhaps they have the best chance of all the other parties of winning.

- A woman tells us that she ordered shrimp salad in a restaurant because she likes it. However, the reason is probably more complicated. Her response may depend on contextual factors. She may actually prefer other dishes to shrimp salad, but they are not on the menu; she only likes shrimp salad relative to the restricted choice that the menu offers. Or, shrimp salad was the best liked dish within a certain price range; or there were other things on the menu that she liked equally well but had eaten them recently. These additional possibilities must be explored in the interview to ascertain the full, true motive for the behavior.

- Similarly, when we ask a friend why he came to visit us late at night and he replies he was lonely, the reason may be much more complicated. Why did he visit me rather than someone else? There may be something about me that led him to visit, in addition to his loneliness. Furthermore, why did he visit anyone instead of going to a movie, as many people would do? Posing these questions would provide more insight into his reasons.

Mirra Komarovsky (1940/1955) employed this kind of analytical discerning very effectively in interviews that she conducted. She undertook to analyze the impact of the 1930s depression on social relationships within the family. Of special interest to her was the impact of unemployment on the loss of family authority by the head of the household. Komarovsky recognized that discussing this issue is subject to two possible sources of error. The family changes indicated may not have taken place, and if they have they may not have been due to unemployment.

Komarovsky developed criteria to determine whether unemployment had fostered psychological and behavioral changes. The most basic criterion is that subjects' statements must specifically state that unemployment caused a change in behavior, for example, "I lost my love for my husband because he turned out to be a failure;" "Unemployment made me lose faith in myself;" "My wife lost respect for me because I failed as a provider;" "My husband nags since unemployment because he has nothing to do all day."

If a statement describes a sequence of behaviors without specifically indicating that unemployment caused them, the causal influence of unemployment cannot be accepted without further evidence. Examples are: "Prior to unemployment the children used to go to my husband's church. Now they go with me to the Catholic Church;" "My husband has been drinking since he has been unemployed;" "I used to enjoy sexual relations with my husband. I don't any more;" "We don't talk to each other as often as we used to." In these cases, we have merely a sequence of unemployment and the change. If she adds, "because I am too disgusted with him being out of work to bother talking to him," this is a clear expression that unemployment fostered the change.

One way to illuminate causal interconnections is to ask the respondents as to possible motives by which unemployment and the change in question could be linked. For instance, if it has been established that a man goes to church more often, does he know why he goes more often now and what it has to do with being unemployed?

Similarly questions might be directed to find out what feature in unemployment appears to the respondent as the cause of the change. It has been established that a man reads fewer books since he became unemployed. What in the unemployment situation has been the decisive causal feature of this decrease? No longer having any access to the factory library? Spending all his time on job hunting? Losing interest in books because of worry?

Another kind of specifying question that explores the link between unemployment and family change—for example, between unemployment and being ignored in the family—inquires when the subject recognized the fact, how he recognized it, what he did about it, and how members of the family reacted to it.

Submitting the original statements of the respondent to the above-described questioning may in some cases serve completely to eliminate alleged causal relationships. In other cases, if we succeed in transforming statements of sequence into statements of a causal relationship, we have a more satisfactory kind of evidence. The woman who said that since her husband's unemployment her children had been going to the Catholic Church may confess that prior to unemployment she had had to acquiesce to her husband's demands because otherwise he threatened to withdraw his support from the family. Now she no longer depends on him for support and can do whatever she wants to. This data illuminates how unemployment has led to the change.

Another criterion for whether unemployment influenced family changes is whether they always occurred in tandem or whether one occurred without the other. Komarovsky looked at the following situations as tests of the validity of the causal explanation offered by the informant.

A woman says that it is natural that unemployment would make her lose all respect for her husband, that a man who is a failure cannot be respected. Yet there is evidence that her unemployed brother still has her respect and affection. Therefore, there may be reasons other than unemployment for disrespecting her husband.

Conversely, the personal relationship may have existed previously in the life of the informant even when the alleged causal factor (unemployment) was absent. A woman says that it is only unemployment that keeps the family together, that they are very unhappy, and if it were not for their poverty, they would break up the family. But the couple stayed together prior to unemployment when they could afford to maintain separate homes, although evidence shows that their relationships were not better then.

A wife says that she despises the fact that since his unemployment began, her husband reads all evening without paying attention to her. On analysis it may appear, however, that he always was fond of reading in the evening and never paid any more attention to her than at the time she made the statement. The fact is that for one reason or another, she has refused to tolerate this situation since he has been unemployed.

The problem of alternative explanations is particularly important in the consideration of parent–child relationships. Loss of paternal authority that is attributed to unemployment may actually be due to normal developmental processes such as a growing child's demands for autonomy. How can we decide whether the loss of authority is due to unemployment or to the social maturation of the child?

A factor such as unemployment can be assumed to effect a result such as loss of authority if three conditions are met:

1. If the conflict that precipitated loss of control was an aspect of unemployment, for example, if the conflict was about some aspect of unemployment such as blaming the father for a reduced standard of living.
2. If the father felt that unemployment undermined his power in dealing with the child, or if the father felt that his personality had changed due to unemployment.
3. If the child explicitly utilized unemployment in his struggle for emancipation.

Cases in which loss of authority is observed, but in which the conditions, (1), (2), and (3) do not exist, would not be regarded as due to unemployment. Alternative explanations for changes in parent–child relationships may be stated as follows:

1. Possible changes in folkways may have affected the problem. Since times have changed, children may perhaps demand greater freedom from regulation.

2. Aging of parents may have fostered the change being studied. Perhaps they are less patient and more irritable with the younger children, which in turn causes conflict. Even if there are no older children for purposes of comparison, the informant should be asked whether the mere fact of the children's growing older may not offer a complete explanation of the change. Can he be sure that the disciplinary problems would not have arisen had there been no depression?

3. Differences in the personalities of the children may have affected the problem. It may be that the differences between the older and the younger children are the result, not of the depression, but of differences in personalities such as the fact that the younger ones may be more stubborn or rebellious.

In determining whether unemployment caused a particular family change, Komarovsky also considers whether the statements of the respondents were psychologically consistent with the total evidence of the case. A woman may deny that loss of earning ability has undermined her respect for her husband. This statement may be inconsistent with what is known about her values of life, her attitude toward her husband at the time of their marriage, and her present behavior toward him.

There were cases in which it was not possible to get the respondent to state what the causal link was between unemployment and the change. A woman maintained that she did not know why she ceased to enjoy sexual relations with her husband since unemployment. In this case and a few others, however, the causal link between the two phenomena seemed highly probable to Komarovsky in spite of the fact that the respondent had not admitted it. Other information indicated that the failure of the husband as a provider was a sharp blow to the wife. She was disillusioned in the husband. His continuous presence at home revealed to her, as she said, that he had no personality. She blames him for unemployment and feels that a real man should be able to provide for his family. Our general experience with human reactions suggests that there might be a causal link between these attitudes and the decline in this woman's response to her husband in the sexual sphere.

The interview techniques of Komarovsky, Lazarsfeld, and Merton were designed to aid individuals in identifying influences on their psychology and behavior. These techniques are vital for detecting influences that experiments cannot reveal. It would be nearly impossible to obtain baseline measures of family interactions before and after unemployment to see the variation that was caused by changes in job status. The reason is that we would have no way of knowing which individuals would eventually be fired and so we would not know which employed laborers to interview to obtain our comparative data. We would have to interview many employed workers at random and then wait for perhaps years until some of them happened to lose their jobs, upon which we would obtain our "post-test" measures. It may also turn out that only a very few of our sample actually lost their jobs and we would thus have very few suitable subjects to study. It would also be extremely difficult to employ a different experimental procedure, namely matching employed and unemployed individuals on all factors except for their job status and then comparing family interactions. Even if we could do so, the internal relationship of unemployment and family interactions would be mystified. We would not know how and why unemployment had the effects it did. However, when a wife states in an interview that she has lost respect for her husband *because* he has no job (thereby implicitly blaming him for the loss), then the actual cause of her new relationship with him is clear.

Cultural psychologists can utilize probing interviews to investigate the impact of social activities, concepts, and artifacts on psychology. We can ask individuals to reflect, as best they can, on how these impact their emotions, motives, attitudes, problem solving, and mental illness just as the social psychologists inquired about reasons for voting, purchasing products, or having family difficulties. Where individuals cannot connect their psychological phenomena to social activities, artifacts, and concepts, the procedures of the 1940s social psychologists must be supplemented with other ones to detect cultural aspects.

Two procedures can serve this function. The first one entails presenting subjects with various cultural issues and observing their reactions. If their reactions are affected by variations in the cultural issues, then we can identify the cultural issues that produced the effect. I have employed this procedure in a study of moral reasoning that is described in Chap. 6. I asked subjects to offer judgments about morally appropriate behavior in relation to a family member, a stranger, and a pet in situations of poverty and wealth. When subjects endorsed different morally appropriate behaviors toward a stranger and toward a family member, then it became obvious that their moral judgment was shaped by the sharp cultural distinction between family and stranger. Structuring the interview around particular cultural issues led to disclosing cultural concepts that probably would not have been expressed if I had asked subjects to "identify important cultural concepts that affect your moral judgments," or even if I had asked, "Is the cultural distinction between family member and stranger fundamental to your moral judgments?" Subjects do not spontaneously think about cultural concepts that underlie their moral judgments; however, when an interviewer introduces such concepts into a discussion format, the subjects respond differentially to them, thereby indicating their importance.

Another way to elucidate cultural aspects of psychological phenomena is to elicit extensive statements (and behaviors) that are so rich in content that the researcher can identify their cultural origins, characteristics, and functions. The interviewer must probe for subjects' thoughts and feelings and then identify cultural aspects embodied within them. This procedure has led researchers to identify Protestant values in North American symptoms of mental illness; Catholic values in the symptoms of Latin American patients; the recapitulation of a split between private and public life in schizophrenic symptoms; female stereotypes in the hysterical symptoms of 19th century middle-class women; and bourgeois values and activities such as competition, individualism, and materialism in the pathogenic behavior of parents toward their children (Ratner, 1991, pp. 259–261, 264–278). The next chapter describes this cultural analysis (interpretation) of interviews.

5

A Procedure for Analyzing Cultural Themes in Verbal Accounts

After verbal accounts have been obtained (from interviews, narratives, and self-reports), we explicate the cultural features of psychological phenomena expressed therein. This means identifying forms of social activities, artifacts, and concepts that are embedded in the subjects' statements. Such an interpretive act is subject to mistakes unless it is performed in a rigorous and systematic manner. This chapter outlines a detailed procedure for analyzing cultural themes in verbal accounts.

To justify the need for this procedure, I would like to demonstrate the errors that can arise when a rigorous analysis is not employed. An illustrative example comes from research on agoraphobia by Capps and Ochs (1995, pp. 100–101). The authors interviewed agoraphobic individuals and drew a conclusion about the psychological gain that the disorder provides. I will present their interpretation of an interviews with a patient named Meg, then examine whether it corresponds with her statements. The authors state:

> In attempting to understand and treat psychological disturbances, clinicians ask how a client may be benefiting from a particular disorder ... Meg's narratives suggest that agoraphobia provides a medical reason for neither accommodating nor even negotiating demands and desires imposed or promoted by others. Following this line of reasoning, agoraphobia spares her from having to say "I would rather not," or "I can't, for these reasons," or "I have other obligations or priorities at this time." More crucially, Meg does not have to engage in the usual give-and-take negotiations that characterize decision making about plans. She does not have to explain herself or lobby for engaging in a joint activity when or where it is more convenient for her. In this perspective, agoraphobia is a warrant for avoiding confrontation and disappointment, and not having to accommodate.

Meg's interview protocol is this:

Meg: Like for instance the other day I got an invitation in the mail to attend a friend's graduation from State College. And I'm thinking, well

167

that's out of my safety zone. I can't go over there because—(.4-second pause) There again it's another one of those can'ts. I can't drive to Hamilton.
Lisa: Um-hm.
Meg: It's out of my boundaries and I'll just have to find a way to explain.
Lisa: What will you tell her?
Meg: I think she knows she's not a real close friend that I've confided in a lot about this. But I think she knows I have some anxiety problems.

Comparing Meg's statements with the authors' interpretation, we can see that the latter is inaccurate. Meg never says or even implies any of the points that the authors assert. Her words do not indicate that agoraphobia spares her from accommodating, negotiating, explaining, confronting, and rejecting requests by others. One of her statements flatly contradicts the contention that she is trying to avoid explaining herself. Meg explicitly states that she *will* have to find a way to explain.

While this kind of misinterpretation seems easily avoidable in short protocols such as Meg's, it commonly occurs. It is even more common in analysis of lengthier, complex protocols. The prevalence of misinterpretation in qualitative research calls for a procedure that can aid in accurately identifying and summarizing themes in verbal accounts. I will enunciate such a procedure. It draws on the pathbreaking work of researchers in the tradition of phenomenology (Creswell, 1998, pp. 271–295; Fischer & Wertz, 1979; Giorgi, 1975a,b, 1994) and grounded theory (e.g., Strauss, 1987; Strauss & Corbin, 1990). These authors focused on elucidating personal meanings from verbal accounts. As stated in Chap. 3, this is a crucial first step in a qualitative cultural psychological analysis. Only if psychological qualities are fully manifest can they be compared to cultural activites, artifacts, and concepts. After I describe a procedure for identifying psychological themes I will explain how cultural features can be detected within them.

A PHENOMENOLOGICAL PROCEDURE FOR IDENTIFYING PSYCHOLOGICAL THEMES IN VERBAL ACCOUNTS

Interpreting psychological qualities involves boiling down an account to essential themes that can then be summarized. The final summary must accurately reflect all the major themes of the original protocol, and it must reflect only those themes. We do not want to overlook any themes. Nor do we want to add (impose) themes that are foreign to the subject's statement.

The first step is to identify "meaning units" within the document. These are coherent and distinct meanings embedded within the protocol. They can be composed of any number of words. One word may constitute a meaning unit. Several sentences may also constitute a unit. A meaning unit may contain a complex idea. It simply must be coherent and distinctive from other ideas. The meaning unit must preserve the psychological integrity of the idea being expressed. It must neither fragment the idea into meaningless, truncated segments nor confuse it with other ideas that express different themes.

It will be instructive to illustrate this point by identifying the meaning units in an actual interview protocol. I will use as data an account that was published by Higgins, Power, and Kohlberg (1984). The subject was asked whether a student is morally obliged to offer a ride to another student in the school (whom he did not know) who needs a ride to an important college interview. I shall bracket meaning units that express issues related to the moral obligation of doing favors for strangers.

> [I don't think he has any obligation]. If I was in his place and I [didn't know the kid too well], [if I wanted to sleep late], [I don't feel that it is my responsibility] to go drive somebody to their interview, [it is up to them, they are responsible]. If I were going there, [if I had an interview there at the same time, sure I would]. But if I had the opportunity to sleep late and didn't know the kid at all, I wouldn't...
>
> [People seem to think as long as you have a car they have a ride], and in my opinion it doesn't operate that way. [If I wanted to give him a ride, I will give him a ride], [if I am going there and they want to go there]. It is [my car and I am the one who is driving], and I don't see why I should give him a ride.
>
> It doesn't mean I shouldn't give them a ride, but [if I don't know them well enough], I think [just out of protection for myself and my property], I wouldn't. I think people may say that [being responsible to yourself is more important than other people]. I think there is [an extent where you put yourself first]. And when you [believe in putting yourself first, like I do]... [I don't feel I should be obligated to somebody else's work, especially if I don't know them], I don't think I should give them a ride.

Identifying meaning units requires interpretation about what constitutes a coherent and distinct theme. This can be done only after the researcher has become familiar with the entire protocol and comprehends what the speaker is saying. Then the researcher can go back to identify particular themes *of this* account. The meaning units are meaningful only in relation to the structure of all the units—that is, in terms of the entire (whole) narrative of which they are parts (see Ratner, 1997a, pp. 136–138).

The selection of meaning units is also guided by the research question. If the question is the relation of fathers and children, then responses that pertain to this issue should be highlighted. Other responses irrelevant to the question should not be identified as meaning units in this research. For example, if the subject says, "We moved to San Francisco in 1994," this has no explicit or implicit significance for his relationship with his child. Accordingly, it should not be a meaning unit in this particular research. Of course, if the subject indicates that the move did have some bearing on his relationship with his child then it should be part of a meaning unit that expresses its importance for this relationship.

Rigorously identifying meaning units is crucial because it serves as a basis and justification for all further interpretations that the researcher makes. Any interpretations that the researcher makes can be referred back to these original meaning units. This helps to avoid arbitrary, subjective impressions being imposed on the subject. The misinterpretation of Meg's protocol committed by Capps and Ochs would have been avoided if meaning units had been carefully identified.

After the meaning units have been identified, they are paraphrased by the researcher in "central themes." If the meaning unit is "Oh hell," the researcher may construe this as "anger." "Anger" will be the theme, or central theme, of the unit.

The meaning units of the statement on moral reasoning can be represented by the following central themes:

- No moral obligation to drive/help (meaning unit: "I don't think he has any obligation")
- Don't help distant social relations (meaning unit: "Don't know him well")
- Self-gratification (meaning unit: "Sleep late"; "Put yourself first")
- Self-responsibility (meaning unit: "Everyone responsible for own self"; "Not responsible for others")
- Help if it's convenient for self (meaning unit: "If he and I were going to the same place")
- People use each other (meaning unit: "People think as long as you have a car they have a ride")
- Private property can be used as one desires without obligation (meaning unit: "It's my car")
- Self-protection (meaning unit: "Don't know people well"; "Out of protection for myself")

The central themes should represent the psychological significance of the meaning units. For instance, when the subject surmises that if he wanted to sleep late he need not worry about driving a schoolmate to an interview, it seems that he is emphasizing his own desire over other people's and that this is a form of self-gratification. Similarly, when he says that it's his car and he is the one driving, the implication is that he can use his property however he wishes and is under no obligation to use it to help another person. Central themes involve interpreting the psychological significance of the meaning unit which is often not explicitly stated. However, the inference must be consistent with the body of statements.

Identifying central themes requires sophisticated interpretation of the meaning unit. The following example from Shweder and Much (1987) illustrates the process of identifying a statement as "an accusation": Alice (4 years of age) is seated at a table. She has a glass full of water. Mrs. Swift (the teacher) approaches and addresses Alice: "That is not a paper cup." "While there is no formal, abstract, or logical feature of the utterance that marks it as an 'accusation,' the context, the discourse, and certain background knowledge makes the teacher's utterance readily identifiable as an accusation" (ibid., p. 209). The teacher is clearly implying that Alice was wrong to have used a glass and should have used a paper cup instead. Both Alice and the observer realize that the teacher was making an accusation based on this implicit rule.

The authors (ibid., pp. 210–211) note that

> Determining the meaning of a stretch of discourse is no formal or mechanical matter, but is objectively constrained. It calls for a good deal of prior cultural knowledge ... The utterance 'That is not a paper cup' is basically a category contrast, meaning 'That is not a paper cup, it is a glass.' It refers the meaning of the event to what is assumed to be known about the relevant differences between paper cups and glasses (a potential for harm through breakage) ...

The teacher's statement will be recognized as an accusation only if the listener realizes the implicit distinction between glasses and paper cups, the implicit knowledge that glasses can break and cause injury, and the implicit assumption that young children are insufficiently competent or conscientious to be trusted with the unsupervised use of fragile and potentially harmful materials. A listener who does have knowledge of these background cultural assumptions and distinctions can readily identify the teacher's statement as an intended accusation.

The meaning (which is summarized in the central theme) is not transparent in the explicit words people use. It must be inferred from knowledge of complex implicit rules, assumptions, and distinctions. "We must be concerned not only with what was said but also with what was presupposed, implied, suggested, or conveyed by what was said" (ibid., 212). The implicit rules, assumptions, and distinctions may refer to unnamed events, rules, beliefs, roles, statuses, and other phenomena.

After the central themes have been identified, several related central themes are organized into a category called "general theme." The general theme names the meaning of the central themes. Central themes from throughout the protocol may be related into one general theme.

TABLE 5.1. THE PHENOMENOLOGICAL METHOD

Statement	Central theme	General theme		General structure	General summary
Xxx [xxxxxxxxx]	1	C.T. 1 C.T. 3	Gen. theme 1	Xx xxxx xxxxxxxx xx xxxxx.	Xx xxxx xx x xxxxxx xxxxx.
Xxxx xxxxx xxxxxxx [x] xxxx	2	C.T. 5			
xx [xxx xxxxx x xxxxxxx]	3			Xxxx xxx xxxxxxx x xxx.	
[Xxxx xxxx xxxxxx] [xxx]	4 5	C.T. 2 C.T. 4	Gen. theme 2		Xxxxxx xxxxxx xx xxx.
xxxxxxx [xxxx xxx xxxxxxx]	6	C.T. 6	Gen. theme 3	Xx xxxxx xxxxxxx xxxxxxxxx. Xxxx xxxxxx.	

Each general theme is explained or amplified in a "general structure."
All the general structures are integrated—compared and explained—
in a summary statement, the "general summary."

Table 5.1 depicts the phenomenological procedure just described.

AN APPLICATION OF THE PHENOMENOLOGICAL PROCEDURE TO CULTURAL PSYCHOLOGY

A useful example of the phenomenological method applied to cultural psychology is Chao's (1995) research on Chinese and American mothers' beliefs about childrearing. Although Chao did not follow my procedures, her method is similar in many respects. She asked the mothers to write about their childrearing values. From the protocols, Chao noted significant phrases (meaning units), identified themes ("central themes"), and combined these into broader general themes. Central themes from American mothers were "nurturing and patient," "separate the child's behavior from the person" (i.e., criticize behavior but not the child), and "love." Chao categorized these three "central themes" as expressing a general theme "self-esteem." Her work can be organized into my phenomenological system in Table 5.2.

TABLE 5.2. CENTRAL AND GENERAL THEMES

American mothers		Chinese mothers	
Central themes	General themes	Central themes	General themes
Nurturing and patient. Separate behavior from person. Love.	Independent self-esteem.	Encourage learning new things. Encourage trying new things by self.	Independence.
Respect others. Respect work. Respect money.	Instilling values.	Good person. Good judgment Honesty. Responsible. Adaptable.	Instilling moral character.
Fulfill child's needs. Make child happy.	Love.	Talk to kids. Listen to kids. Being a friend. Sacrifice. Devotion.	Love.
Getting in touch with feelings. Labeling feelings. Expressing feelings.	Process feelings.	Share toys. Politeness. Avoid envy.	Teach respect for others.

Chao explained the significance of the general themes in general structures. She pointed out that independence in children was valued by American mothers for the purpose of encouraging children to separate from the family. Independence was valued by Chinese mothers for the opposite purpose of helping children become successful so they could contribute more to the family. In the same way, love was valued by American mothers as a means to foster self-esteem in their children. For Chinese mothers, love was a means to foster an enduring social relationship with their children.

General themes and structures of Chao's work are systematized and diagrammed in Table 5.3.

In the phenomenological analysis, every stage preserves and illuminates the meaning of the earlier stages. Central themes express the specific psychological meaning of the meaning units; general themes express the meaning of central themes; general structures convey the meaning of general themes; and the general summary explains how all the general structures are interrelated. The summary explains whether structures complement or contradict each other.

TABLE 5.3. GENERAL THEMES AND GENERAL STRUCTURES

American		Chinese	
General themes	General structures	General themes	General structures
Independent self-esteem.	Independence in order to live on one's own. Separating self from behavior insulates. self from criticism. directed at behavior.	Independence.	Independence in order to better provide for family.
Love.	Love is valued to foster self-esteem in child.	Love.	Love is valued to foster enduring social relationship with child.
Process feelings.	To know self better; not to understand other people better.		

Because each higher level of analysis elucidates the specific quality of the lower level, a general theme may have a very different name from the central theme. For example, for American mothers the central theme of love connoted the general theme of independent self-esteem; thus, the general theme is not love. Instead, the general theme "love" was used to express the central theme of "make child happy."

The psychological significance of a central theme, rather than the bare words, determines the terminology that is used to identify general themes. For example, when a factory worker says he uses all the bathroom breaks he can take, it is necessary to identify the specific psychological meaning of this in a central theme. If other parts of the text indicate that he uses breaks to combat management control and exploitation, then this sense should be identified in the central theme. It might be stated as: "Uses breaks to retaliate against management control and exploitation."

When the phenomenological procedure is employed to analyze cultural–psychological phenomena, all the levels of analysis—central themes, general themes, general structures, and the general summary—should denote specific psychological characteristics that can be linked to cultural activities, artifacts, and concepts. Chao indicated the specific quality of independence and love in her general structures. Gee illuminated the specific character of marriage for one woman in his interpretation of her statement which I cited in Chap. 1. Recall that the "meaning unit" was "Why in the world would you want to stop and not get the use out of all the years you've already spent together?" Gee designates the "central theme" (meaning) of this statement as: "Time spent in marriage is being treated as an 'investment'." Investment denotes a particular kind of transaction or relationship. It could be amplified in a general structure such as: "In terms of the investment metaphor, if we invest money/time, we are entitled to a 'return.' So according to this model, it is silly not to wait long enough, having made an investment, to see it 'pay off' and be able to 'get the use out of' the time/money that has been invested."

Lystra identified specific characteristics of romantic love in a phenomenological analysis of love letters (see Ratner, 1997a, pp. 135–136). From meaning units such as "Regard me as one with yourself," she identified central themes such as "Love is a merging of personal identities," "Love is exclusive," "Love is a rare match between unique individuals," "Love involves revealing personal thoughts and feelings." These phrases denote specific qualities of self, thoughts, emotions, and the interpersonal relationship of lovers.

Another example of elucidating concrete psychological qualities in narratives is Sobel's analysis of self-concept in narratives written between 1740 and 1840. Sobel concludes that

> At the outset of the eighteenth century most people seemed to regard themselves as having porous boundaries and as part of a wider or 'we–self.' It was in the hundred-year period between 1740 and 1840 that many people in America first came to accept that they had an inner self that controlled their emotions and actions and to believe that they themselves might alter this self. In this period, and as part of this process of change, the churches and then the new state encouraged the written reevaluation of life experiences in journals and in autobiographies (ibid., p. 3). By the close of this period, the ideal white male was individuated, self-concerned, and determined to succeed in a rapacious market economy. (Sobel, 2000, p. 4)

Sobel arrived at this conclusion by discerning specific characteristics of self in the narrators' descriptions. For instance, the early narratives depicted life as a sum of events such as hardships endured, marvels witnessed, crops harvested, animals killed, material possessions accumulated, and ceremonies accomplished. When dreams were mentioned in narratives, they contained other people and events acting on the dreamer, but the dreamer did not initiate action or even envision himself in his own dreams (pp. 21–22). Sobel interprets these details as indicating a particular kind of self that accepts life events and manifests little personal agency or choice: "The narratives written by people who had a porous sense of self were generally repetitive tales of events the narrators passively endured. They did not see themselves as having fashioned their lives or as being responsible for their selves" (ibid., p. 19).

Cultural psychologists strive to avoid abstract terminology because it precludes apprehending their specific psychological and cultural character.

For example, if the worker's statement, "Uses all the bathroom breaks he can," is parsed abstractly as "Attends to bodily needs" this would obscure the cultural significance that the breaks have for the worker. Literal paraphrasing of a statement similarly expunges its psychological and cultural significance. If the worker's statement, "Uses all the bathroom breaks he can," were paraphrased as "Takes many bathroom breaks" its psychological and cultural significance would be obfuscated.

Most qualitative researchers are not interested in culture and therefore most of their codes are abstract. For instance, in analyzing a job, Strauss codes it as: information passing, attentiveness, efficiency, monitoring, providing assistance, conferring (Strauss & Corbin, 1990, pp. 64–73). None of these codes elucidates the content or quality of the work. They could refer to a nurse or prison guard equally well (both do all of these things) and fail to distinguish the vastly different ways that a nurse and prison guard treat people. Strauss turns even further in the direction of abstractness when he advocates dimensionalizing these codes in terms of their frequency, intensity, and duration. Instead of revealing what the subject concretely does, how she treats people, what her objectives are, and what the institutional pressures are, Strauss's procedure leaves us with the abstract knowledge that the subject passes information frequently and for short durations each time.

Miles and Huberman (1994, pp. 54–72) continue this trend in their guidebook on qualitative data analysis. In a study on schools the authors found that "Ken decides not to tell teachers ahead of time about transfers [of pupils into and out of the school] 'because then we'd have a fait accompli'." Miles and Huberman (p. 54) code this segment as "plan for planning/time management." This code obscures Ken's thoughts and emotions about the teachers, and his interpersonal relationships with them. Evidently he has misgivings and fears about their reactions to knowing about transfers. He therefore withholds from them vital information regarding the number and composition of students in their classes. These vital social psychological issues are suppressed in the abstract code "time management." Abstract codes eliminate details and stifle further inquiry. If Ken's action is simply a form of time management there is nothing more to say about it. The code squelches interest in exploring the teachers' concrete thoughts, emotions, and relationships, and tracing these to structural aspects of educational activity such as the internal division of labor into roles with different rights, responsibilities, opportunities and rewards, budgetary constraints, and pressures from governmental bureaus and parents' groups.

Even Chao uses abstract terms such as "processing feelings," "respect work," "instilling values," "moral character," "good person," "adaptable," "talk to kids," "respect others," "honest," "patient." All of these express no specific cultural–psychological content, for example: In what ways does one respect others (by questioning them closely to find out their feelings or by allowing them a great deal of privacy)? How does one talk to kids (as mature adults or as immature children; patiently or impatiently)? How does one respect work (to earn money or to build character)?

Chao could have avoided this problem by identifying concrete meanings at every level of analysis. The central theme "Respect work" should have been "Respect work to become wealthy" or "Respect work to develop a strong ethical code," or "Respect work to contribute to society." Providing concrete information in the central themes is the ultimate "thick description" that Geertz and Ryle have espoused. "Thick description ... entails an account of the intentions, expectations, circumstances, settings, and purposes that give actions their meanings" (Greenblatt, 1999, p. 16).

A Cultural Analysis of Psychological Themes

Using concrete terms for all the codes enables the cultural psychologist to relate each one to cultural activities, artifacts, and concepts. In the case of Chao's data, we can see the homology between the general structure "Independent self in order to live on one's own" and the widespread American value of individual autonomy and the free market where individuals must make their own decisions. This kind of cultural analysis allows us to conclude that certain childrearing values recapitulate and reinforce cultural concepts, activities, and artifacts outside the family.

Gee's interpretation of marriage as an investment similarly allows us to note that commercial concepts and practices have penetrated the formerly distinct domain of family life. Sobel's concrete analysis of self concept enabled her to observe that the changes in self-concept during the Revolutionary era were related to practices and concepts of the Protestant church. Protestant sects fostered the individuated self by requiring members to analyze and control their selves. Protestantism also encouraged people to regard life as consisting of crossroads at which choices are made by individuals who are responsible for the direction they take (Sobel, 2000, pp. 24–25, 28, 32).

We can similarly trace the cultural activities and concepts that influenced the central themes of the young man (mentioned previously) who denied any moral obligation to drive a schoolmate to an interview. The specific content of the central themes allows us to see that they embody responsibility for oneself, individual gratification, private property that is controlled exclusively by the owner, an antipathy to social obligations, a strict demarcation between self and others, and a deep suspicion of strangers. These are all major principles of capitalist economic relations (see, Ci, 1999a). Thus, bourgeois economic relationships and concepts constitute the staple of Jay's moral code—the specific character that it has by virtue of existing in the United States today. If this cultural character of moral reasoning were found in a large number of individuals we would conclude that moral reasoning in this country has largely been coopted by bourgeois economic principles and that it will direct people to evaluate and treat each other according to these principles. Of course, Jay's moral tenets may have roots in cultural activities and concepts besides economic ones. A thorough cultural analysis would ascertain the concordance or discordance between Jay's moral tenets and a wealth of cultural activities and concepts.

Engestrom (1993) performed a similar analysis of medical interactions between a doctor and patient in a health center in Finland. He recorded behavioral and verbal interactions and then questioned the doctor at a later point to obtain more information about his thinking. Although Engestrom did not rigorously analyze the interactions into meaning units, he did summarize their psychological meanings. In a second step, Engestrom compared the doctor's thinking and behavior to business principles and organizational structure of corporate medical activity. He identified the doctor–patient interactions as expressing either a biomedical, psychosocial, life–world, or medical/administrative–authority orientation within corporatized medicine. For example, the medical–authority orientation reflects an emphasis on rational, cost-efficient, productivity. A biomedical orientation reflects a preoccupation with technical analyses and solutions.[1]

Relating psychological themes to cultural activities and concepts is a significant advance over simply describing psychological themes that are expressed in different societies. Whereas the latter kind of description identifies *psychological differences within culture*, elucidating the congruence between psychology and cultural activities and concepts illuminates the ways in which *culture (activities, concepts, and artifacts) is embedded within psychology*.

A cultural psychological analysis transcends the subject's knowledge. The subject is aware of details of her psychological functions; however, she is not aware of how these details reflect cultural activities and concepts. The task of the cultural psychologist is an objective comparison of the characteristics of psychology and the characteristics of cultural concepts and activities (Ratner, 1997a, Chaps. 3, 4, 5). We may say that a cultural psychological analysis goes beyond describing manifest psychological themes that individuals are aware of and delves into latent cultural themes that pervade individuals' psychological phenomena but remain outside the individuals' awareness (see Ratner, 1994).

This requires great sensitivity because the researcher must remain faithful to the subjects' statements, yet must also explicate cultural issues in the statements that subjects are not fully aware of. In other words, statements contain cultural information that is recognizable only by someone who is knowledgeable about cultural activities and concepts. The researcher brings this knowledge to bear in analyzing cultural aspects of the statements. The researcher must use the statements as evidence for cultural issues. Any conclusion about cultural aspects of psychology must be empirically supported by indications in the verbal statements. At the same time, the cultural aspects are not transparent in the statements and cannot be directly read off from them because the subjects have not themselves explicitly reflected on or described these aspects. They are embedded in the statements and must be elucidated from them. The task of analyzing descriptive data is to remain faithful to what the subjects say, yet also transcend the literal words to apprehend the cultural meanings embedded in the words—just as the physician listens to the patient's report of symptoms and then utilizes his medical knowledge to identify what disease the patient has (see Schutz, 1967, p. 6).

OBJECTIVE DETERMINATION OF MEANINGS

The goal of understanding other people's cultural psychology is to be objective. To understand the cultural psychology of other people is to understand a reality—a psychological reality, to be sure—that exists independently of the researcher. The cultural psychologist must find a way to understand that reality as it exists for other people just as any natural scientist must understand a reality that exists independently of himself. It is just as disastrous to misapprehend people's cultural psychology as it is to misapprehend the nature of physical things. Labeling an individual or a group as mentally ill, stupid, aggressive, lazy, unemotional, or sexist when he or she is not has terrible practical consequences. The whole point of developing a rigorous procedure for interpreting verbal accounts is to avoid these errors.

Attempting to make interpretations objective may seem oxymoronic. The dominance of positivism in psychological research had led many qualitative researchers to question whether interpretations of meaning can be objective. Because objectivity has long been defined as quantifying simple, overt behaviors and employing statistical criteria to determine psychological conclusions, any sort of interpretation appears subjective and arbitrary. Many qualitative researchers accept this positivistic notion and deride the possibility of objectively interpreting subjective meanings.

However, the positivistic denigration of interpretation is a caricature of science. Science is not reducible to sense data of immediately experienced things. All science interprets sensory data as indicating unsensed, unexperienced phenomena (Ratner, 1997a). Physicists and astronomers interpret light and dark areas on a photograph as indicating subatomic particles, the birth or death of distant stars, and the existence of galaxies. Vygotsky (1997b, pp. 271–273) explained that interpretation in the natural sciences is as common and indispensable as it is in psychological science:

> The use of a thermometer is a perfect model of the indirect method [of interpretation]. After all, we do not study what we see—the rising of the mercury, the expansion of the alcohol—but we study heat and its changes which are indicated by the mercury or alcohol. We interpret the indications of the thermometer, we reconstruct the phenomenon under study by its traces, by its influence upon the expansion of a substance ... To interpret means to re-create a phenomenon from its traces and influences relying upon regularities established before (in the present case—the law of the extension of solids, liquids, and gases during heating). There is no fundamental difference whatsoever between the use of a thermometer on the one hand and interpretation in history, psychology, etc. on the other. The same holds true for any science: it is not dependent upon sensory perception. (ibid., p. 273)

Gould (2000, p. 20) explains that systems of biological classification are forms of interpretation. He says that "All systems of classification must express theories about the causes of order and must therefore feature a complex mixture of concepts and percepts—that is, preferences in human thinking combined with observations of nature's often cryptic realities."

The fact that all scientific analysis is based on theory and interpretation does not preclude it from being objective. The natural sciences are tremendously objective even though they are based on theories and interpretations. Theoretical conclusions about the big bang, evolution, and other natural phenomena command widespread support although they are based on inferences and deductions and are not directly visible through the senses. Of course, interpretations *may* be inaccurate on any particular occasion. However, they are not intrinsically distorting of truth.

The positivistic antimony between interpretation and objectivity rests on a false distinction between sense experience and cognition. Positivists assume that objectivity requires the pure reception of physical data via sense organs. Cognition—including interpretation—is presumed to distort this pure sensory process. The truth of the matter is quite the opposite. Cognition is indispensable for comprehending reality in an objective manner (i.e., as it exists). Mere sense impressions receive only fragmentary, superficial, ambiguous information. By themselves they can never comprehend reality. Cognitive interpretation holds the only possibility of objectively comprehending reality. The difference between objective and erroneous conclusions is not that the former derives directly from sense impression while the latter derives from cognition. Rather, the former derives from logical, comprehensive, analytical reasoning while the latter derives from superficial, fragmented, impressionistic thinking.

Many scholars in the humanities have emphasized the necessity and possibility of objective interpretation. The philosophical tradition of hermeneutics is a case in point (Ratner, 1997a, pp. 59–64). Hermeneutics originally developed as a subdiscipline of philology to clarify the authentic meaning of religious documents. The need for this was especially intense in the 16th century when Catholics and Protestants debated over competing interpretations of the bible. In the 18th century, hermeneutics was expanded to ascertain the meaning of art works and historical events. Schleiermacher further extended hermeneutics to comprehend the spirit (Geist) of an age and the cultural experiences of different populations.

The anthropologist Shweder believes that "Objective determinations of meaning are possible." "Given sufficient prior knowledge of context, background assumptions, usage, etc., it is possible to distinguish between valid and invalid inferences about what an utterance means, to recognize improper or implausible deductions about what was left unstated, presupposed or assumed in the communication, etc." (Shweder & Much, 1987, p. 209).

Objectivity is a vital goal in qualitative research because it means faithfully representing the speaker's meanings. If we respect others and desire to know them, we want to objectively comprehend what they say without distortion. If we disregard this point and impose our assumptions on people's words, we are being ethnocentric and egocentric; we fail to respect their point of view.

Although an extended discussion of objectivity in cultural psychological interpretation is beyond the scope of this chapter (see Ratner 1997a for such a discussion), we may say that an essential criterion of objectivity is the congruence of an interpretation with the psychological meanings of the original statement. This is not as difficult or mysterious as it may appear. Researchers can agree whether an interpretation is congruent with particular statements in a definite context or whether it superimposes assumptions that are not indicated by the protocol. Earlier we saw that Capps and Ochs' analysis of agoraphobia was patently discrepant with a patient's statements. It is also easy to detect inappropriate coding of meaning units and central themes in content analysis.

Consider, for example, the following statement about the significance of health: "Well, I link personally to health: The complete functionality of the human organism, all the biochemical processes of the organism included in this all cycles but also the mental state of my person and of Man in general." The speaker is expressing two main meanings: Health is a personal issue for him; and he defines health broadly including physical processes, his mental state, and even the state of Man. The speaker seems to be expressing two meaning units: (1) "I link personally to health." (2) "The complete functionality of the human organism, all the biochemical processes of the organism included in this all cycles but also the mental state of my person and of Man in general." Each of these meaning units contains enough information to be psychologically meaningful, expresses a coherent meaning that runs throughout all the elements in the unit, and is distinctive from other unit.

Flick (1998b, p. 181), who provided this example, arrived at a different analysis of meaning units. He segmented it into 15 meaning units: "Well I/link/personally/to health/: the complete functionality/of the human organism/all/the biochemical processes/of the organism/included in this/all cycles/but also/the mental state/of my person/and of Man in general." We can see that these meaning units are so truncated as to be deprived of psychological significance. "To health," "but also," "of the organism," express no identifiable meaning. Flick mechanically segmented words without conveying the psychological significance of what the speaker was saying. Flick's misidentification of meaning units leads inexorably to misidentifying central themes. He claims that the meaning unit "personally" denotes the subject's self in contrast to others. However, a single word may mean many things and there is no indication from the surrounding context that it has an individualistic significance in the speaker's statement. Actually, the subject later links his own health to that of Man in general, which contradicts Flick's interpretation that he contrasts himself to other people.

Similarly, Flick codes "the biochemical processes" as "prison, closed system, passive, other directed." However, the mere mention of biochemical processes does not confirm this interpretation. The meaning depends on related phrases which Flick has erroneously divorced from "biochemical processes." Actually, the related phrases indicate that biochemical processes include the mental state of the subject and Man in general—quite the opposite of a closed system and passive. Flick codes "the mental state" as "mechanistic, negative taste, abuse, static" simply because the subject uses the term "state." Again, a single, isolated word is no grounds for imputing this host of pejorative attributes. Perhaps the most egregious misinterpretation is Flick's contention that the simple phrase "of my person" means that the subject "produces a distance, talks very neutrally about what concerns him, defense against too much proximity to the female interviewer and to himself." Here Flick invents defenses against women and self on the basis of the words "my person."

It is not difficult to conclude that Flick has imposed assumptions on the phrases that are not indicated by the speaker's words and meanings. Flick evidently imposed dictionary-type meanings on words such as "state" and "biochemical processes." The reader can easily perceive that these meanings were not expressed by the speaker.[2]

Faithfully representing another person's meanings is quite possible with the aid of the phenomenological method outlined herein. The procedure enhances objectivity by (1) directing the researcher to comprehend the meaning of particular phrases through their interrelationship with other phrases in the context of the entire narrative; (2) elucidating the psychological significance of "lower," "earlier" levels of analysis in "higher," "later" levels—for example, central themes express the significance of meaning units, general themes express the significance of central themes, etc.; and (3) proceeding from lower to higher levels of analysis in small, controlled steps. Each new paraphrase, interpretation, categorization, and summary can be checked against earlier, original ones. The general summary is based on this carefully constructed sequence of interpretations, categorizations, and summaries. We can retrace the general summary to evaluate its faithfulness and completeness in representing all the earlier steps. Proceeding in small steps to arrive at the general summary guards against jumping to conclusions from the original protocol. These procedures help ensure that the researcher's description respects and represents the speaker's meanings and psychological qualities.

My procedure can be adapted to the complexity of the verbal account that is being analyzed. If the central themes are few in number and easily interpretable they can be readily summarized without going through general themes and structures. The full procedure is necessary when the verbal account is complex and ambiguous and the researcher needs a structured sequence of steps to objectively understand the themes.

QUANTIFICATION

When groups of people are studied, it is very useful to calculate the percentage of individuals in each group who express various central themes, general themes, general structures, and summaries. It is informative to learn that 40% of American mothers encourage their children to process feelings while none of the Chinese mothers do. Quantification is also indispensable for identifying diverse responses within a group of people. No group is homogeneous, and quantifying the percentage of subjects who express different themes is the most informative way to express differences. It is far more informative (and objective) than presenting some scattered responses to represent different trends.

Quantification can be applied to the different stages of analysis. The general summaries can be categorized into types and the number of each type can be presented. It would be interesting to know that 42% of the general summaries expressed a certain pattern of themes while 4% expressed a different pattern of themes, and 64% still another pattern of themes. Central themes can be compared quantitatively as well. If a certain transcript yielded 27 central themes, we could compute the percentage of subjects who expressed each one. The same can be done for general themes.

The researcher must wait until the entire phenomenological procedure has been completed before performing any calculations on the lower levels. It is pointless and misleading to calculate the percentage of parents who express a central theme or a general theme before its meaning has been established. For example, in Chao's study, American and Chinese mothers both valued love in their relationship with their children. However, the quality of love differed. American mothers emphasize love to enhance the self-esteem of their children, which would help the child to become an autonomous individual. Chinese mothers want their love for children to promote a long-lasting relationship with them. In this case, comparing the percentage of Chinese and American mothers who value love has to include the caveat that love is rather different for the two groups. Quantitative comparisons must not obscure qualitative differences in the phenomenon.

Quantification is quite compatible with qualitative methods if one waits until the cultural quality of themes has been established. Quantification computes numbers of people; it does not measure psychological phenomena, for example, the degree or strength of psychological phenomena.

Once we know the number of individuals who manifest different cultural psychological phenomena, these numbers should be subjected to statistical tests of significance. Such tests are vital with small sample sizes that are subject to sampling artifacts. Even large differences in numbers—for example, 20% vs. 80%—may reflect chance sampling artifacts with no substantive meaning in the larger population from which the sample was drawn.

Quantification is not the enemy of qualitative methods. If it is done correctly, it complements them. Quantification is misleading only when it is used incorrectly to measure psychological phenomena rather than numbers of people. When psychologists attempt to quantify the amount of a phenomenon, such as intelligence, logical reasoning, introversion, or collective personality, they obscure their quality as we have seen in Chap. 3, note 3. Quantifying psychological phenomena is as foolhardy as quantifying beauty or creativity. However, it is useful to count the number of people who are mentally ill, violent, criminal, intelligent, and creative once these characteristics have been ascertained by qualitative methods. Because qualitative methods use quantification, it is incorrect to counterpoise qualitative and quantitative methods. It is correct to counterpoise qualitative methods with the philosophy of positivism which misuses quantification (Ratner, 1997a). Repudiating quantification, per se, is too sweeping and superficial. Attacking quantification does not attack the epistemological and ontological assumptions of positivism that underlie the misuse of quantification. Repudiating quantification is akin to repudiating industrialization because it is polluting and impersonal. Such a critique is superficial because it attacks the end-product of a social system but does not investigate the social system that structures industrialism in a deleterious way. The problem with industrialism is the social relationships that shape it, just as the problem with quantification is the philosophical principles that dominate it. In these cases, the immediate, overt target (quantification, industrialism) is not inherently deleterious; it can be retained and improved by altering the principles that structure it.

NOTES

1. While Engestrom's study is a valuable contribution to qualitative cultural psychological research from the perspective of activity theory, I would suggest a more detailed methodology. His interviews could have been more extensive and detailed. This would provide more information for obtaining a thorough and accurate interpretation of the personal and cultural qualities of the interactions. For example, he interprets an instance of a doctor's abruptness to his being under time pressure in the cost-efficient health center. However, this interpretation is not supported by verbal data. Engestrom should have directly asked the doctor why he was abrupt, what he was thinking when he acted this way, whether he feels any pressure to produce from the organization of the center, what the basis of this pressure is (profit, etc.), and how the pressure is exerted. Fuller data would provide for more objective interpretations and it would protect against alternative interpretations. An additional improvement to Engestrom's study would be to present a quantitative comparison of the various kinds of interactions between patients and the doctor. This would allow us to determine which aspects of medical activity are most influential on the interactions. It would be quite informative to know whether commercial, administrative, or humanitarian aspects of this activity are more influential in the exam room.

2. This kind of critique is performed on interpretations in the natural sciences as well. In a brilliant article on classification in biology, Gould (2000) observes that organisms can be classified in all sorts of ways; however, some are artificial, some are downright fallacious, while others represent real genealogical relationships among organisms. An example of a fallacious classification is: Corals were categorized as plants when, in fact, they are animals. An example of an artificial classification would be a zoo director housing all animals of the same size together (for practical purposes) despite the fact that they are genealogically and physiologically quite different. Similarly, Agassiz classified jellyfish and starfish together for their common property of radial symmetry, whereas they are actually members of two genealogically distant phyla. An example of superior and inferior classifications is classifying whales genealogically with mammals as opposed to amalgamating them with squids, sharks, and other animals that swim in the ocean.

This evaluation of biological classifications as useful, fallacious, or artificial can be directly applied to psychological interpretations, as I have done with Flick, Capps and Ochs.

6

An Empirical Investigation into the Cultural Psychology of Children's Moral Reasoning

This chapter presents a design for empirically investigating the cultural psychology of children's moral reasoning. It presents a theoretical framework for conceptualizing moral reasoning as mediated by cultural concepts, and it formulates procedures for elucidating and recording cultural concepts that mediate moral reasoning. The study has not been conducted, so no results are reported.

Theoretical Framework

A cultural–psychological analysis of children's moral reasoning elucidates the cultural activities and concepts that mediate and organize morality. For example, one will regard teachers spanking students as morally right or wrong according to one's concept of the authority, rights, and responsibilities of teachers vs. children; the best way to promote learning; bodily privacy; psychological effects of corporal punishment; and diverse other things. Similarly, a person's moral evaluation and reasoning about one issue, such as abortion, are related to her reasoning about other issues, such as premarital sex, gender roles, or her concept of whether an embryo has the status of a person (Jensen, 1997, pp. 328–329). All of these concepts are socially constructed, and shared across large segments of the population.

In the same vein, one's judgment about the moral obligation of helping someone depends on cultural concepts of personal responsibility. If one adopts the belief that people are responsible for themselves, this may absolve one from the moral obligation to help people. Cultural concepts stipulate which social relationships between individuals deserve to receive help as well as the kind of help that is morally appropriate. In the

United States it is morally imperative that a parent help a child but this does not extend to strangers (Miller & Bersoff, 1992; Miller, Bersoff, & Harwood, 1990).

Among the Oriya of India, cultural concepts stipulate that stealing is generally wrong, but it is condoned in certain restricted situations. One can steal to help someone if the robber derives no personal gain whatsoever. I can steal to help a stranger who has no personal relationship to me. I cannot steal to help myself. This encompasses stealing to help family or friends who have a personal relationship with self and are part of self (Shweder & Much, 1987, p. 43). This principle is exactly opposite the Confucian code which condones stealing to help a family member. According to Confucian ethics, filial duty is a person's first priority and it supercedes a social sanction against stealing. According to Confucianism, people feel close to family members, depend on them, and need to spend their limited resources helping them even when this duty conflicts with broader social policies (Hwang, 1998).

Moral judgments, or standards, also depend on legalistic concepts of justice, for example, how one conceptualizes a promise, law, the social good, obligation, and even morality itself.

For example, since the 18th century, capitalist countries have adopted and enforced a legal concept of promises as being a voluntary agreement between individuals. Promises that are coerced are not legally or morally binding. Once a promise has been voluntarily offered it is legally and morally binding regardless of subsequent conditions that may arise— such as misfortune that befalls the promisor and prevents him from fulfilling the agreement. In medieval times, promises did not have this individual, volitional character. A promise was binding only if it conformed to an existing custom. Individual promises to do things outside of established customs were not legally or morally binding (Haskell, 1985). The legal and moral implications of breaking an individual promises were inconsequential for medieval people while modern Westerners consider breaking promises to be immoral in accordance with our legal concept.

Prasad (1999) found that American men legitimate prostitution as a moral act because (1) it represents a voluntary, mutual agreement on the part of the customer and the prostitute; and (2) it is straightforward and unambiguous, and does not involve dishonesty among the two parties. Prasad observes that these values are the values of free market commodity exchange (see also Ci, 1999a). Commodity exchange involves selling a service for a price; the buyer and seller volunatarily agree to the terms; each honestly says what he wants (service, money) and provides what he promised (money, service); and no other considerations (outside the immediate economic transaction) are relevant, for example, personal feelings, social relationships, social consequences, other people's opinions. The principles of commodity exchange on the free market thus comprise the elements of moral reasoning that justify buying and selling sex for money.

A cultural–conceptual approach to morality is rather novel. "In psychology, the dominant approach emphasizes a separation of moral reasoning from more comprehensive worldviews" (Jensen, 1997, p. 325). Morality is typically understood in terms of abstract values such as "avoiding punishment," "upholding rights," "respecting authority," "honoring contracts," "concern for all people." Kohlberg (1981, 1984) regarded morality as consisting of such general values. He was not concerned with the specific cultural conceptions that children had of entities such as friendship, family, person, child, and promises.

According to Kohlberg, if you consider intentions as relevant you are defined as reasoning at a certain stage. If you consider social rules as relevant you are defined as reasoning at a different stage. The considerations you use have no specific content: It is not what you think authority consists of that defines your moral level (e.g., is authority totalitarian or based on wisdom and reason?); it is whether you think authority at all should govern behavior that defines your moral level.

Even when Kohlberg's moral dilemmas elicited cultural concepts from subjects, he analyzed the responses according to abstract features. For example, the famous dilemma of Heinz asks whether he should steal medicine for his wife, a sick stranger, a sick animal pet, and a wife whom Heinz does not love. However, Kohlberg did not consider the content that subjects expressed—for example, that animals are not as important as humans and therefore do not justify breaking the law, or strangers are less important to one's well being than family so one should not steal for them. Kohlberg was interested only in whether subjects referred to intentions, reciprocity, a social contract, authority, the social good, etc.

Gilligan criticized Kohlberg's categories and proposed different ones that were more applicable to women. Gilligan (1982) argued that Kohlberg's principles of justice (reciprocity and equality of rights, dignity of individuals) are not the only (universal) components of moral development. She maintains that women use other considerations such as caring for people, meeting social obligations (such as loyalty to one's spouse), and discerning and alleviating trouble as the basis for their moral judgements. However, Gilligan's categories are as abstract as Kohlberg's. For Gilligan, the particular concept of what loyalty involves in particular situations is not relevant. All that matters is that women refer to loyalty when they discuss morality.[1]

Abstract, general moral categories appear to be divorced from social processes and seem instead to spring from universal, internal processes.

Abstract, general categories of morality lend credence to the idea that they are intrinsic to individual minds and develop in a universal sequence according to maturational principles.

The exclusion of sociohistorical issued in the structuralist viewpoint is illustrated in one of Kohlberg's discussions about children's responses to the dilemma of Heinz. One child stated, "That must be a pretty terrible druggist. A druggist is like a doctor; he's supposed to save people's lives." Kohlberg classified this response as stage three because it refers to a sense of social goodness, badness, and deservingness (Kohlberg, 1984, p. 630). Another child said that Heinz should steal because he was poor and needed the medicine to help his dying wife. Kohlberg classified this response as stage 4 because the subject exempted Heinz from social laws that applied to other people.

In response to the question "Did the druggist have the right to charge that much?" a child responded, "No, for him to make that much profit is ignoring his responsibility to people." Kohlberg (1984) classified this as a stage 4 judgment because it linked property rights to social responsibility.

Kohlberg's classifications disregard specific concepts that underlie the children's judgments. For example, the first subject believed that it is important for druggists to help people in need. He held a specific belief about the occupation of being a pharmacist. He did not mention an abstract notion that one should act for the social good. Similarly, the second child believed that it is morally acceptable for a poor person to violate social norms to save the life of a loved one. He did not endorse a general principle that individuals are above the law. Likewise, the third subject expressed a specific view of profit—that it should be moderate so that people can afford to buy necessary goods. He did not expound an abstract view of social responsibility.

Kohlberg's general categories are too abstract to account for specific moral judgments. Simply knowing that subjects have some sense of social good that informs their thinking about morality is insufficient to understand or predict specific moral judgments. We must know what people think about the social good (as well as loyalty, authority, reciprocity, intentions, laws, and promises) to understand or predict their moral evaluation of the druggist (see Ratner, 1991, pp. 113–131, 1997a, pp. 209–213; Simpson, 1974).

Consider the moral judgment about abortion. Two individuals may share the general notion that all human beings should be protected by equal rights (stage 6 of Kohlberg). However, within this categorical/ structural understanding, one person may believe that an embryo is a person while the other believes it is not. The two will arrive at opposite moral evaluations of abortion on the basis of their concept of a person even though they are at the same "structural level" of moral reasoning

(Jensen, 1997, p. 329). Similarly, the framers of the American Constitution were fierce defenders of individual liberty; however, they considered slaves as subhuman and therefore not covered by individualistic moral and legal codes. The sanctioning of slavery rested on the cultural concept of "human being," not on a stage of moral reasoning.

Likewise, two individuals may share a general belief in justice that all individuals should be protected from harm. One believes that pornography is psychologically damaging while the other believes it is innocuous entertainment. Their different concepts of the issue lead to opposite moral evaluations about displaying pornography despite the general ideal of justice that they share (Nisan, 1984, pp. 213–216, 219).

Thus, Jensen is correct to observe that adopting conservative or progressive moral codes is not a function of formal thinking processes (structures) but of content: "No matter how much reversibility of thought orthodox and progressivist adults engaged in, they would not be likely often to arrive at similar moral reasoning. This is because their worldviews are markedly different. Their divergent views of human nature, reality, suffering, and how to overcome suffering often lead them to different understandings of the viewpoints of subjects in a moral situation" (Jensen, 1997, pp. 341–342; see also Shweder & Much, 1987, pp. 225–231).

Kohlberg's abstract stages disregard and obscure concrete moral values and reasoning. They collapse vastly different values into common categories that promote the false appearance of similarity. They are impoverished, incomplete descriptions of people's real moral values and reasoning. This is clear when we consider concrete responses such as the following. An Israeli man, living on a kibbutz, said that Heinz should steal the drug because the druggist had no right to control its price: "The medicine should be made available to all in need; the druggist should not have the right to decide on his own ... the whole community or society should have the control of the drug." A New Guinea man argued that Heinz's stealing the drug reflects a social failure of the community to provide for his wife: "If nobody helped him [save his dying wife] and so he stole to save her, I would say *we* had caused that problem." An Indian man said that Heinz should steal the drug to save his pet's life because "The basic unity of life cannot be denied ... All of life, human or non-human, is divine, sacred, and a manifestation of the Supreme reality" (Snarey, 1985, pp. 222–225). Subsuming these responses in any of Kohlberg's stages or categories—for example, "postconventional reasoning" (Kohlberg's stages 5 and 6)—expunges them of interesting, important, concrete views of life and fosters the erroneous impression that they are "basically" similar. In fact, the specific values and views that constitute the subjects' moral reasoning are far more interesting, important, and real than notions such as postconventional reasoning.

Kohlberg is not alone in eliminating concrete cultural content from moral reasoning. This tendency is pervasive. For example, a collection of studies in Tappan and Packer (1991) coded narratives about morality. The codes identified the presence of "recurrent words," "emotional resonances," "inconsistencies in style," "shifts in narrative position—the use of first-, second-, or third-person voice," "the voice of the 'I' speaking in the story," "wishes and concerns about listening and being listened to," "concerns about fairness between people" (pp. 46–47), "turn taking," "granting and questioning authority," "a directedness that organizes activity" (p. 78). Now, noting that an individual manifests an emotional resonance, inconsistency in style, or speaks from the first or third person perspective obfuscates the cultural content of the moral belief.

Even studies that seek to elucidate specific social concepts often fail to do so. In Miller, Bersoff, and Harwood's study (1990) some subjects replied that if a person had a strong need for something it was immoral to deprive her of it. The authors coded this response as an example of "welfare considerations." Other subjects replied that a person was morally obliged to help because she had plentiful resources that she could have offered. This was also categorized as a welfare consideration. This category obscures the cultural issue that moral obligation depends on the helper's wealth and the receiver's poverty.

Disregarding the cultural content of moral concepts can lead to pernicious conclusions. A gangster who dutifully killed people whom the gang leaders had targeted might be categorized as recognizing a social contract, keeping promises, or even interpersonal trust. He would be classified as stage 3 or 4 on Kohlberg's scale. However, this abstract classification would disregard the immoral homicidal nature of his behavior. Abstract, a priori categories leave us with very little insight into people's view of the moral order (Shweder & Much, 1987, p. 226).

An important difference between the structuralist and cultural–psychological approach to morality is the way immoral thinking is explained and corrected. If cultural concepts mediate children's moral codes, the latter can become more socially and personally responsible by altering their conceptual basis. For example, if we find that the cultural concept of competition justifies children's loose moral code concerning classmates (e.g., "I didn't help her understand the material because I wanted her to do worse than me on the test"), this concept can be critiqued and replaced.

In contrast, Kohlberg's structuralist approach attributes immoral judgments to developmental retardation. Young children's inferior moral reasoning is accepted as natural for their age. They are just too young to achieve a higher level. The structuralist approach is child centered and protective (passive) with regard to young children. Older children who produce inferior moral judgments would be regarded as developmentally impaired (for some reason) and they would be taught abstract ideas such as social goodness and individual rights. However, the effectiveness of this strategy is questionable because content is ignored. Even if older children learn the value of respecting individual rights, they may concretize such abstract notions with very immoral content, as illustrated in the foregoing examples. To enhance moral thinking and action, content must be emphasized. That is, children must be taught specific concepts of cooperation, compassion, altruism and justice.

Cultural psychology is interested in discovering the ages at which children learn concrete cultural concepts that generate particular moral evaluations. For example, when do children acquire the concept that inflating the price of medicine and making it unaffordable to people is wrong? When do children learn that promises to friends and relatives should be kept while promises to strangers are not so important? When do they learn that human rights apply to certain kinds of people but not to others? When do they learn particular concepts about what constitutes the social good?

Leahy's (1990) study of the development of concepts of economic and social inequality in children is germane to the current study of the development of moral concepts. Leahy found that young children (ages 6–11) explained wealth and poverty primarily in terms of social–structural or political factors such as differences in possessions and inheritance. Between ages 11 and 17, children explained inequality as due to psychological causes (individual factors) such as effort and intelligence (see Leahy, 1983 for additional examples of developmental trends in children's conceptions of social issues). The situations in which children learn cultural concepts are also important to study.

The cultural–psychological approach draws on the work of sociologists such as Durkheim and Weber which linked morality to worldviews. Durkheim maintained that belief systems not only make things intelligible by understanding and explaining their relationships; belief systems also prescribe the ways that things should be and the manner in which people should act to make these outcomes occur. This prescriptive function of belief systems comprises moral judgments.

Durkheim further linked moral judgments to social activity. He argued that people who live in societies with different degrees of division of labor have different worldviews. Their different worldviews, in turn, give rise to different forms of moral reasoning. According to Durkheim, members of societies with a low degree of division of labor identify strongly with each other. This "collective consciousness" leads to an understanding of moral laws as transcendent, absolute, and inviolable, and of moral transgressions as subject to "repressive" punishment driven by the need for revenge. In societies with a high degree of division of labor, collective consciousness diminishes and members see individual differences as salient. This leads to an emphasis on individual rights and "restitutory" punishment primarily aimed at restoring societal order rather than inflicting painful suffering on the transgressor (Jensen, 1997, pp. 326–327).

Morality ultimately depends on social systems. This is the fundamental insight of cultural psychology.

PROCEDURE

This study seeks to empirically elucidate cultural concepts that underlie children's moral reasoning. I undertake this by introducing cultural issues into Kohlberg's scenarios. For example, in the famous story of Heinz stealing medicine for his dying wife, I will ask whether he should steal for his wife, a stranger, an important person, and a pet. The responses to these cultural issues reveal cultural distinctions and concepts. If a subject says that Heinz should steal for his wife but not for a stranger, because stealing is justified only to protect strong personal bonds, we can see that the subject is invoking a cultural distinction between family members and strangers. She is valuing personal bonds over social laws against stealing. Varying the issues in the stories (e.g., wife, stranger) enables us to see which variations make a difference to moral judgments. I do not simply ask for simple, discrete responses such as, Should Heinz steal or not? I ask subjects to explain *why* they offer different moral judgments to different issues/situations. The explanations contain cultural concepts about the issues, for example, what it is about family relationships that justifies stealing and what about strangers does not justify stealing.

In my procedure, the researcher structures the interview around preconceived cultural issues such as wife, stranger, pet. This ensures that, with appropriate probing, the subjects will express cultural concepts about these issues. A less structured format that employed general questions about morality—such as "Please tell me what you think Heinz should do," or "What are the issues that affect your moral judgments?"—would undoubtedly fail to elicit specific cultural concepts such as "Personal bonds supercede social laws against stealing; however, casual relationships among strangers do not." Such concepts are not uppermost in peoples' minds and would not be spontaneously expressed. Social concepts need to be specifically elicited, as we have seen in Chap. 3. Of course, preselecting cultural issues limits them to a fairly arbitrary set. To compensate for this limitation I shall employ two stories to present additional issues and elucidate additional concepts that may underlie moral judgments. Of course, additional research is encouraged to elucidate additional concepts.

One point of interest in this study is whether different concepts are at play in older and younger children, and in boys and girls. Consequently, subjects will be six 8-year-old boys, six 8-year-old girls, six 15-year-old boys, and six 15-year-old girls. The rationale for these two age groups is that Kohlberg (1963, p. 16) found a dramatic shift in moral codes at 10 years of age. My age groups will straddle this age to ascertain whether cultural concepts about morality manifest the same dramatic shift that Kohlberg found. All subjects are Caucasian, middle-class children matched for family income to eliminate confounding effects of social class and ethnicity. Other ethnicities and classes will be explored in later studies.

The younger subjects will be asked only one of the stories, but the older subjects will be asked both.

Because each subject will be asked a number of hypothetical questions that constitute different versions of the stories (wife, stranger, pet), this research is a repeated measures design. To avoid practice effects and order effects, the order of the stories and the questions (or versions of each story) must be counterbalanced or asked in a different order.

To elucidate the social concepts underlying morality, I utilize specific procedures for interviewing the subjects and for analyzing their responses, which have been described in Chaps. 4 and 5. Because I have preselected the issues of the study, the questions call for limited responses that are fairly easy to interpret. It is therefore possible to utilize a limited form of phenomenological analysis to content-analyze children's statements. It is not necessary to use the full phenomenological method described in Chap. 5 to explicate the concepts.

From a pilot study, I learned that many American children conflated morality with practical and legal issues. Although they were asked to explain whether certain actions were morally correct, they actually discussed whether actions were practical or legal to do. They frequently said that Heinz should not steal the medicine because he might get caught. They failed to consider moral principles as such. Consequently, I tried to encourage subjects to focus on morality, not on legality or practicality. I specifically instructed them to focus on morality in the introductory material I read. I also asked them to explain what they meant by morality and whether it was similar to or different from practical/legal. My goal was to help the subjects (Ss) clarify for themselves what morality is; then they could use this notion in answering the questions. After most questions I asked whether their answers referred to moral issues as opposed to practical–legal ones.

I also altered the wording of many of Kohlberg's questions. He used terms such as "Is it important to do …?" or "Should X do …?" He rarely used the term "moral" in his questions. I am sure that the absence of the term "moral" allowed Kohlberg's Ss to confuse legal/practical issues with moral ones. I believe that much of Kohlberg's data expressed legal/practical thinking more than moral reasoning. I replaced "important" and "should" with "morally correct" to keep the issue of morality in the forefront of the Ss' thinking. And after each answer, I asked whether they had considered moral or legal/practical issues.

The pilot Ss' responses also made me alter, add, and delete several questions. Many of the pilot Ss thought Heinz was a peculiar name so I changed it to George.

Introduction to Subjects

"I am interested in the way in which young people of your age think about moral issues. I'm going to present two stories to you which deal with moral issues. Then I want to ask you a few questions to see how you think about these stories. I'm especially interested in what you think the proper action should be. I'm also very interested in the reasons you have for thinking this way. Since I want to understand your thinking I may ask some picky questions to clarify just what your reasons are. I'm not trying to doubt you or annoy you with these questions. I'm really trying to understand how you think. Sometimes the thoughts behind words are not easy to comprehend by someone who doesn't know you very well. This is why I may sometimes ask questions to clarify the underlying thoughts. Occasionally I will ask you to compare your answer on one question to that of another question. I may say, "Oh, you seem to be saying … Now, in another question you said … Do you mean the same thing in both cases or are you expressing a different thought/reason/principle?"

Before reading you the first story, I'd like to clarify what the word morality means to you. What makes something a moral problem? A specific question for you to consider is whether morality is the same as legality. In other words, is everything that is legal to do also moral, and is everything that is illegal also immoral? Are moral and legal synonymous or different? Similarly, do you think that moral is the same as practical? In other words, if something is not practical to do—if it is risky or difficult, for example—then is it also immoral? Conversely, if something is practical is it moral? Are the two similar or different?

As you answer the questions to the stories, I may occasionally repeat these questions so that I can clarify how you think about moral issues."

Kohlberg's Story No. 3 (Kohlberg, 1984)

In Europe, a woman was near death from a particular form of cancer. There was one drug that the doctors thought might save her. It was a form of radium that a druggist in the same town had recently discovered. The drug was expensive to make, but the druggist was charging ten times what the drug cost him to make. He paid $400 for the radium and charged $4000 for a small dose of the drug. The sick woman's husband, George, went to everyone he knew to borrow the money and tried every legal means, but he could get together only about $2000, which is half of what it cost. He told the druggist that his wife was dying, and asked him to sell it cheaper or let him pay later, but the druggist said, "No, I discovered the drug and I'm going to make money from it." So, having tried every legal means, George becomes desperate and considers breaking into the man's store to steal the drug for his wife.

1. Please tell me the right and wrong actions of each person in the story.
2. Is it moral for George to steal the drug? Why or why not?
3. If George doesn't love his wife, is it moral for him to steal the drug for her? (Does it make a difference in what George should do whether or not he loves his wife?) Why or why not?
4. Suppose the person dying is not his wife but a stranger. No one else can get the medicine for this person. Is it moral for George to steal the drug for the stranger? Why or why not?
5. If the dying person was an important member of society, or an especially kind person, would that make it morally correct to steal the drug in order to help her? Or if she were cruel would that make it less morally correct to steal for her?
6. Suppose it's a pet animal he loves. Is it moral for George to steal to save the pet animal? Why or why not?
7. It is against the law for George to steal. Does this mean that it is immoral for George to steal it to save his dying wife? Why or why not? Is illegal synonymous with immoral?
8. The druggist inflates the price of the drug and made exorbitant profit from it. Is it morally right or not for George to steal the drug since the price was inflated?

George did break into the store. He stole the drug and gave it to his wife. George was arrested and brought to court. The jury finds George guilty. It is up to the judge to determine the sentence. The judge knows that George's wife is dying and needs the drug but can't afford it.

9. Is it moral for the judge to consider the wife is ill and has little money in his sentencing? Is it moral that he give George some sentence, or should he suspend the sentence and let George go free? Why is that best?

The issues involved in the questions of George are:

- Morality of saving a family member vs. obeying laws against stealing (1, 6, 8)
- Stranger (3)
- Pet animal (5)
- Love for wife (2)
- Inflating the price to earn exorbitant profit (7)
- Qualities of the dying person (4)

Kohlberg's Story No. 2 (Kohlberg, 1984)

Judy was a 12-year-old girl. Her mother promised her that she could go to a special rock concert coming to their town if she saved up from babysitting and lunch money to buy a ticket to the concert. She managed to save up the $15.00 the ticket cost plus another $5.00. But then her mother changed her mind and told Judy that she had to spend the money on new clothes for school. Judy was disappointed and decided to go to the concert anyway. She bought a ticket and told her mother that she had only been able to save $5.00. That Saturday she went to the performance and told her mother that she was spending the day with a friend. A week passed without her mother finding out. Judy then told her older sister, Louise, that she had gone to the performance and had lied to her mother about it. Louise wonders whether to tell their mother what Judy did.

1. Please tell me the right and wrong actions of each person in the story.
2. The mother promised Judy she could go to the concert if she earned the money. Was it morally right for Judy to go because her mother originally agreed?
3. Does the mother's breaking her promise justify Judy's lying and going to the concert.
4. Was it morally right for the mother to break her promise and request Judy spend the money on clothes?

5. Does the fact that Judy earned the money herself justify disregarding her mother and lying to her? Why or why not?

6. If Judy's uncle had given her the money (instead of her earning it) should she be allowed to use it as she wishes or should she have to give it to her mother? In other words, does earning money vs. receiving it as a gift affect the morality of the mother's request?

7. Is it morally necessary to keep a promise to someone you don't know well and probably won't see again? Why or why not? How about to a family member? Why/why not?

8. Does Judy's mother have the moral right to control the way she spends money?

9. Is it moral for Louise, the older sister, tell their mother that Judy lied about the money or should she keep quiet? Why?

10. In wondering whether to tell, Louise thinks of the fact that Judy is her sister. Should that make a difference in Louise's decision?

11. Is it more or less moral for Louise to tell on her sister than on a friend or stranger? Why or why not?

12. Does telling have anything to do with being a morally good daughter? Why or why not?

13. If the family was poor and mother needed the money for basic goods can the mother require Judy to use the money for that, instead of using it to go to the concert?

14. If Judy had committed a crime—rather than lied to her mother—should Louise have told her mother?

Issues in the questions of Judy are:

- Relationship of mother's promise to Judy's behavior (1, 2, 3)
- Right to spend earned money (4)
- Right to spend earned money vs. gift (5)
- Promise to stranger vs. to close relative (6)
- Mother's authority over daughter's spending money (7)
- Loyalty to Judy vs. telling truth to mother (8, 11)
- Informing on a sister (9)
- Informing on a stranger (10)
- Poverty (12)
- Different infractions (13)

Interview procedures will carefully probe subjects to articulate their cultural concepts. If a child says that it's wrong for George to steal the drug for anyone, including his wife, then we should probe the social concept that underlies, or mediates, this idea. "Why should everyone adhere to the same moral standard? Why shouldn't we allow certain people in special relationships or situations to break a law?" If S says, "because we should treat everyone alike" this is a social concept. We might ask, "Why?" to get more detail, and we might be told "because it doesn't matter how you differ from other people in terms of your relationship or position; all people have the same rights and the same feelings—therefore, acting immorally towards one kind of person will make him feel bad (e.g., stealing from George will make him unhappy)." This answer indicates a specific social concept about human nature, that everyone has similar feelings and will feel bad when hurt. Individual differences are superceded by similar feelings/needs.

If a subject says that X should be severely punished for committing a serious crime and cause suffering, the interviewer should explore the reasoning behind this judgment. "Why should committing a crime be met with a serious punishment?" "What is the point of punishment?" "Is there a principle of exchange/equity such that causing a given amount of suffering should receive an equal amount of suffering in the form of punishment?"

If the subject says X should be punished because he deliberately caused suffering, the interviewer should ask about intention and responsibility as a value for assessing crime: "Why is it important that X deliberately hurt someone as opposed to accidentally hurting him? Why does deliberateness raise the seriousness of the crime?" What does this tell us about the subject's concept of action, suffering, agency?

In addition to asking subjects to explain particular responses, the experimenter should ask subjects to compare responses. If a subject says it's alright to steal for a family member but in another place says it's wrong to steal for a stranger, it's important to ask for an explanation for the differences. This explanation will reveal a concept—for example, a family helps one so it's important to protect the family, whereas strangers rarely help so it's not so important to protect them.

Another valuable source of cultural concepts is probing contradictory responses. "Earlier you said that Louise should not tell her mother because it would break the trust with Judy. Now you say that Louise can tell her mother if she did not explicitly promise not to tell her. Which principle is more important?"

The point is to try to discover concepts about the nature of people, things, social relationships, etc. The experimenter must continually ask himself after every question, "Did the subject indicate a definite concept?" If the answer is yes, the experimenter paraphrases it to the subject to ensure that this is what the latter means: "Are you saying that the mother's breaking her promise justified the daughter's lying?" If the experimenter is not convinced that a definite cultural concept has been expressed, he should ask additional questions to elicit such. This requires practice to identify concepts and probe for them.

RESULTS

Results will consist in six kinds of data:

1. Data for each subject that presents each issue in a story (wife, stranger), the behavior that is deemed morally appropriate (steal, don't steal), and the reasons for its appropriateness (stealing will help the wife more than hurt the drug store; stealing is wrong because it hurts other people; don't steal because he might get caught). The reasons for the action are cultural concepts. One subject may give several reasons for an action, and several subjects may give the same reason.

Subjects' responses to the story of George are summarized in Table 6.1.

TABLE 6.1. DATA TABLE FOR THE STORY OF GEORGE

Issue	Morally appropriate action/No. of Ss	Cultural concepts: reason the action is appropriate
Wife	Steal	
Wife	Don't steal:	
Unloved wife	Steal	
Unloved wife	Don't steal:	
Stranger	Steal	
Stranger	Don't steal:	
Profit	Don't steal:	
Profit	Steal	
Negative qualities of the patient	Steal	
Negative qualities of the patient	Don't steal	
Positive qualities of patient	Steal	
Positive qualities of the patient	Don't steal:	
Pet	Steal	
Pet	Don't steal	
Judge	No leniency	
Judge	Leniency: Fine, not jail:	
Legal = moral	No:	
Legal = moral	Yes:	

Subjects' responses to the story of Judy are summarized in Table 6.2.

2. For each issue, the number of subjects who advocate a certain action (e.g., 14 Ss approved of stealing to help the stranger, 10 Ss disapproved of stealing to help the stranger).

3. For each issue, the number of subjects who give a particular reason for why a behavior should be undertaken.

4. Eight year olds will be compared with 15-year-olds on the behaviors and reasons that are endorsed.

5. Boys and girls will be compared regarding the behaviors and reasons that are endorsed.

TABLE 6.2. DATA TABLE FOR THE STORY OF JUDY

Issue	Morally appropriate action/no. of Ss	Cultural concepts: reason the action is appropriate
Mom breaks promise.	J. can't go or lie.	
Mom breaks promises.	J. can go and lie.	
Daughter's right to spend earned money	Shouldn't go to concert.	
Daughter's right to spend earned money	Can go to concert.	
If $ was a gift	Don't go to concert.	
If $ was a gift	Go to concert.	
Promise to stranger vs. relative	Don't break promise to either one.	
Promise to stranger vs. relative	Can break promise to stranger.	
Mother's authority over $	Can't go to concert.	
Mother's authority over $	Can go to concert.	
L's loyalty to J. vs. telling truth	Don't tell mom.	
L's loyalty to J. vs. telling truth	Tell mom.	
Tell on sister	Tell mom.	
Tell on sister	Don't tell mom.	
Tell on stranger	Don't tell.	
Tell on stranger	Tell.	
Poverty	J. can't go to concert.	
Poverty	J. can go to concert.	
Serious crime	Tell.	
Serious crime	Don't Tell.	

6. The number of subjects who did not discuss moral issues and who responded in terms of practical/legal or other considerations. The nonmoral reasons they give are calculated. If a large percentage of Ss replace moral principles with practical thinking, despite the interviewer's diligent effort to keep the focus on moral issues, this would indicate an important trend in the social evolution of morality.

Notes

1. Gilligan's insistence on gender differences altogether is dubious. Seventeen cross-cultural studies conducted in 15 countries compared male and female subjects on moral reasoning, and 14 of these 17 studies found no significant sex differences. In contrast, 10 of 11 studies found class differences in moral reasoning (Snarey, 1985, p. 218).

REFERENCES

Barber, B. (1984). *Strong democracy: Participatory politics for a new age*. Berkeley: University of California Press.

Bartlett, F.C. (1932/1967). *Remembering: A study in experimental and social psychology*. New York: Cambridge University Press.

Baxandall, M. (1988). *Painting and experience in fifteenth-century Italy*. New York: Oxford University Press.

Belek, I. (2000). Social class, income, education, area of residence, and psychological distress: Does social class have an independent effect on psychological distress in Antalya, Turkey? *Social Psychiatry and Psychiatric Epidemiology, 35*, 94–101.

Bergesen, A. (1993). The rise of semiotic Marxism. *Sociological Perspectives, 36*, 1–22.

Bhaskar, R. (1989). *The possibility of naturalism: A philosophical critique of the contemporary human sciences* (second edition). New York: Harvester Weatsheaf.

Blumer, H. (1969). Fashion: From class differentiation to collective selection. *Sociological Quarterly, 10*, 275–291.

Bordo, S. (1993). *Unbearable weight: Feminism, Western culture, and the body*. Berkeley: University of California Press.

Bourdieu, P. (1977). *Outline of a theory of practice*. New York: Cambridge University Press.

Bourdieu, P. (1978). Sport and social class. *Social Science Information, 17*, 819–840.

Bourdieu, P. (1990a). *In other words: Essays toward a reflexive sociology*. Stanford: Stanford University Press.

Bourdieu, P. (1990b). *The logic of practice*. Stanford: Stanford University Press.

Bourdieu, P. (1993). The field of cultural production. New york: Columbia University Press.

Bourdieu, P. (1996). *The rules of art: Genesis and structure of the literary field*. Stanford: Stanford University Press.

Bourdieu, P. (1998a). *On television*. New York: New Press.

Bourdieu, P. (1998b). *Practical reason*. Stanford: Stanford University Press.

Bourdieu, P. (2000). *Pascalian meditations*. Stanford: Stanford University Press.

Branco, A., & Valsiner, J. (1997). Changing methodologies: A co-constructionist study of goal orientations in social interactions. *Psychology and Developing Societies, 9*, 35–64.

Brandist, C. (2000). Neo-Kantianism in cultural theory: Bakhtin, Derrida, and Foucault. *Radical Philosophy, 102*, 6–16.

Briggs, C. (1983). Questions for the ethnographer: A critical examination of the role of the interview in fieldwork. *Semiotica, 46*, 233–261.

Brison, K. (1998). Giving sorrow new words: Shifting politics of bereavement in a papua new Guinea village. *Ethos, 26*, 363–386.

205

Brooks-Gunn, J., Kelbanov, P., & Duncan, G. (1996). Ethnic differences in children's intelligence test scores: Role of economic deprivation, home environment, and maternal characteristics. *Child Development, 67,* 396–408.

Brown, A., Susser, E., Jandorf, L., & Bromet, E. (2000). Social class of origin and cardinal symptoms of schizophrenic disorders over the early illness course. *Social Psychiatry and Psychiatric Epidemiology, 35,* 53–60.

Bruner, J. (March 9, 2000). Jot talk. *New York Review of Books,* pp. 27–30.

Bruner, J. (1982). The language of education. *Social Research, 49,* 835–853.

Bruner, J., & Amsterdam, A. (2000). *Minding the law.* Cambridge: Harvard University Press.

Capps, L., & Ochs, E. (1995). *Constructing panic: The discourse of agoraphobia.* Cambridge: Harvard University Press.

Capshew, J. (1999). *Psychologists on the march: Science, practice, and professional identity in America, 1929–1969.* Cambridge: Cambridge University Press.

Cayton, M. (1997). Who were the Evangelicals?: Conservative and liberal identity in the Unitarian controversy in Boston, 1804–1833. *Journal of Social History, 31,* 85–108.

Chao, R. (1995). Chinese and American cultural models of self reflected in mothers' child-drearing beliefs. *Ethos, 23,* 328–354.

Ci, J. (1999a). Justice, freedom, and the moral bounds of capitalism. *Social Theory and Practice, 25,* 409–438.

Ci, J. (1999b). Disenchantment, desublimation, and demoralization: Some cultural conjunctions of capitalism. *New Literary History, 30,* 295–324.

Costa, P., McCrae, R., & Dembroski, T. (1989). Agreeableness versus antagonism: Explication of a potential risk factor for CHD. In A. Siegman & T. Dembrowski (Eds.), *In search of coronary-prone behavior: Beyond type A* (pp. 41–63). Hillsdale, NJ: Lawrence Erlbaum.

Cott, N. (2000). *Public Vows.* Boston: Harvard University Press.

Cressy, D. (1983). The environment for literacy: Accomplishment and context in seventeenth-century England and New England. In D. Resnick (Ed.), *Literacy in historical perspective* (pp. 23–42). Washington, DC: Library of Congress.

Creswell, J. (1998). *Qualitative inquiry and research design: Choosing among five traditions.* Thousand Oaks, CA: Sage.

Cushman, P. (1991). Ideology obscured: Political uses of self in Daniel Stern's infant. *American Psychologist, 46,* 206–219.

Daly, K. (2001). Reconstructing family time: From ideology to lived experience. *Journal of Marriage and Family, 63,* 283–294.

D'Andrade, R. (1987). A folk model of the mind. In D. Holland & N. Quinn (Eds.), *Cultural models in language and thought* (pp. 112–148). New York: Cambridge University Press.

Derne, S. (1994). Hindu men talk about controlling women: Cultural ideas as a tool of the powerful. *Sociological Perspectives, 37,* 203–227.

Dewey, J. (1910). *The influence of Darwin on philosophy and other essays on contemporary thought.* New York: Holt.

Dobb, M. (1963). *Studies in the development of capitalism.* New York: International.

Durkheim, E. (1953). Individual and collective representations. In E. Durkheim, *Sociology and philosophy* (pp. 1–34). Glencoe, II: Free Press. (Originally published 1898)

Durkheim, E. (1995). *The elementary forms of religious life.* New York: Free Press. (Originally published 1915)

Eckert, P. (1989). *Jocks and burnouts.* New York: Teachers College Press.

Edwards, D. (1999). Emotion discourse. *Culture and Psychology, 5,* 271–291.

Emirbayer, M., & Mische, A. (1998). What is agency? *American Journal of Sociology, 103,* 962–1023.

Engestrom, Y. (1993). Developmental studies of work as a testbench of activity theory: The case of primary care medical practice. In S. Chaiklin & J. Lave (Eds.), *Understanding practice: Perspectives on activity and context* (pp. 64–103). New York: Cambridge University Press.

Ermarth, M. (1981). The transformation of hermeneutics: 19th century and 20th century moderns. *The Monist, 64(2)*, 175–194.

Exoo, C. (1994). *The politics of the mass media.* Minneapolis: West.

Fabrega, H. (1989) On the significance of an anthropological approach to schizophrenia. *Psychiatry, 52*, 45–65.

Fischer, C. & Wertz, F. (1979). Empirical phenomenological analyses of being criminally victimized. In A. Giorgi, R. Knowles, & D. Smith (Eds.), *Duquesne studies in phenomenological psychology* (vol. 3, pp. 135–158). Pittsburgh: Duquesne University Press.

Flick, U. (1998a). *The psychology of the social.* New York: Cambridge University Press.

Flick, U. (1998b). *An introduction to qualitative research.* Thousand Oaks, CA: Sage.

Fowler, W. (1986). Early experiences of great men and women mathematicians. In W. Fowler (Ed.), *Early experience and the development of competence* (pp. 87–109). San Francisco: Jossey-Bass.

Garbarino, J., Kostelny, K., & Barry, F. (1997). Value transmission in an ecological context: The high-risk neighborhood. In J. Grusec & L. Kuczynski (Eds.), *Parenting and children's internalization of values* (pp. 307–332). New York: John Wiley & Sons.

Gardner, H. (Oct. 19, 2000). Paroxysms of choice. *New York Review of Books*, pp. 44–49.

Gartman, D. (2000). Why modern architecture emerged in Europe, not America: The new class and the aesthetics of technocracy. *Theory, Culture, and Society, 17*, 75–96.

Garvey, E. (1996). *The adman in the parlor: Magazines and the gendering of consumer culture, 1880s to 1910s.* New York: Oxford University Press.

Gaudio, R. (1998). Male lesbians and other queer notions in Hausa. In S. Murray & W. Roscoe (Eds.), *Boy-wives and female husbands: Studies of African homosexualities* (pp. 115–128). New York: St. Martin's.

Gauvain, M. (1993). The development of spatial thinking in everyday activity. *Developmental Review, 13*, 92–121.

Gauvain, M. (1998a). Historical footprints of psychological activity. *Cross-Cultural Psychology Bulletin, 32(3)*, 10–15.

Gauvain, M. (1998b). Cognitive development in social and cultural context. *Current Directions in Psychological Science, 7*, 188–192.

Gee, J. (1992). *The social mind: Language, ideology, and social practice.* New York: Bergin & Gervey.

Gee, J. (1999). *An introduction to discourse analysis: Theory and method.* New York: Routledge.

Gerris, J., Dekovic, M., & Janssens, J. (1997). The relationship between social class and childrearing behaviors: Parents' perspective taking and value orientations. *Journal of Marriage and the Family, 59*, 834–847.

Gerth, H., & Mills, C. W. (1953). *Character and social structure: The psychology of social institutions.* New York: Harcourt, Brace.

Giddens, A. (1987). *Social theory and modern sociology.* Stanford: Stanford University Press.

Giddens, A. (1995). *Politics, sociology, and social theory.* Stanford: Stanford University Press.

Gilligan, C. (1982). *In a different voice: Psychological theory and women's development.* Cambridge: Harvard University Press.

Giorgi, A. (1975a). Convergence and divergence of qualitative and quantitative methods in psychology. In A. Giorgi, C. Fischer, & E. Murray (Eds.), *Duquesne studies in phenomenological psychology* (vol. 2, pp. 72–79). Atlantic Highlands: Humanities Press.

Giorgi, A. (1975b). An application of phenomenological method in psychology. In A. Giorgi, C. Fischer, & E. Murray (Eds.), *Duquesne studies in phenomenological psychology* (vol. 2, pp. 82–103). Atlantic Highlands: Humanities Press.

Giorgi, A. (1994). A phenomenological perspective on certain qualitative research methods. *Journal of Phenomenological Psychology, 25*, 190–220.

Goldhagen, D. (1996). *Hitler's willing executioners: Ordinary Germans and the holocaust.* New York: Knopf.

Goldstein, L. (1988). *The social and cultural roots of linear perspective.* Minneapolis: MEP.

Gould, S. J. (Sept. 2000). Linnaeus's luck. *Natural History,* 18–76.

Greenblatt, S. (1999). The touch of the real. In S. Ortner (Ed.), *The fate of "culture": Geertz and beyond* (pp. 14–29). Berkeley: University of California Press.

Grogan, S. (2000). *Body image: Understanding body dissatisfaction in men, women, and children.* London: Routledge.

Hacking, I. (1999). *The social construction of what?* Cambridge: Harvard University Press.

Hadden, R. (1994). *On the shoulders of merchants: Exchange and the mathematical conception of nature in early modern Europe.* Albany: State University of New York Press.

Halliwell, R. (1998). *The Mozart family.* New York: Oxford University Press.

Harre, R. (1984). Some reflections on the concept of "social representation." *Social Research, 51*(4), 927–938.

Harrington, A. (2000). Objectivism in hermeneutics? *Philosophy of the Social Sciences, 30*(4), 491–508.

Harris, T., Brown, G., & Bifulco, A. (1987). Loss of parent in childhood and adult psychiatric disorder: The role of social class position and premarital pregnancy. *Psychological Medicine, 17,* 163–183.

Hartmann, M. (2000). Class-specific habitus and the social reproduction of the business elite in Germany and France. *Sociological Review, 48*(2), 241–261.

Haskell, T. (1985). Capitalism and the origins of the humanitarian sensibility. *American Historical Review, 90,* 547–566.

Higgins, A., Power, C., & Kohlberg, L. (1984). The relationship of moral atmosphere to judgments of responsibility. In W. Kurtines & J. Gewirtz (Eds.), *Morality, moral behavior, and moral development* (pp. 74–106). New York: John Wiley & Sons.

Hogan, R., & Emler, N. (1978). The biases in contemporary social psychology. *Social Research, 45,* 478–534.

Holland, D., Lachicotte, W., Skinner, D., & Cain, C. (1998). *Identity and agency in cultural worlds.* Cambridge: Harvard University Press.

Horwitz, M. (1977). *The transformation of American law, 1780–1860.* Cambridge: Harvard University Press.

House, J. (1981). Social structure and personality. In M. Rosenbery & R. Turner (Eds.), *Social psychology: Sociological perspectives* (pp. 525–561). New York: Basic Books.

Howe, D. (1970). *The Unitarian conscience: Harvard moral philosophy, 1805–1861.* Cambridge: Harvard University Press.

Howe, M. J. A. (1999a). *The psychology of high abilities.* New York: New York University Press.

Howe, M. J. A. (1999b). *Genius explained.* New York: Cambridge University Press.

Hwang, K. K. (1998). Two moralities: Reinterpreting the findings of empirical research on moral reasoning in Taiwan. *Asian Journal of Social Psychology, 1,* 211–238.

Illouz, E. (1997). *Consuming the romantic utopia: Love and the cultural contradictions of capitalism.* Berkeley: University of California Press.

Jackson, N., & Oates, G. (1998). *Violence in intimate relationships.* Woburn, MA: Butterworth-Heinemann.

Jadhav, S. (1996). The cultural origins of depression. *International Journal of Social Psychiatry, 42,* 269–286.

Jensen, L. (1997). Different worldviews, different morals: America's culture war divide. *Human Development, 40,* 325–344.

Kandyoti, D. (1988). Bargaining with patriarchy. *Gender and Society, 2,* 274–290.

Kasson, J. (1990). *Rudeness and civility: Manners in nineteenth-century urban America.* New York: Hill & Wang.

Katz, E., & Lazarsfeld, P. (1955). *Personal influence: The part played by people in the flow of mass communications.* Glencoe, IL: Free Press.

Kaye, J. (1998). *Economy and nature in the fourteenth century: Money, market exchange, and the emergence of scientific thought.* New York: Cambridge University Press.

King, A. (2000). The accidental derogation of the lay actor: A critique of Giddens' concept of structure. *Philosophy of the Social Sciences, 30,* 362–383.

Kohlberg, L. (1963). The development of children's orientations toward a moral order. *Vita Humana, 6,* 11–33.

Kohlberg, L. (1981). *The philosophy of moral development.* New York: Harper.

Kohlberg, L. (1984). *The psychology of moral development.* New York: Harper.

Komarovsky, M. (1940/1955). The technique of "discerning." In P. Lazarsfeld & M. Rosenberg (Eds.), *The language of social research: A reader in the methodology of social research* (pp. 449–457). Glencoe, II: Free Press.

Kornhauser, A., & Lazarsfeld, P. (1935/1955). The analysis of consumer actions. In P. Lazarsfeld & M. Rosenberg (Eds.), *The language of social research: A reader in the methodology of social research* (pp. 392–420). Glencoe, II: Free Press.

Kulick, D. (1992). *Language shift and cultural reproduction: Socialization, self, and syncretism in a Papua New Guinea village.* New York: Cambridge University Press.

Kvale, S. (1996). *InterViews.* Thousand Oaks, CA: Sage.

Lazarsfeld, P. (1941/1955). Evaluating the effectiveness of advertising by direct interviews. In P. Lazarsfeld & M. Rosenberg (Eds.), *The language of social research: A reader in the methodology of social research* (pp. 411–419). Glencoe, III: Free Press.

Lazarsfeld, P. (1934/1972). The art of asking why? In *Qualitative analysis: Historical and critical essays* (pp. 183–202). Boston: Allyn & Bacon.

Lazarsfeld, P. (1944). The controversy over detailed interviews—An offer for negotiation. *Public Opinion Quarterly, 8,* 38–59.

Leach, W. (1980). *True love and perfect union: The feminist reform of sex and society.* New York: Basic Books.

Leach, W. (1993). *Land of desire: Merchants, power, and the rise of a new American culture.* New York: Pantheon.

Leahy, R. (1983). *The child's construction of social inequality.* New York: Academic Press.

Leahy, R. (1990). The development of concepts of economic and social inequality. In V. McLoyd & C. Flanagan (Eds.), *Economic stress: Effects on family life and child development* (pp. 107–120). San Francisco: Jossey-Bass.

Lears, T. J. (1985). The concept of cultural hegemony: Problems and possibilities. *American Historical Review, 90,* 567–593.

Leontiev, A. (1978). *Activity, consciousness, and personality.* Englewood Cliffs, NJ: Prentice-Hall.

Leontiev, A. (1979). The problem of activity in psychology. In J. Wertsch (Ed.), *The concept of activity in Soviet psychology* (pp. 37–71). Armonk, NY: Sharpe.

Leontiev, A. (1981). *Problems of the development of the mind.* Moscow: Progress.

Leo-Rhynie, E. (1997). Class, race, and gender issues in child rearing in the Caribbean. In J. Rooparine & J. Brown (Eds.), *Caribbean families: Diversity among ethnic groups* (pp. 25–56). Greenwich, CT: Ablex.

Leventhal, T., & Brooks-Gunn, J. (2000). The neighborhoods they live in: The effects of neighborhood residence on child and adolescent outcomes. *Psychological Bulletin, 126,* 309–337.

LeVine, R., Miller, P., Richman, A., & LeVine, S. (1996). Education and mother–infant interaction: A Mexican case study. In S. Harkness & C. Super (Eds.), *Parents' cultural belief systems: Their origins, expressions, and consequences* (pp. 254–269). New York: Guilford.

Lightfoot, C., & Valsiner, J. (1992). Parental belief systems under the influence: Social guidance of the construction of personal cultures. In I. Sigel, A. McGillicuddy-DeLisi, & J. Goodnow (Eds.), *Parental belief systems: The psychological consequences for children* (pp. 393–414). Hillsdale, NJ: Lawrence Erlbaum.

Likert, R. (1951). The sample interview survey as a tool of research and policy formation. In D. Lerner & H. Lasswell (Eds.), *The policy sciences: Recent developments in scope and method* (pp. 233–251). Stanford: Stanford University Press.

Linde, C. (2001). The acquisition of a speaker by a story: How history becomes memory and identify. *Ethos, 28,* 608–632.

Luker, K. (1984). *Abortion and the politics of motherhood.* Berkeley: University of California Press.

Luker, K. (1996). *Dubious conceptions: The politics of teenage pregnancy.* Cambridge: Harvard University Press.

Lystra, K. (1989). *Searching the heart: Women, men, and romantic love in nineteenth-century America.* New York: Oxford University Press.

Marcuse, H. (1964). *One-dimensional man.* Boston: Beacon.

Marcuse, H. (1987). *Hegel's ontology and the theory of historicity.* Cambridge: The MIT Press. (Originally published 1932)

Martin-Baro, I. (1994). *Writings for a liberation psychology.* Cambridge: Harvard University Press.

Marx, K., & Engels, F. (1975). *Collected works* (vol. 4). New York: International.

Merton, R. (1972). Insiders and outsiders: A chapter in the sociology of knowledge. *American Journal of Sociology, 78,* 9–47.

Matsuki, K. (2001). Negotiations of memory and agency in Japanese oral narrative accounts of wartime experiences. *Ethos, 28,* 534–550.

Mauss, M. (1938/1985). A category of the human mind: The motion of person; the motion of self. In M. Carrithers, S. Collins, & S. Lukes (Eds.), *The category of the person: Centhropology, philosophy, history* (pp. 1–25). New york: Cambridge University Press.

Mayfield, D., & Thorne, S. (1992). Social history and its discontents: Gareth Stedman Jones and the politics of language. *Social History, 17,* 165–188.

Maynard, A., Greenfield, P., & Childs, C. (1999). Culture, history, biology, and body: Native and non-native acquisition of technological skill. *Ethos, 27,* 379–402.

McChesney, R. (1999). *Rich media, poor democracy.* Champaign, IL: University of Illinois Press.

McCrae, R., Yik, M., Trapnell, P., Bond, M., & Paulhus, D. (1998). Interpreting personality profiles across cultures: Bilingual, acculturation, and peer rating studies of Chinese undergraduates. *Journal of Personality and Social Psychology, 74,* 1041–1055.

Merton, R. (1968). *Social theory and social structure.* New York: Free Press.

Merton, R., & Kendall, P. (1946). The focused interview. *American Journal of Sociology, 51,* 541–557.

Miles, M., & Huberman, A. (1994). *Qualitative data analasis: An expanded source book.* Thousand Oaks, CA: Soge.

Miller, J., & Bersoff, D. (1992). Culture and moral judgement: How are conflicts between justice and interpersonal responsibilities resolved? *Journal of Personality and Social Psychology, 62,* 541–554.

Miller, J., Bersoff, D., & Harwood, L. (1990). Perceptions of social responsibilities in India and in the United States: Moral imperatives or personal decisions. *Journal of Personality and Social Psychology, 58,* 330–47.

Mirowsky, J., & Ross, C. (1989). *Social causes of psychological distress.* New York: de Gruyter.

Mishler, E. (1986). *Research interviewing: Context and narrative.* Cambridge: Harvard University Press.

Nadel, S. (1952). Witchcraft in four African societies: An essay in comparison. *American Anthropologist, 54,* 18–29.

Nadel, S. (1957). *The theory of social structure* Mleveoe: free Press.

Naoi, M., & Schooler, C. (1990). Psychological consequences of occupational conditions among Japanese wives. *Social Psychology Quarterly, 53,* 100–116.

Nisan, M. (1984). Content and structure in moral judgement: An integrative view. In W. Kurtines & J. Gewirtz (Eds.), *Morality, moral behavior, and moral development* (pp. 208–224). New York: John Wiley & Sons.

Nisbett, R., & Wilson, T. (1977). Telling more than we can know: Verbal reports on mental processes. *Psychological Review, 84,* 231–259.

Noble, D. (1998). Selling academe to the technology industry. *Thought and Action (The National Educational Association Journal), 14*(1), 29–40.

Norenzayan, A., & Nisbett, R. (2000). Culture and causal cognition. *Current Directions in Psychological Science, 9,* 132–135.

Nunner-Winkler, G. (1994). The growth of moral motivation. *Moral Education Forum, 10,* 8–20.

Ogbu, J. (1987). Opportunity structure, cultural boundaries, and literacy. In J. A. Langer (Ed.), *Language, literacy, and culture: Issues of society and schooling* (pp. 149–177). Norwood, NJ: Ablex.

Ogbu, J., & Stern, P. (2001). Class status and intellectual development. In R. Sternberg & E. Mrigorenko (Eds.), *Environmental effects on cognitive abilities* (pp. 3–37). Mahwah, NJ: Lawrence Erlbaum.

Ohmann, R. (1996). *Selling culture: Magazines, markets, and class at the turn of the century.* New York: Verso.

Oyserman, D., & Markus, H. (1998). Self as social representation. In U. Flick (Ed.), *The psychology of the social* (pp. 107–125). New York: Cambridge University Press.

Pelton, L. (1994). The role of material factors in child abuse and neglect. In G. Melton & F. Barry (Eds.), *Protecting children from abuse and neglect* (pp. 131–181). New York: Guilford.

Pendergast, T. (2000). *Creating the modern man: American magazines and consumer culture 1900–1950.* Columbia, MO: University of Missouri Press.

Phillips, D. C. (2000). *The expanded social scientist's bestiary: A guide to fabled threats to, and defenses of, naturalistic social science.* Lanham, MD: Rowman & Littlefield.

Porter, R. (2000). *The creation of the modern world: The untold story of the British Enlightenment.* New York: Norton.

Powell, W., & DiMaggio, P. (1991). *The new institutionalism in organizational analysis.* Chicago: University of Chicago Press.

Prasad, M. (1999). The morality of market exchange: Love, money, and contractual justice. *Sociological Perspectives, 42,* 181–214.

Ratner, C. (1991). *Vygotsky's sociohistorical psychology and its contemporary applications.* New york: Plenum.

Ratner, C. (1993a). Review of D'Andrade and Strauss, Human motives and cultural models. *Journal of Mind and Behavior, 14,* 89–94.

Ratner, C., (1993b). Contributions of sociohistorical psychology and phenomenology to research methodology. In H. Stam, L. Moss, W. Thorngate, & B. Kaplan (Eds.), *Recent trends in theoretical psychology* (vol. 3, pp. 503–510). New York: Springer-Verlag.

Ratner, C. (1994). The unconscious: A perspective from sociohistorical psychology. *Journal of Mind and Behavior, 15,* 323–342.

Ratner, C. (1997a). *Cultural psychology and qualitative methodology: Theoretical and empirical considerations.* New york: Plenum.

Ratner, C. (1997b). In defense of activity theory. *Culture and Psychology, 3,* 211–223.

Ratner, C. (1998). The historical and contemporary significance of Vygotsky's sociohistorical psychology. In R. Rieber & K. Salzinger (Eds.), *Psychology: Theoretical–historical perspectives* (pp. 455–474). Washington, DC: American Psychological Association.

Ratner, C. (1999). Three approaches to cultural psychology: A critique. *Cultural Dynamics, 11,* 7–31.

Ratner, C. (2000a). Outline of a coherent, comprehensive concept of culture. *Cross-Cultural Psychology Bulletin, 34*(1 & 2), 5–11.

Ratner, C. (2000b). A cultural–psychological analysis of emotions. *Culture and Psychology, 6*, 5–39.

Risman, B. (1987). Intimate relationships from a microstrutural perspective: Men who mother. *Gender and Society, 1*, 6–32.

Rogler, L. (1989). The meaning of culturally sensitive research in mental health. *American Journal of Psychiatry, 146*, 296–303.

Rohner, R. (1984). Toward a conception of culture for cross-cultural psychology. *Journal of Cross-Cultural Psychology, 15*, 111–138.

Roseberry, W. (1982). Balinese cockfights and the seduction of anthropology. *Social Research, 49*, 1013–1028.

Rothbaum, F., Weisz, J., Pott, M., Miyake, K., & Morelli, G. (2000) Attachment and culture. *American Psychologist, 55*, 1093–1104.

Saltman, K. (2000). *Collateral damage: Corporatizing public schools—A threat to democracy.* Lanham, MD: Rowman & Littlefield.

Sameroff, A., & Fiese, B. (1992). Family representations of development. In I. Sigel, A. McGillicuddy-DeLisi, & J. Goodnow (Eds.), *Parental belief systems: The psychological consequences for children* (pp. 347–369). Hillsdale, NJ: Lawrence Erlbaum.

Sameroff, A., Seifer, R., Barocas, R., Zax, M., & Greenspan, S. (1987). Intelligence quotient scores of 4-year old children: Social-environmental risk factors. *Pediatrics, 79*, 343–350.

Sartre, J-P. (1963). *Search for a method.* New York: Knopf.

Saxe, G. (1999). Cognition, development, and cultural practices. In E. Turiel (Ed.), *Development and cultural change: Reciprocal processes* (pp. 19–36). San Francisco: Jossey-Bass.

Schmidt, L. (1995). *Consumer rites: The buying and selling of American holidays.* Princeton: Princeton University Press.

Schooler, C. (2001). The intellectual effects of the demands of the work environment. In R. Sternberg & E. Mrigorenko (Eds.), *Environmental effects on cognitive abilities* (pp. 363–380). Mahwah, NJ: Lawrence Erlbaum associates.

Schutz, A. (1967), *Collected papers* (vol. 1). The Hague: Nijhoff.

Scribner, S. (1997). *Mind and social practice.* New York: Cambridge University Press.

Seeley, K. (2000). *Cultural psychotherapy.* Northvale, NJ: Aronson.

Seidman, S. (1991). *Romantic longings: Love in America, 1830–1980.* New York: Routledge.

Sherif, M., & Sherif, C. (1969). *Social psychology.* New York: Harper & Row.

Sherif, M., Harvey, O., White, J., Hood, W., & Sherif, C. (1988). *The Robber's Cave experiment: Intergroup conflict and cooperation.* Middletown, CT: Wesleyan University Press. (Originally published 1954).

Shweder, R., & Much, N. (1987). Determinations of meaning: Discourse and moral socialization. In W. Kurtines & J. Gewirtz (Eds.), *Moral development through social interaction* (pp. 197–244). New York: John Wiley & Sons.

Simpson, E. (1974). Moral development research: A case study of scientific cultural bias. *Human Development, 17*, 81–106.

Sklair, L. (1998). The transnational capitalist class and global capitalism: The case of the tobacco industry. *Political Power and Social Theory, 12*, 3–43.

Smail, J. (1994). *The origins of middle-class culture: Halifax, Yorkshire, 1660–1780.* Ithaca, NY: Cornell University Press.

Snarey, J. (1985). Cross-cultural universality of social-moral development: A critical review of Kohlbergian Research. *Psychological Bulletin, 97*, 202–232.

Sobel, M. (2000). *Teach me dreams: The search for self in the Revolutionary Era.* Princeton: Princeton University Press.

Southall, R. (1973). *Literature and the rise of capitalism.* London: Lawrence & Wishart.

Spring, J. (1998). *Education and the rise of the global economy*. Mahwah, NJ: Lawrence Erlbaum.

Stearns, P. (1993). Girls, boys, and emotions: Redefinitions and historical change. *Journal of American History, 80*, 36–74.

Stearns, P. (1997). *Fat history: Bodies, and beauty in the modern West*. New York: New York University Press.

Strauss, A. (1987). *Qualitative analysis for social scientists*. New York: Cambridge University Press.

Strauss, A., & Corbin, J. (1990). *Basics of qualitative research: Grounded theory procedures and techniques*. Newbury Park, CA: Sage.

Swartz, D. (1997). *Culture and power: The sociology of Pierre Bourdieu*. Chicago: University of Chicago Press.

Tappan, M., & Packer, M. (1991). *Narrative and storytelling: Implications for understanding moral development*. San Francisco: Jossey-Bass.

Tavris, C. (1992). *The mismeasure of woman*. New York: Simon & Schuster.

Thompson, E. P. (1967). Time, work-discipline, and industrial capitalism, *Past and Present, 38*, 56–97.

Thompson, J. (1990). *Ideology and modern culture*. Stanford: Stanford University Press.

Tomasello, M. (1994). On the interpersonal origins of self-concept. In U. Neisser (Ed.), *The perceived self: Ecological and interpersonal sources of self-knowledge* (pp. 174–184). New York: Cambridge University Press.

Tomasello, M. (1998). Social cognition and the evolution of culture. In J. Langer & M. Killen (Eds.), *Piaget, evolution, and development* (pp. 221–246). Hillsdale, NJ: Lawrence Erlbaum.

Tomasello, M. (1999). *The cultural origins of human cognition*. Cambridge: Harvard University Press.

Tomasello, M. (2000). Culture and cognitive development. *Current Directions in Psychological Science, 9*, 37–40.

Valsiner, J. (1998). *The guided mind: A sociogenetic approach to personality*. Cambridge: Harvard University Press.

Van der Veer, R., & Valsiner, J. (1994). *The Vygotsky reader*. Cambridge: Blackwell.

Vasconcellos, V., & Valsiner, J. (1998). Making of a personal place at 18 months of age. In M. Lyra & J. Valsiner (Eds.), *Construction of psychological processes in interpersonal communication* (pp. 85–101). Stamford, CT: Ablex.

Volosinov, V. (1973). *Marxism and the philosophy of language*. Cambridge: Harvard University Press. (Originally published 1929).

Vygotsky, L. S. (1971). *The psychology of art*. Cambridge: The MIT Press. (Originally published 1925)

Vygotsky, L. S. (1987). *Collected works* (vol. 1). New York: Plenum.

Vygotsky, L. S. (1997a). *Educational psychology*. Boca Raton, FL: St. Lucie Press. (Originally written 1921)

Vygotsky, L. S. (1997b). *Collected works* (vol. 3). New York: Plenum.

Vygotsky, L. S. (1998). *Collected works* (vol. 5). New York: Plenum.

Vygotsky, L. S. (1999). *Collected works* (vol. 6). New York: Plenum.

Werner, E. (April, 1989). Children of the garden island. *Scientific American, 260*, 106–111.

Wertsch, J. (1998). *Mind as action*. New York: Oxford University Press.

White, L. (1949). *The science of culture*. New york: Farrar, Straus.

Whitrow, G. (1973). Time and measurement. In P. Wiener (Ed.), *Dictionary of the history of ideas* (pp. 398–406). New York: Scribner's.

Williams, R. (1977). *Marxism and literature*. New York: Oxford University Press.

Wright, R. (1945). *Black boy*. New York: Harper & Row.

Zilsel, E. (2000). *The social origins of modern science*. Dordrecht, Netherlands: Kluwer.

INDEX

Abstract categories, 189n
Abstract features, 112, 189
Abstract stages, 191
Abstract terminology, 143, 175n
Abstract values, 189, 193
Advertisements, 37, 38, 45, 46
Alienation, 78, 90, 96
American social psychologists and sociologists, 142, 145, 156, 158
Antisemitism, 126
Architecture, 31–34, 68
Assertiveness, 39, 64, 68
Attachment, 110–112

Bhaskar, R., 16, 59
Blumer, H., 84
Body image, 37–40, 49–50
Bourdieu, P., 60-62, 67, 71, 85, 91, 98, 101
Bruner, J., 75–78, 81–83, 89, 97, 100

Central themes, 170n
Child rearing, 10, 12, 15, 17, 19–20, 23, 27, 30ff, 41, 45, 56, 70–73
Choice, 23
Choice, 84, 86
Clinical psychology, 6, 94
Clocks, 10, 32
Collective, 10, 12–13, 33–36
Commerce, 43, 52–53
Commodity, 15, 20, 34, 66
Competition, 22, 25, 40, 89, 92
Consistency of experience, 18n, 68
Context, 146, 149, 161
Conversation analysis, 108
Cooperation, 14, 25, 36, 46, 56, 71, 73

Creative agency, 63, 65, 66, 73
Critical realism, 101
Cross-cultural psychology, 106, 141
Cultural capital, 19
Cultural-psychological hypotheses, 109, 156

Definition of psychological issues, 109
Degrees of institutionalization, 13
Depression, 30, 50 51
Dewey, J., 3, 11, 47
Dilthey, W., 123, 134, 136
Discourse analysis, 70–71, 99, 127n
Diverse experience, 18n, 68, 72
Domestic violence, 30
Durkheim, E., 193

Eclecticism, 5
Education, 19, 20, 23, 27, 28–30, 43, 46, 55–56, 70–71, 74
Elites, 13, 19, 47
Emotions, 18, 30, 36, 44, 50 51, 56, 65
Ethnomethodology, 108
Experiments, 151, 164
Expert knowledge, 130n, 178
Exploratory studies, 109

Family, 93n
Formal thinking processes, 191
Frame of reference, 148–149
Free market, 13–15, 25, 33, 39, 42, 43, 48, 68, 71
Freud, S., 56–57

Gardner, H., 86
Gee, J., 19, 47, 56, 70, 127–129, 174, 177

Gender, 37–39, 116
General features of psychological phenomena,
    7, 12–14, 16, 22, 31, 42, 52, 107, 110, 139
Gerth, H., & Mills, C., 15, 16, 21, 36
Giddens, A., 100
Gilligan, C., 189
Goffman, E., 100, 108
Goldhagen, D., 113, 123n

Hegemony, 47
Hermeneutics, 122, 123, 129, 134, 136

Ideology, 11, 35, 41–42, 46, 48, 67, 85, 91, 152
Idiosyncratic traits, 86, 91n
Implications of an opinion, 148
Inconsistent responses, 149
Individual person, 12, 13, 14, 16, 18, 22, 36, 51,
    60–61, 63, 73–74
Individualism, 9, 14, 32–34, 36, 41n, 47, 48,
    52, 54, 55, 62, 64, 68, 70, 72
Institutions, 13, 21, 22, 33, 35, 37, 42, 47, 61–
    62
Internal relations, 105, 106, 121, 127, 143
Interpretation, 112, 122, 123, 134, 138, 141,
    179n
Interview procedures, 194, 199
IQ, 22, 27n

Justice, 189n.

Kagan, J., 95
Kohlberg, L., 189n

Language, 27, 36, 44n, 61–63, 72
Legal concepts, 15, 35, 43, 71
Leontiev, A., 10, 36
Linear concepts, 42
Linear perspective, 53

Martin-Baro, I., 90
Marx, K., 36, 49, 55, 60–62
Mathematics, 22, 48, 52–54, 67
Meaning unit, 169n
Mental illness, 31, 35, 50, 51, 65
Micro-sociology, 108
Miles, M., & Huberman, A., 176
Mozart, W., 67

Narratives, 83, 87, 99, 167, 175
Natural science, 17, 47, 49, 71

News, 37, 39, 46, 68, 71

Objectivity, 125–127, 149, 164, 179n
Ogbu, J., 22, 74
Ontogenetic development, 57–58
Opinion poll, 146
Order effects, 149
Order, 68

Painting, 52
Perceptual illusions, 32
Personal identity, 84
Personal meanings, 75, 80n, 91, 92, 100
Phylogenetic, 57–58
Positivism, 5, 140, 142, 151, 179–180, 185
Postmodernism, 5, 132, 144
Poverty, 28–31, 40, 59, 66
Psychological development, 30

Quantification, 183
Quasi-experiments, 117, 120

Reading, 19, 21, 23n, 27
Romantic love, 9, 56, 68–69, 115, 117, 156

Scholasticism, 98
Schools, 19, 20, 22, 27, 57, 70, 86
Science, 5
Scribner, S., 78, 81, 87
Self-concept, 175n
Shame, 51
Sherif, M., 25
Shopping, 21–22
Social class, 9, 17–22, 27–31, 47, 50, 56, 61,
    62, 64, 66, 70, 72, 86, 91, 93, 100, 114,
    117, 119, 122, 128, 129
Social construction, 35, 46, 65
Social institutions, 77, 81n, 90, 91
Social life in contemporary societies, 4
Social models, 73
Social role, 11, 15n, 37n, 55, 64, 65, 70–73
Social unconscious, 152
Sociology, 16, 35
Space, 31–34, 46, 53–54
Specialization of psychology as an academic
    discipline, 4
Statistical analysis, 119
Strauss, A., 168, 176
Structuralism, 190, 192

Studying individual psychology, 107, 112, 114n, 123
Suffering, 38, 50, 65
Superficial responses, 147

Teen motherhood, 65n
Time, 16, 32, 34, 42n
Tomasello, M., 15, 58, 73, 83

Unit of analysis, 16

Universals, 12–14, 51, 62, 72
Unobservables, 140
Unstructured interview, 154, 155

Valsiner, J., 79n, 86, 132
Vygotsky, L., 10, 11, 18, 31, 35, 63, 92, 138

Wertsch, J., 85
Witchcraft, 118
Word meanings, 145